D1570471

SPOTLIGHT ON THE CHILD

Recent Titles in
Contributions in Drama and Theatre Studies
Series Editor: Joseph Donohue

SPOTLIGHT ON THE CHILD

Studies in the History
of
American Children's
Theatre

Edited by ROGER L. BEDARD and C. JOHN TOLCH

CONTRIBUTIONS IN DRAMA AND THEATRE STUDIES,
Number 28

GREENWOOD PRESS
New York • Westport, Connecticut • London

Library of Congress Cataloging-in-Publication Data

Spotlight on the child : studies in the history of American children's
    theatre / edited by Roger L. Bedard and C. John Tolch.
    p.   cm.—(Contributions in drama and theatre studies, ISSN
    0163–3821 ; no. 28)
      Bibliography: p.
      Includes index.
      ISBN 0–313–25793–0 (lib. bdg. : alk. paper)
      1. Children's plays—Presentation, etc.—United States—History.
    I. Bedard, Roger L.   II. Tolch, C. John.   III. Series.
    PN3159.U6S66   1989
    791'.0226'0973—dc19   88–21336

British Library Cataloguing in Publication Data is available.

Library of Congress Catalog Card Number: 88–21336
ISBN: 0–313–25793–0
ISSN: 0163–3821

First published in 1989

Greenwood Press, Inc.
88 Post Road West, Westport, Connecticut 06881

Printed in the United States of America

The paper used in this book complies with the
Permanent Paper Standard issued by the National
Information Standards Organization (Z39.48–1984).

10 9 8 7 6 5 4 3 2 1

Contents

SPOTLIGHT ON THE CHILD

1

Introduction

ROGER L. BEDARD AND
C. JOHN TOLCH

It is a sometimes precarious balance of interests that has perpetuated theatre with and for young people both in this culture, as well as in cultures throughout the ages. It is well documented that children, when left to their own devices, will turn to things mimetic. Yet for children to go to the theatre, or even to participate in formal drama or theatre activities, adults must not only sanction the activity, they must also design and implement such programs. Throughout the history of this country, adults have held differing views on the morality, the appropriateness and the makeup of theatre with and for children.

Theatre has been a part of the American culture from the beginning, and its fortunes and various manifestations are well known. But in the story of this development of a theatrical heritage, it is not always easy to discern a through-line of theatre activity with and for children. This is true, in part, because historians have not always taken special note of the child as audience member. (After all, didn't nineteenth-century audiences of all ages attend such plays as Joseph Jefferson's *Rip Van Winkle* in much the same manner that contemporary audiences of all ages have flocked to *Annie* and *Cats*?) But, more important, children's theatre has been, historically, more the product of the educator and the social worker than the producer or the theatre artist. Theatre with and for young people has thus not been included in traditional theatre history studies.

Yet, one can find American theatre and children as companions virtually from the beginning, and this relationship has taken many forms. It was in 1792, only eighteen years after "the Continental Congress passed a declaration to discourage 'every species of extravagance and dissipation, especially all horse-racing, and all kinds of gaming, cock-fighting, exhibition of shews, plays, and other expensive diversions and entertainments' ''[1] that Charles Stearns began creating his plays (dialogues) for school children. The traditions, successes and possibilities of eighteenth-century school drama (which remain largely undocumented) inspired social workers a century later to explore similar activities in their playground and settlement house work. In that context, the processes of informal dramatizations *by* young people as well as the practice of adults performing specialized dramatic fare *for* young people were explored in many settings throughout the country.

At the end of the nineteenth and beginning of the twentieth century one can find the professional producers experimenting more vigorously with the commercial possibilities of the child as audience member. At the same time, George Pierce Baker, through his work at Radcliffe and Harvard, was training an influential new generation of theatre artists. Children's playwright Charlotte B. Chorpenning was one of his prized students, and Edith King and Dorothy Coit, of the noted King-Coit Children's Theatre and School, benefited from his counsel and support. In fact, Baker himself, on at least one occasion, taught a class wherein "special attention" was "given to the staging of plays for school children."[2]

Children's theatre in the first half of the twentieth century was carried forward primarily by educators and by amateur theatre artists; both groups attempted to strike a balance between the requirements of the classroom and the stage. Theatre activities with and for children, whether performed by the Junior League, by the students themselves in "auditorium" sessions, or by such specialized institutions as the King-Coit Theatre, differed markedly from group to group. During this period, the children's theatre field also began to find definition, as theorists and writers such as Winifred Ward and Charlotte Chorpenning strove to articulate those differences, in theory and practice, between the child as participant in creative drama and the child as audience member.

Many artists and educators have subsequently tested and refined these ideas. The publisher Sara Spencer nurtured the artistic in children's theatre by guiding and supporting several generations of playwrights, from Chorpenning to Aurand Harris. The Federal Theatre Project introduced professional theatre artists to young audiences on a large scale. And artist/managers such as John Clark Donahue developed comprehensive theatres and schools to entertain and to train young people.

The work accomplished by these people is but a small sampling of that throughline of the history of American theatre with and for young people. Historians have only begun to discover and illuminate the many pieces to this picture and understand how they work together as a whole—as a heritage for the field today.

This heritage is primarily one of strong-willed individuals—educators, social workers and artists—who have shaped institutions or organizations to serve the dramatic in the child. Generally they have worked in isolation from one another, though, at least in the later years, there are many connections. We can see connections between the progressive educators of the eighteenth and nineteenth centuries, who led their students to see moral truth by using the drama that many considered immoral. We can see connections in the influential people who studied with George Pierce Baker and made solid contributions to the children's theatre field. We can see connections in the practice and philosophies of the progressive social workers who insisted that drama was an important tool in treating the child. We can see connections in the scores of amateur actors and directors—working under the auspices of the Junior League and other community organizations—who brought live theatre into the schools throughout the country. And we can see connections in those who persisted in the call for theatre "art" for children in the face of heavy pressure from those who felt that theatre for children must teach.

The following chapters illuminate some of the many facets of the rich and varied history of American theatre with and for children. It is hoped that these will serve as a beginning to a fuller understanding of the history of the field and as a challenge to others to search for the many missing pieces.

NOTES

1. Garff B. Wilson, *Three Hundred Years of American Drama and Theatre* (Englewood Cliffs, N.J.: Prentice-Hall, 1973), p. 17.

2. Cecil Hinkel, "An Analysis and Evaluation of the 47 Workshop of George Pierce Baker," Ph.D. diss., Ohio State University, 1959, Volume 1, p. 273.

2

The Dramatic Dialogues of Charles Stearns: An Appreciation

JONATHAN LEVY

> It is to no purpose to attempt to write or preach down an amusement [the theatre] which seizes so forcibly upon all the powers of the mind.
> (Benjamin Rush, *A Plan for the Establishment of Public Schools and the Diffusion of Knowledge in Pennsylvania*, 1786)

Historians will probably never know the true extent of theatrical activity in American schools between the end of the eighteenth century and the middle of the nineteenth, for performances and recitations of one kind or another were simply too common to be taken special note of. Although plays done on ceremonial school occasions were sometimes recorded, performances done in connection with the study of rhetoric (then normally part of the curriculum) were not, any more than were exercises or examinations in arithmetic or Latin. To complicate matters further, plays done in schools were often not called "plays," lest they be confused in parents' minds with that seminary of vice, the professional stage.

Still, there is good evidence that there was a great deal of theatrical activity in American schools in this period; and the influence of that activity on American life has yet to be fully explored and understood.

The relationship between acting and action is cloudy. How thought and character are formed, by playing life as well as by living life, is not now and may never be clear. What is clear is that rhetorical style can be formed early and that style affects substance. One key to the public tone of pre–Civil War America, as reflected in the bar, the pulpit and the Congress, might well be found in the dramatic activity in its schools.

Most of the dramatic pieces done in American schools, then as now, were adaptations and borrowings. They were parts from plays for adults, English or continental plays for children or translations of European plays, either for adults or children. However, a few Americans did turn their hands at writing children's plays. Occasionally, these were professional writers who were persuaded to write a play for a particular school occasion. More often, as in England two hundred years earlier, they were schoolmasters and schoolmistresses who wrote plays for their own pupils.

Charles Stearns is perhaps the first, probably the most gifted and certainly the most prolific of these American schoolmasters. The thirty dramatic dialogues he wrote for his pupils in Lincoln, Massachusetts, at the very end of the eighteenth century, constitute the first substantial body of plays for young people written by an American. What is more, many of the dialogues are good plays, still stageworthy today. For both reasons, the *Dialogues* and their author deserve an extended study, for which, it is hoped, the following essay will provide a beginning.

Charles Stearns, the son of Thomas Stearns and Lydia Mansfield Stearns, was born on July 19, 1753, at Lunenberg, Massachusetts, and grew up in the nearby town of Leominster.[1] He entered Harvard College in 1769 and distinguished himself "for vigorous and successful application to study."[2] He graduated in 1773 and spent the next several years studying theology and teaching school. He received an M.A. from Harvard in 1776 and was appointed tutor in the college in 1780.[3] He resigned his tutorship eighteen months later to become the pastor of Christ Church in Lincoln, where he remained for forty-five years.

On December 4, 1781, he married Susanna Cowdry of Reading, a descendent of the first minister of that town. They had eleven children, six boys and five girls, seven of whom lived to their majority.[4]

In 1792, twenty-one prominent citizens of Lincoln organized themselves as the Associated Proprietors of the Liberal School in Lincoln, where Stearns taught and of which he became the first principal. It was for his pupils at the Liberal School that Stearns, over the next six years, wrote his *Dramatic Dialogues*.[5]

As both minister and teacher, Stearns was "emphatically the person—parson— of the town. . . . Everybody went to him for advice. He seemed to be invested with a kind of magisterial dignity."[6] In time, Stearns grew very fat. But despite occasional serious illnesses, he "retained his bodily and mental facilities in a remarkable degree" and preached his last sermon in the same month he died.[7]

In 1809, Stearns was elected a member of the American Academy of Arts and Sciences,[8] and in 1810 he received an honorary doctorate from Harvard. About this time, he was apparently approached about accepting the presidency of Harvard, but declined on the grounds that "he was content with his parish and that he could not maintain his family and meet the increased expenses at Cambridge on the president's salary."[9] He died on July 26, 1826, in his seventy-fourth year. He is buried in Lincoln, between his wife, who outlived him by eight years, and his daughter Eliza.

On May 27, 1827, the Town of Lincoln allotted $50.00 to erect a monument to Stearns: "a slab supported by three pillars . . . with a suitable inscription on the same."[10] The original monument was destroyed and replaced by the town in 1972. The inscription reads:

He was distinguished for high attainments in various branches of science; for strength and soundness of mind; for method and accuracy in reasoning, and facility in communicating knowledge. By his piety, benevolence, and learning he gained the affection and respect of his beloved people, the esteem and confidence of his numerous friends, and the well deserved honors of literary societies. His life was full of practical goodness; the genuine fruit of deep felt piety, and his death, of religious hope and peace. By the habitual exercise of faith, humility, patience and charity, he exhibited Christianity, in a strong and permanent light, and is gone, it is believed, to enjoy the rewards of a good and faithful servant of Jesus Christ.

Stearns left four kinds of written works: plays, in the *Dramatic Dialogues*; a poem, *the ladies' philosophy of love*; a religious textbook, *Principles of Religion and Morality*; and several sermons.[11] The sermons and textbook are interesting chiefly for the light they shed on the plays. The poem is a touching oddity, interesting in its own right.

We have, complete or in part, eight sermons Stearns wrote over a period of thirty-two years.[12] They are well written and closely reasoned, rhetorically formal and theologically orthodox. "The word," Stearns wrote, "is unchangeable, forever settled in heaven. It must then be a rule absolute in itself."[13] He extols the unglamorous virtues. He praises patience, by which "we are active under the leaden repetition of ordinary duties and labours, that we conflict with bodily sickness, infirmity and pain, for hours, days, weeks, months, and sometimes years, that we eradicate the vices we love, and plant virtues which are most severe in their stead. . . . "[14]

And, again and again, he recommends a stern variety of temperance:

You must distrust yourself. You must be jealous of your favourite hypothesis, and your preconceived opinions. Every favorite system, hypothesis, and opinion, creates a strong interest. It becomes a Delilah, and you must sleep upon her lap. You . . . must dread your own favourite authors, lest they deceive you. You must cleave to the scriptures, allow no paramount authority, and tremble lest you pervert them.[15]

Stearns, in short, preached the most stringent of New England orthodoxies, in a pulpit tone that combines the oppositions of Eccelesiastes with the gravity of Dr. Johnson. Indeed, if all we had of Stearns were the sermons, we would have very little inkling of the originality and variety of his mind.

For Stearns' pulpit tone is only one of his tones, his pastor's voice only one of his voices. His voice and tone are quite different in the expository prose and the little of his recorded conversation we have. And the *Dramatic Dialogues* includes all these, and many others.

Stearns was not a hypocrite or a fraud. He clearly believed what he preached
and believed it unwaveringly throughout his life. But Stearns was, even in the
pulpit, always an artist—specifically, an artist of the theatre—whose instinct
caused him to find the most appropriate voice for each character he created
(including the Reverend Charles Stearns, D.D.) in order to make the words that
character speaks not only more effective, but more true.

Principles of Religion and Morality is the only one of Stearns' works besides
the *Dramatic Dialogues* written in dialogue. It resembles the *Dramatic Dialogues*
in no other way. It was written as a textbook for his pupils and was only printed,
Stearns explains in his preface, because it was simpler to print the book than to
have his students keep copying it out.[16]

The work is divided into three parts: Part One is "Of the Evidence of Religion," Part Two is "Principles of Religion," and Part Three is "Principles of
Morality." Each section is divided into subsections, which, like the catechism,
take the form of dialogues, here between a Preceptor and his Scholar. The
Preceptor asks a rote question to which the Scholar gives a rote answer:

Preceptor
Was the true God known to the Patriarchs?

Scholar
Yes, he revealed himself to them often.[17]

The rhythm and tone of these dialogues are, throughout, those of the old-fash-
ioned classroom, the cadence of the question rising, the cadence of the answer
falling. Indeed, they seem examples of the rote religious instructious which
Hannah More, twenty years earlier, wrote her biblical dramas to supplant.

But for Stearns, the Bible's "Word was unchangeable"; which is to say, it
could not be paraphrased or translated, even into another genre. Thus, none of
his dialogues is on a biblical subject. The religious instruction he gave his pupils
was pure and undoctored, both in his sermons and in his *Principles of Religion
and Morality*.

Stearns did not intend his *Principles of Religion and Morality* to be a brilliant
book. He meant it, he said, to be useful rather than eminent. And useful it seems
to have been. It ran to four editions.

Stearns' only extant poem is *the ladies' philosophy of love*. He wrote it in
1774, the year after he graduated from Harvard, but did not publish it until 1797.
As is sometimes the case, the author's reasons for writing the work and his
reasons for publishing it were quite different.

Stearns, twenty-two and "under no obligation to any of the fair but mere good
will,"[18] got the idea of writing the poem from a young lady his own age, who
observed "that nothing could be more useful to young ladies than to know
precisely the sentiments of the young Gentlemen concerning them."[19] "The
idea," Stearns writes, "strongly possessed the author's imagination."[20] The

result was a philosophic-romantic poem in four cantos of heroic couplets, explicated by Stearns' own learned footnotes.

Canto I introduces Stearns' subject and examines "the moral qualities which render women amiable to the other sex." There are no surprises in the qualities the young divinity student recommends—"fair modesty," "blest education" and "compliance":

> She in the blissful enterprize succeeds,
> Who follows, modest, while her hero leads.[21]

However, the qualities Stearns warns *against* are surprising, both for the vehemence with which they are expressed and for their particularity. Stearns counsels, in a general way, against modesty and vanity. But what really seems to irk him are sharp-tongued, complaining women:

> In woman's heart, when lust of satire burns,
> The angel to a hissing serpent turns . . .
> All swains abhor the fretful, whining strain,
> Of nymphs, whose only joy is to complain.[22]

Canto II treats women's "personal and external accomplishments." Stearns counsels balance informed by education, especially the moral lessons to be learned from great literature:

> Despise not then, the wisdom of the schools,
> But plan thy life by sage and equal rules . . .
> Learn from grave Homer, midst his thundering arms,
> The fate of *Troy;* and HELEN's vicious charms;
> Observe in faithful, sweet PENELOPE,
> What now thou art, and what thou still must be.[23]

He also recommends a variety of social accomplishments: physical grace, dress, diction and pronunciation. Of grace, he writes:

> Learn dextrous to retire, and to advance
> In all the mazes of the figured dance,
> Enter the social scene with modest grace;
> Withdraw with looks composed, and decent pace.[24]

And he observes of dress:

> The short, on towering buskins raised appear
> Majestic, and their port our hearts revere;
> The small are better by a fuller dress;
> The thick, by drapery light, their taste
>   express. . . .[25]

But he gives his most vivid advice about diction, pitch and pronunciation:

> Free from impatience and with happy choice,
> Learn the just modulation of thy voice.
> Clear, sweet, distinct, let all the accents sound
> Not lisping, whispering, or with shrilling scream,
> Nor faint, like accents in a muttered dream.[26]

These social accomplishments translate, in theatrical terms, into movement, costume and vocal production, to the nuances of which Stearns showed himself very sensitive very early.

Canto III treats ways of "discerning men's characters and the means of fixing attachments," particularly how a young woman may learn to know a "scribbler," who is "according to Addison . . . a man who practices the forms of courtship to a lady, without any real design of marrying her."[27] And Canto IV describes "the means of securing Reputation; with an encomium on women—Marriage— American Treatment, and Education of Women—with the conclusion of the poem."[28]

The poem *the ladies' philosophy of love* is, then, self-important, endearing, silly stuff. Although Stearns gained something of a reputation as a poet by it, it is less interesting as a poem than as a document on the history of New England sensibility. Still, it is an ambitious piece of writing and, in technical terms, a respectable apprentice work.

It seems clear why Stearns wrote the poem. It gave the young scholar a chance to write on Ovid's subject in Pope's meter; and it gave the young man a chance to put himself in the role of a teacher with women his own age, to strut his learning and his rectitude, and, legitimately, to spend most of his waking hours thinking about the opposite sex. That is, it gave him the occasion to ruminate on eternal questions, as Stearns himself describes them:

> Hence when the boy has fifteen summers known,
> And on his cheek appears the springing down,
> A gentle fever thrills along his veins;
> Quick beats his heart, he wonders what it means.[29]

That is surely why Stearns wrote the poem, but not why he published it. When he did publish it, he was in his late forties and had been "a lover—a husband— a father of numerous family—a pastor—a preceptor for many years to youth of both sexes."[30] Experience had only confirmed to Stearns the truth of what he had written at twenty-two. And at forty-four, he was convinced such work was needed, since

it is certain fact, that neither the penalties of law, or ecclesiastical Censures; have prevented ill conduct between the sexes in early life—not the scheme of some to keep them in ignorance of love-matters. Invincible curiosity will . . . be perverted by . . . silly Novels. . . . But in all places where *education* of young ladies has been attended to properly, *debauchery* has vanished before *learning*, like fog before the ascending sun.[31]

Thus, though the poem may have been written as a divinity student's *Art of Love*, it was printed as an experienced teacher, minister and father's advice to young women on what is always a delicate subject—behavior between the sexes before marriage—in the deep belief that "a true and philosophical idea of the passion of LOVE—and of the rights of women—and not IGNORANCE, is the cause of proper behaviour in women. . . . "[32]

Dramatic Dialogues for the Use of Schools is Stearns' major work. It consists of thirty plays, eleven "single pieces"—set pieces for individual speakers—and an introduction, which is surely one of the most thoughtful and practical documents in the history of theatre for children in America.

The plays are short. Though they are, typically, written in three or five acts, they rarely run to more than ten pages of printed text. Stearns cautioned that a school exhibition should contain between four and six plays and no more than five single pieces and should not run longer than four-and-one-half or five hours. Thus, allowing for set changes between pieces, it would seem that the running time of any single piece was rarely as long as an hour and was more usually closer to half an hour.

Stearns took his plots where he found them and wrote in the most conventional genres of his century—romanoid tragedies, history plays, Eastern tales, comedies of manners and *comedies larmoyantes*.[33] But the best of his plays are the ones he drew from life: scenes of New England town, farm and school life at the very end of the eighteenth century.

An anonymous critic wrote of the *Dramatic Dialogues*, a century after it was printed:

The work seems to us very crude and simple, and often wanting of *finesse,* but we must bear in mind that, a hundred years ago, school exhibitions and the dramatic art had not made much progress in these parts. The book was a great novelty . . . [and] met with such favor that several towns subscribed for a hundred copies each. It must be regarded as a pioneer in the field of dramatic text-books in New England.[34]

This judgment is probably right in its assessment of the *Dialogues*' originality and wrong in its assessment of its quality. Few playwrights, and fewer critics, transcend the conventions of their times. Stearns' plays have, undeniably, the defects of their eighteenth-century models. They are sometimes woodenly high-classical. They are sometimes sentimental, or as sentimental as Lincoln, Massachusetts, allowed. Sometimes, there is a too obvious *raisonneur* in them, to draw the moral for the audience in the event they missed it in the action. Frequently, they are divided into abrupt French scenes.

Yet they also contain undeniable virtues, which are in part the virtues of their period, in part the particular virtues of their author and in part the virtues which arose perforce from the conditions under which Stearns wrote them.

The plays are wonderfully compact. Because the playing time for each was short, Stearns was forced to distill and compress, omitting the merely decorative and discursive, and beginning the action of each play, and the action of each scene, close to the point of its climax. Here, for example, is the opening of *A Woman of Honor*:

Belinda (Running in)
Lucy, do you not intend to go to the ball?

Lucy
What ball do you mean?

Belinda
Cousin Fireflash this day is twenty one; and he gives a splendid Ball to all his acquaintance.

Lucy
I am invited and mean to go.

Belinda
Mean to go! And here you sit drudging like some tame old house wife, with a dozen children.[35]

But the two chief qualities of the *Dialogues* for the modern reader are, first, at such an early point in the country's history, how American the American plays are; and, second, despite Stearns' lack of practical theatrical experience, how theatrical they are.

The American plays are American first in their language. The tragedies and histories could have been written by anyone with a literary knowledge of English. But the comedies, even when not set in America, sound American. And the New England plays, particularly the dialogue of the farmers and children, are American to their core.

Stearns' educated characters speak with simplicity and reserve, even (or especially) when moved or hard pressed. Here, the teacher, Mr. Treadwell, is speaking to his student, Juliet:

Treadwell
There is a very particular reason [for his speaking to her]. Your excellent mother, that bright example of all the virtues, in the last moments of her life, affectionately grasped my hand—I am, said she, on the confines of the world of the spirits—My husband must serve the states in this necessary war—Juliet is left and extremely exposed—look after her; direct her; keep her, if possible, from error or vice. This is my dying request. Could I fail to regard it? This is the cause of all the attentions which I have given to your affairs.[36]

The uneducated speak with a fine exuberance, even when not moved at all:

Mrs. Ironsides (from within)
RUN, Jule, Mr. Butterford is coming. Put up and look as smart as you can—put on your new moroker shoes, and clean shawl, quick, quick.[37]

And here is an interview between Jule and Mr. Butterford:

Jule
If I marry you for your money, I must know whether I may spend it or not—if that be the only motive I must spend the whole.

Mr. Butterford
You are all upon the joke now—
(Slaps her on the arm and chucks her under the chin) hoh! hoh! hoh!

Jule
Positively, if you will not be decent I will withdraw from the room.

Mr. Butterford
How shall I be decent, hoh! hoh! hoh!

Jule
Sit peaceably in your own chair, that will please me most—then answer to such questions as I ask you—or ask me such questions as I can answer with propriety.

Mr. Butterford
(Sits confused for a few moments, then bursts into a great laugh) Hoh! hoh! hoh!

Jule
What makes you so merry sir?

Mr. Butterford
'Tis darn clever, hoh! hoh! hoh!

Jule
What is that which is so clever; will you not let one partake of your mirth?

Mr. Butterford
Fayther's got all the advantage of uncle Sye . . . Uncle Sye's land lies on the hill, and fayther's land lies all below. Uncle Sye carries out all manner of *nasty truck* on his land for manyure, and fayther's land gets all the wash of it. So fayther has *clean* the advantage of uncle Sye.[38]

Stearns, here as elsewhere, ridicules boorish manners but not uneducated speech. Indeed, he often shows a particular affection for his uneducated characters and a particular pleasure in writing dialogue for them; just as, surely, his students must have taken a special pleasure in acting these characters. For both author and actors, these characters offered an escape from civility and propriety: a chance to sprawl, dress outlandishly, talk common and cut up.

For Stearns, inventing characters unlike himself gave him not only a brief liberation from the authority and respectability, as a minister and schoolmaster, he embodied; it also gave him occasions to speak his mind, in public, in ways he surely could not in his own person.

He could, first of all, speak intimately and personally here of the fleeting pleasures of fatherhood: "She was about three years old—when I went aways, a little proud Sylph—I remember how she would caper when she was dressed up."[39]

He could also speak critically, sometimes scathingly, about insufferable little children:

Your children are the most disorderly crew that ever were hatched, when they are out of humor they are always bawling—There will be half a dozen of them turning up at once—They are ever fighting and clawing at one another—When they are in good humor they play with excessive noise and violence as if the house were going out the windows—Then they are upsetting everything thro the whole house—They are ever breaking their own shins or one another's noses—They are ever losing their hats and their shoes—One falls down stairs and is taken up half dead—One is burnt and another is scalded—Another cuts his leg or hand, and is bleeding to death. . . . [40]

He could exhibit the less-than-admirable qualities of some of the students he was paid to teach. The boys could be fops and bullies:

But then how you dress [one says to a new boy at school], as far from the fashion as from Nova Scotia to Georgia—What do you mean wearing that old bayonet hat—Your coat is half a yard too short—oh! fun indeed! this is pretty! what a coat!—and then your hair tied up with a leather—whang—you look like old Jeremy—fact. . . . [41]

The girls could be calculating and cold-blooded:

I consider a suitor as worth nothing, unless you can treat him in as many ways as you can dress a fish; and still find him humble and passive—A fish you know may be baked, broiled, roasted, boiled, smoked and dried—may be dressed with sauce, or without, and every way makes a good dish. So a lover suitable to my taste, must broil with resentment, must be roasted with anger, must be baked with the heat of constant affection, must broil with jealousy, must be smoked with contempt—and his very marrow must be dried up with anxious expectation. . . . [42]

And he could speak frankly of his own condition:

I have read of the trial of fire ordial [sic]—A lady whose character was suspected, walked barefoot among red hot ploughshares, with scarcely room to set her feet to the ground; and if she burned her feet in the least, it was concluded that she was guilty. Such is the life of a minister in a parish.[43]

But the fact that Stearns found relief in writing *louche* and boorish characters and putting controversial opinions in their mouths is, in the end, incidental. What is central is that Stearns's powers of observation and breadth of sympathy allowed him to draw a large and varied cast of characters—the old, the young, the rich, the poor, the proper and improper, the good and the not-yet-good; and, in so doing, preserve for us a detailed picture of American life, at one time, in one place, nearly two hundred years ago.

It is less surprising that the *Dialogues* are so American than that they are so theatrical. One would not expect a clergyman and scholar to have such a command of the realities and practicalities of the stage.

That Stearns had such a command is probably as much due to the conditions under which he worked as to the natural theatrical instinct, which he clearly had. Like many teachers after him, he was obliged to understand and perform, or at least supervise, every aspect of every production.

He had to develop an audience and consider his budget: "Let not exhibitions be too expensive—People are generally hurt by expence, and will not long love that which draws their money from them."[44]

He was theatre architect and set designer. He advised that every school house where plays were to be done should have "a small esplanade or stage," and he offered instructions for such:

If no one be made in the construction of the house you may erect a temporary one. It will be very convenient to have a room behind the stage to which the performers can withdraw, when they should be supposed absent. About this stage, on a frame erected for the purpose, you may draw curtains to conceal the stage, occasionally, from the audience. This will give opportunity, to represent different scenes of action. Then by tables, books, &c. the stage may represent a study—by national arms, the emblems &c. a court—by military trophies, an encampment or field of war. . . . Thus on a stage of no more than twelve feet by eight. . . . Beside the curtains which are drawn around the stage, there should be one drawn across from side to side, which may totally hide the back scene.[45]

Stearns cast the plays, cannily: "For the principal character in each piece you will doubtless select a speaker on whom you can depend for steadiness of temper, and complete self command. . . . Scholars uniformly perform best in the character which is natural to them, or that which is directly the opposite."[46] And he directed, apparently in the mechanical fashion of the period: "Persons engaged in opposite parties, sentiments, or interests, or who are in any way at variance, should enter on opposite sides of the stage. If during the representations they be not reconciled they should also depart on opposite sides, if they become friends they should go off on the same."[47]

The fact that Stearns knew his actors and his audience, knew the physical limitations of his theatre and knew when he wrote his plays that he would be directing them, all helped him to transcend literature and become the expert playwright he was.

For expert he was. He wrote dialogue which not only conveyed sense and displayed character, but which created tension by its rhythm and form:

Emily
Did your husband ever put on high airs of authority?

Mrs. Easy
Yes.

Emily
Did he ever talk with passion, and be saucy to you?

Mrs. Easy
Yes.

Emily
Was he ever cross and ill humored?

Mrs. Easy
Yes.

Emily
Was he ever in a passion with you?

Mrs. Easy
Yes.

Emily
Did he ever leave you, or go into company abroad?

Mrs. Easy
Yes.

Emily
Was he ever suspicious of you?

Mrs. Easy
Yes.

Emily
Was you ever afraid that he might leave you to distress and want?

Mrs. Easy
Yes.

Emily
He had a great many faults then?

Mrs. Easy
Yes.

Emily
And could you be happy with such a man?

Mrs. Easy
Yes.

Emily
O admiration. Had I such a husband I must die out-right—Do you not think I should?

Mrs. Easy
No.[48]

And Stearns used the stage admirably, even when his characters were not speaking. Indeed, his stage directions give a vivid sense of how effective his plays must have been in performance:

Mr. Tiptoe
MADAM your most obedient humble servant.

Miss Bridget (Receding to the farthest part of the stage)
Sir?—
(Seats herself prim and bridles up)

Mr. Tiptoe
Madam if conversation could be tho't agreeable.
(Offers to seat himself by her; she removes, places an empty chair between him and her, with the back towards him, and draws another chair before her, and says)

Miss Bridget
Sir? [49]

Here is another example of his physical use of the stage:

Mrs. Fortinbras
Well sir, you got home very late last night. It was but one of the clock in the morning.

Colonel Fortinbras
I hoped, madam, to have met with a kind reception from you. I did not think it was very late.

Mrs. Fortinbras
But I know it was late—and it was a pretty fancy indeed, if one must marry and expect to find a friend in a husband, and have him leave one in utter contempt, and tarry out late.
(The Colonel takes up an old fiddle and plays)

Colonel Fortinbras
Tum tum diddle de dum dum dum.

Mrs. Fortinbras
You pretend to have your soldier frolics—who knows what you are about when you are abroad?

Colonel Fortinbras
Tum dum &c. (Plays)

Mrs. Fortinbras
No woman of spirit can bear such treatment, I protest.

Colonel Fortinbras
Tum dum diddle, &c (Plays)

Mrs. Fortinbras
You have not bought me a new gown this twelve month.

Colonel Fortinbras
Tum dum, &c. (Continues playing)

Mrs. Fortinbras
I won't bear this treatment—it is intolerable.

Colonel Fortinbras
Tum dum diddle, &c. (Still continues)

Mrs. Fortinbras
If ever there was a woman so abused by her husband.

Colonel Fortinbras
Tum dum diddle. (He pursues her with his music till she is off the stage) [50]

There is, clearly, a pervasive playfulness in the best of the dialogues, which makes them attractive and which makes them play. But, for Stearns, playfulness and theatricality were not ends in themselves. They were means toward the deep education he believed the theatre provided. The theatre, he thought, could show moral dilemmas *in action*, and thus teach them thoroughly and memorably. Thus, he gave each of the *Dialogues* a subtitle which made plain the particular problem it explored and resolved: "The quarrels of married persons are generally frivolous," to *The Discontented Wife*; "The folly of local prejudice," to *The Wooden Boy*; and so on. Indeed, there is no dialogue in which a dilemma is not posed and examined, and only one in which a dilemma is not resolved. It is *The Insolvable Question,* and its subtitle explains its title: "Prudery and forwardness are equally pernicious to women." Yet the didactic format of the dialogues has been so established that, in *The Insolvable Question*, characters actually step out of the action to condemn the author for his irresolution, before, finally, excusing it and admitting that for once he had posed a problem which had equally good arguments for each side.

Given the view of his age, Stearns would have had to argue the moral benefits of the *Dialogues* even if he had not believed in them, which he clearly did. The common view of school exhibitions in his time, as Stearns summarized it, was that:

they are expensive, that they encourage profanity and vice; that the feelings of students are often hurt by the distribution of parts—or their parents cruelly mortified—that the students acquire by them an indecent confidence, and that they intrude upon studies more necessary and useful . . . and they are imitations of a theatre, which is always a seminary of vice.[51]

Stearns, of course, summarized this view in order to contradict it. When school exhibitions are properly conducted, he wrote:

[T]hey enlarge the ideas and polish the manners of students. They show an example of moral precepts represented in real life. . . . [They] are productive of a most rational amusement, and not only improve the outward carriage of the students; but implant most useful morals in them; and in the minds of their friends, who attend their performance.[52]

They are not an enemy, but an ally of reason. They "awaken the ambition of students, and they become desirous of behaving in a rational manner."[53] Moreover, according to Stearns, "it has often been observed, that where there have been in the same town, schools on the same footing in other respects, yet some have had exhibitions and others not, that the schools in which there have been exhibitions, have not only excelled in the point of exhibitions but in every other."[54] Stearns need not have protested so much. His best argument against what Jonah Barish has called the anti-theatrical prejudice is the *Dialogues* themselves. They are more than "moral lessons brought into action," which is what

Stearns' contemporary, Madame de Genlis, called her plays. The *Dramatic Dialogues* are, at their best, delightful, playable pieces; *paysages* lightly *moralisés*, which preserve for us a detailed picture of life in an American village at the turn of the nineteenth century; and which are at once a foundation and a standard for plays for American children which have been written since.

A note on the text: The *Dramatic Dialogues* was printed from Stearns' manuscript, "about 1,000 pages in quarto, closely written" (*Dramatic Dialogues*, p. 537). Quite naturally, they contained errata. Stearns found and noted twenty-two, but there are more. In my quotations from the *Dialogues*, I have incorporated Stearns' corrections and tried to correct obvious typographical mistakes he missed. Except for putting quotations from the plays in a format more familiar to the modern reader, I have left Stearns' text as it was printed, including his idiosyncratic punctuation.

Material from the Harvard University Archives is cited by permission. I would like to express my thanks to Harley P. Holden, curator of the archives, Jill Erickson of the Boston Atheneum, Louis L. Tucker, director of the Massachusetts Historical Society, and Joel Orlen and Frank Manuel of the American Academy of Arts and Sciences for their help; and to Peg Martin of Lincoln, and Alex Bernhard of Hale and Dorr, Boston, for giving me the benefit of their expertise while I was writing this piece.

NOTES

1. Some sources say he was born at Leominster, and one says he was born in Fitchberg; Stearns' father had lived in both towns before Stearns was born. However, the Harvard Archives, which presumably reflect Stearns' own report, list his birthplace as Lunenberg.

2. William B. Sprague, ed., *Annals of the American Pulpit* (New York: Robert Carter & Brothers, 1865), vol. 7, p. 147. Stearns' early interests were in mathematics, metaphysics and classical, European and English literature, especially poetry. Later, as a tutor at Harvard, he oversaw many "poetical compositions." See "Fac Recs III," pp. 203, 216, 219, 230 and 254, Harvard University Archives; and Zubdiel Adams, *The bishop's office a good work. A sermon preached at the ordination of the Rev. Mr. Charles Stearns, to the pastoral care of the church in Lincoln, November 7, 1781. By Zubdiel Adams* (Commonwealth of Massachusetts: T. & J. Fleet, 1782), p. 26.

3. "A vacancy being made in the Tutorship by the resignation of Mr. Eliot, written votes were bro't in for a tutor, & it appeared that Mr. Charles Stearns was chosen for a term not to exceed three years from the time of his accepting that office." "Fac Recs III," June 15, 1780, p. 87. He received a salary of ten pounds for his half-year. Ibid., pp. 149–50. "Mr Tutor Stearns vacated his office, by taking pastoral charge of the church in Lincoln." Ibid., November 7, 1781, p. 32.

4. Susanna was the daughter of Jonathan and Rachel Cowdry (or Coudry). She was born on July 20, 1755, and died on July 22, 1832. The eleven children were, in order of their births: Susanna (b. October 6, 1782, d. November 7, 1806); Charles (b. February 16, 1784, d. May 5, 1855); Thomas (b. August 8, 1785, d. July 1, 1844); Julia (b. July 14, 1786/87?, d. after May 19, 1819); Sarah (b. July 5, 1789, d. October 8, 1801);

Elizabeth Frances (Eliza) (b. February 12/13?, 1791, d. November 21, 1844); William
Lawrence (b. October 30, 1793, d. May 28, 1857); Daniel Mansfield (b. October 30,
1793, d. October 19, 1847); Rebecca (b. November 15, 1794, d. January 5, 1813);
Samuel (b. August 24, 1796, d. October 20/29?, 1796); Edwin (b. March 13, 1798, d.
June 26, 1798).

5. The Liberal School of Lincoln was one of the first co-educational schools in the
country. It was founded in 1792 on the model of the New Ipswich Academy of New
Ipswich, New Hampshire, opened in the spring of 1793, and "continued in successful
operation for about fifteen years. . . . Instruction was given in rhetoric, astronomy, the
higher branches of mathematics, and in the principles of religion and morality, text-books
being prepared by Dr. Stearns and transcribed by the pupils. Instruction was also given
in Latin and Greek, and particular attention paid to manners and morals of the pupils.
This school gave a new impulse to the cause of education and tended to elevate the
character of the town." D. Hamilton Hurd, ed., *History of Middlesex County, Massachusetts, with biographical sketches of many of its prominent men* (Philadelphia: J. W.
Lewis & Co., 1890), vol. 2, p. 632.

The building was vacated in 1808, rented out as a district school for a year, and sold
to the town in 1810. It was used as a school until 1872.

6. *Proceedings in observance of the one hundred and fiftieth anniversary of the
organization of the first church in Lincoln, Massachusetts, August 21 and September 4,
1898* (Cambridge: The University Press, 1899), pp. 71–72.

7. Sprague, *Annals*, p. 148. For reports of Stearns' various illnesses, see *Proceedings*,
p. 73, and the citation from [Peabody's] *Journal*, vol. 9 in Clifford Kenyon Shipton,
"Shipton's Notes for *Sibley's Harvard Graduates*," Massachusetts Historical Society.

8. He was elected on August 9, 1809, at the academy's 121st meeting, but does not
seem to have taken part in the activities of the academy thereafter.

9. *Proceedings,* pp. 73–74.

10. Lincoln, Massachusetts, town records from 1746 to 1810.

11. In addition, there is a tantalizing reference in Sprague to "six quarto volumes,
containing his Lectures and Addresses to his pupils, and records of their attendance and
acquirements," which, according to Sprague in 1865, were still in existence. Sprague
said that he had "searched diligently for these interesting books . . . but to no purpose."
So have I.

12. Five of Stearns' sermons were printed, two exist in manuscript and one is quoted
at length in a later source, *Collections of the Massachusetts Historical Society*, vol. 3 of
the second series (Boston: 1815), pp. 283–84. There is, in addition, a reference to another
sermon, *The prospect of War, an elegy . . .* , in Joseph Sabin, *Bibliotheca Americana: A
dictionary of books relating to America from its discovery to the present time. Begun by
Joseph Sabin, continued by Wilberforce Eames and completed by R.W.G. Vail, for the
Bibliographical Society of America* (New York: William Erwin Rudge, Printer, 1868–
1936, 29 vols.), (1932–1933), 23: 9087.

13. *A sermon, delivered before the convention of Congregational ministers in Massachusetts, at their annual meeting in Boston, June 1, 1815. By Charles Stearns, D.D.,
pastor of the Church of Christ in Lincoln* (Boston: Charles Callender, 1815), p. 13. See
also *A sermon delivered at Concord, before the Bible Society, in the County of Middlesex,
Massachusetts, 26 April 1815. By Charles Stearns, D.D., pastor of the Church of Christ
in Lincoln* (Cambridge: Hilliard & Metcalf, [1815]), pp. 8–9.

14. *A sermon, at the interment of Mrs. Phebe Foster, consort to the Rev. Edmund*

Foster, preached at Littleton, July 17, 1812. By Rev. Charles Stearns, D.D., Pastor of the Church and Congregation in Lincoln (Boston: Joshua Belcher [1812]), p. 9. See also *A sermon preached November 11, 1806, at the interment of the Hon. Eleazar Brooks, Esq. By Charles Stearns, minister of Lincoln* (Cambridge: William Hilliard, 1807), pp. [3]–4.

15. *Congregational Ministers* sermon, p. 13. Compare with: "There is not a single Appetite or Passion of those arising from the flesh, which is not capable of destroying us; if we give up ourselves to its headstrong impulse," in Stearns' "The Christian's victory: A sermon occasioned by the death of Deacon Samuel Farrar. Preached at Lincoln 1783" (an incomplete MS., n. pag.).

16. *Principles of religion and morality. In three parts. I. Of the evidence of religion. II. Principles of religion. III. Principles of morality; with four lessons on the cardinal virtues. The whole in short lessons, in the form of dialogues; adapted to schools and private instruction in families. By Charles Stearns* (Leominster [Mass.]: Printed by John Prentiss & Co., for the author, 1797), p. iii. According to Stearns, the Rev. Packard had written a collection of dialogues for young children. Stearns' collection was intended for "persons whose minds are nearly arrived at maturity."

17. *Principles*, p. 32.

18. *the ladies' philosophy of love. A poem in four cantos. By Charles Stearns, A.B. . . . Now first published according to act of congress* (Leominster [Mass.]: Printed by John Prentiss & Co., for the author, 1797), preface, p. iv.

19. Ibid., p. [iii].

20. Ibid., p. [iii].

21. Ibid., p. 16. Stearns expands on "the moral qualities which render women amicable in the view of men" in a footnote. They are "good temper, kindness, sensibility, discernment of merit, chastity, compliance with discretion, modesty, genius, spirit, ease of manners, with innocence of heart, prudence in language, sprightliness, and a disposition to contentment—These are all, except genius, attainable qualities. . . . "

22. Ibid., pp. 18, 19.

23. Ibid., pp. 21, 22. Other "personal and external accomplishments" are: "reading, pronunciation, writing, music, dancing, ceremony, delicacy of speech, good breeding, neatness of person, avoidance of base arts, and delicacy of person, taste in dress, easy mode of conversing with men." Pp. 33–34.

24. Ibid., p. 23.

25. Ibid., p. 28. Also: "A dress curtailed, and bosom wide displayed / Denote the misery of a failing maid." P. 27.

26. Ibid., p. 22. "There is scarcely any part of instruction in which ladies are more apt to lose patience than on the correcting of their pronunciation." P. 22.

27. Ibid., p. [35].

28. Ibid., p. [51].

29. Ibid., p. 8.

30. Ibid., p. iv.

31. Ibid., p. iii. The poem *the ladies' philosophy of love* gave Stearns some reputation as a poet. Dr. Oliver Wendell Holmes remembered having, as a boy, seen "bulky Charles Stearns of Lincoln, author of 'The Ladies' Philosophy of Love, A Poem 1797.' How I stared at him! He was the first living person ever pointed out to me as a poet." Quoted in *Proceedings*, footnote to p. 71. But that reputation was not all good. At the time Stearns was given his honorary doctorate, a contemporary wrote of him: "[He] opened

an academy and published a book of nonsense which ruined his finances. His politics have repaired his literary reputation, but he is a man of no extraordinary claims.'' Bentley III, p. 537, in Shipton, "Shipton's Notes."

32. *the ladies' philosophy of love*, pp. [iii], iv.

33. "It may be said that some of the pieces cannot pretend to originality—That there is a resemblence between 'The Triumph of Temper' and Shakespeare's 'Taming of the Shrew;' between the 'Father of a Family[']—and the 'Pere de Famille' of Diederot [*sic*]. That the 'Little Box' is partly taken from the Cistellaria and partly from the 'Poenus' of Plautus—That the 'Captive' favours strongly of the 'Capteivi' [*sic*] or the last mentioned author. That the 'Orphan of China' has been better dramatized by Voltaire and Dr. Murphy. That the discontented wife, is but the enlargement of the 'Uxor Mempsigamos' of Erasmus. The author will deny nothing of this; but say that he has given those pieces a cast better fitted for schools than their originals, and they are so far new he believes that there is not a correspondent page between his book and any other now in print.'' *Dramatic Dialogues for use of schools. By Charles Stearns, A.M. pastor of the church and preceptor of the liberal school in Lincoln* (Leominster [Mass.]: John Prentiss & Co., 1798), preface, p. 30.

34. *Proceedings,* pp. 70–71.

35. *Dramatic Dialogues,* "A Woman of Honor," p. [33].

36. *Dramatic Dialogues,* "The Maid of Groves," p. 209.

37. Ibid., p. 204.

38. Ibid., p. 207.

39. Ibid., p. 215.

40. *Dramatic Dialogues,* "The Mother of a Family," p. 99.

41. *Dramatic Dialogues,* "The Wooden Boy," p. 330.

42. *Dramatic Dialogues,* "The Coquette," p. 221.

43. *Dramatic Dialogues,* "The Maid of Groves," pp. 208–9.

44. *Dramatic Dialogues,* introduction, p. 9.

45. Ibid., p. 10.

46. Ibid., pp. 12, 13. He was also sensitive to the feelings of his students. "To avoid [he wrote] giving offence by distributing the parts; take notice how many performers you have, and let the single pieces be considered. Let each student who desires it have nearly as many lines to speak, as they who perform the single pieces—the least offensive way of disposing of the single pieces which are considered as most *honorary* because in them the whole attention of the audience is turned to the speaker—is to dispose of them in the school by *ballot*. Let the students ballot for the persons to perform them—while the preceptor holds a negative upon their choice in case they choose wrong—In this way all odium of impartiality is avoided. . . . And it is a good exercise to train them to act the part of judicious electors in a free state." Pp. 14–15.

47. Ibid., p. 10.

48. *Dramatic Dialogues,* "The Spring for Flowers," p. 263.

49. *Dramatic Dialogues,* "The Insolvable Question," p. 235.

50. *Dramatic Dialogues,* "The Discontented Wife," pp. 270–71.

51. *Dramatic Dialogues,* introduction, p. [7].

52. Ibid.

53. Ibid., p. 24.

54. Ibid., p. 25. "The first exhibition was given September 27, 1793, Misses Anna Harrington, Hannah Fiske and Sussanah Hoar being assigned the highest parts. The

innovation of allowing young ladies to speak in public caused considerable discussion and some censure. If any other in Middlesex County led the way of allowing young ladies to speak in public on stage, let it be proclaimed. If any one knows of any evils arising from the custom inaugurated here, let him cry out." Hurd, *History of Middlesex County*, p. 632.

BIBLIOGRAPHY

Stearns' Sermons (Chronologically)

[*The prospect of war, an elegy addressed to Mr. Israel Keith. By Mr. Charles Stearns*] N. Pag., 1774. Folio, p. 3. Dated Oct. 14, 1774. From the Heartman catalogue for a sale of October 4, 1923, lot no. 48. Cited in Sabin, *Bibliotheca Americana*, p. 9087

"The Christian's Victory, A Sermon occasioned by the death of Deacon Samuel Farrar. Preach'd at Lincoln, 1783." MS. Incomplete.

Sermon: Preached at an exhibition of sacred musick in Lincoln on the nineteenth of April 1792. By Charles Stearns, A.M., Pastor of the church in Lincoln. Boston: Isaiah Thomas & Ebenezer T. Andrews, 1792.

"Copy of a sermon preached at the Dudleian lecture at the University in Cambridge, Sept. 2d, 1801." MS. Dudleian Lecture, Harvard University, 1801. At head of title, "1801."

A sermon preached November 11, 1806, at the interment of the Hon. Eleazar Brooks, Esq. By Charles Stearns, minister of Lincoln. Cambridge: William Hilliard, 1807.

[Sermon preached at the funeral of Rev. Dr. Cushing, January, 1809]. Boston: 1815. Quoted in part in *Collections of the Massachusetts Historical Society*, Second Series, vol. 3. pp. 283–84.

A sermon, at the interment of Mrs. Phebe Foster, consort to the Rev. Edmund Foster, preached at Littleton, July 17th, 1812. By Charles Stearns, D.D., Pastor of the Church and Congregation in Lincoln. Boston: Joshua Belcher, [1812].

A sermon delivered at Concord, before the Bible Society, in the County of Middlesex, Massachusetts, 26 April, 1815. By Charles Stearns, D.D., pastor of the Church of Christ in Lincoln. Cambridge: Hilliard & Metcalf, [1815].

A sermon, delivered before the Convention of Congregational ministers in Massachusetts, at their annual meeting in Boston, June 1, 1815. By Charles Stearns, D.D., pastor of the Church of Christ in Lincoln. Boston: Charles Callender, 1815.

Stearns' Other Writings (Chronologically)

the ladies' philosophy of love. A poem, in four cantos. By Charles Stearns, A.B. . . . .Now first published according to an act of congress. Leominster, [Mass.]: Printed by John Prentiss & Co., for the author, 1797.

Principles of religion and morality. In three parts. I. Of the evidences of religion. II. Principles of religion. III. Principles of morality; with four lessons on the cardinal virtues. The whole in short lessons, in the form of dialogues; adapted to schools, and private instruction in families. By Charles Stearns. . . . Leominster, [Mass.]: Printed by Charles & John Prentiss for the author, 1798. 2nd ed., Amherst,

Newhampshire: Printed by Samuel Preston—for the author, 1799. 3rd ed., Portsmouth, [New Hampshire]: Printed for the author, 1806. 3rd ed. improved, Portsmouth, [New Hampshire]: Printed for the author, 1807.

Dramatic dialogues for the use of schools. By Charles Stearns, A.M., pastor of the church and preceptor of the liberal school in Lincoln. Leominster, [Mass.]: John Prentiss, & Co., for the author, 1798.

Secondary Sources

Adams, Zabdiel. *The bishop's office a good work. A sermon preached at the ordination of the rev. Mr. Charles Stearns, to the pastoral care of the church in Lincoln, November 7, 1781. By Zabdiel Adams.* Commonwealth of Massachusetts: T. & J. Fleet, 1782.

American Academy of Arts and Sciences, Records of. Vol. 1. MS.

Appleton's cyclopedia of American biography.

The Boston Atheneum, vol. 5, 1888.

Chandler, Charles Henry (with the assistance of Sarah Fiske Lee). *The History of New Ipswich, New Hampshire, 1735–1914 with genealogical records of the principal families.* Fitchburg, [Mass.]: Sentinel Printing Co., 1914.

Harvard University Archives, Pusey Library, Cambridge, MA.

Hurd, D. Hamilton, ed. *History of Middlesex County, Massachusetts, with biographical sketches of many of its prominent men.* Philadelphia: J. W. Lewis & Co., 1890. 3 vols. Vol. 2.

Index to the probate records of the County of Middlesex, Massachusetts, 1648–1876. Cambridge: 1914.

Lincoln, Massachusetts, Town records from 1746–1810.

Lincoln, Massachusetts, Town meeting records from 1754–1806.

Lincoln vital records to the year 1850. Boston: New England Historic Genealogical Society, 1908.

New England Historic Genealogical Society.

Porter, Rev. E. S. "Sermon at Lincoln, MA, 4/9/1898," p. 15. Harvard University Archives.

Probate Court Record of the estate of Charles Stearns, September fifth, 1826 (microfilm).

Proceedings in observance of the one hundred and fiftieth anniversary of the organization of the first church in Lincoln, Massachusetts, August 21 to September 4, 1898. Cambridge: The University Press, 1899.

[Sabin, Joseph]. *Bibliotheca Americana: A dictionary of books relating to America from its discovery to the present time. Begun by Joseph Sabin, continued by Wilberforce Eames and completed by R.W.G. Vail, for the Bibliographic Society of America.* New York: William Erwin Rudge, Printer, 1868–1936. 29 vols. Vol. 23 (1932–1933).

Shipton, Clifford Kenyon. "Shipton's notes for *Sibley's Harvard Graduates.*" Massachusetts Historical Society.

Sprague, William B., ed. *Annals of the American Pulpit. . . .* New York: Robert Carter & Brothers, 1865. Vol. 8.

Van Wegenen, Avis Stearns. *Genealogy and memoirs of Charles and Nathaniel Stearns, and their descendents.* Syracuse, [New York]: Courier Printing Co., 1901. 2 vols. Vol. 2.

3

Theatre for Young Audiences in New York City, 1900–1910: A Heritage of Jolly Productions

Laura Gardner Salazar

Many elements came together in the first decade of this century to raise the profile of theatre for young audiences. The climate was right economically, socially and artistically for theatre for youth to flower; and flower it did. But the theatrical activities engendered were often frivolous and superficial, traits that, for some, became synonymous with children's theatre.

During Easter week in 1900, an adult in New York had the choice of amusing a child at seven different shows recommended by the *New York Times: Jack and the Giant*; *Kindergarten*; *Rip Van Winkle*; Buffalo Bill's Wild West Show; Forepaugh and Sells Brothers Circus; some "clever artists" at Keith's; or Linus II, the equine wonder, at Huber's Museum. From 1900 to 1910, theatre was a place for personal pleasure on the most festive occasions; and dramatic activities in stately mansions or humble halls provided a time to dress in finery, to laugh and to be awed by the magic of entertainment.

Children often celebrated birthdays at the theatre, and several such parties were unusual enough to be noted in the daily papers. Richard Bernard, son of the actor Sam Bernard, asked to have his fifth birthday party on stage following a performance by his father. The wish was granted; and young Richard dined with fifty of his friends, while all of the children in the audience went home with a stick of candy.[1]

Wealthy parents could even summon performances to their own mansions. On March 20, 1908, sixty of little Miss Ava Astor's friends saw *Cinderella up to Date* performed by a group of young society people, who brought the performance, complete with scenery and costumes, to her home from their hotel theatre at the Waldorf Astoria.[2] The Claflins surprised their daughter a week later by smuggling into their house the same troupe, who arrived in a motor car, with costumes under their regular clothing, to perform *The Trundle Bed Cruise*.[3]

Pantomime, a particularly frivolous form of entertainment, became very popular in this country during the nineteenth century:

Perhaps most lavish in their scenic display were the fairy tale plays such as *Aladdin* or *Cherry* and *Fair Star*, which had long and repeated runs throughout the period. *Cinderella* was put on so often that a critic jested, "even rats and mice have become as scarce as pumpkins in the increased demand for the materials whereof fairy coaches and their establishments are made."[4]

For many years, managers considered pantomimes appropriate only for adults and produced them as after-pieces to other theatre attractions. By 1820, pantomimes occasionally ran separately as Christmas features. Between 1806 and 1820, most popular children's stories were "pantomimed," and children, in turn, attended these presentations.[5]

Abounding in special effects and transformations by entortilationists,[6] pantomime's appeals to children were many. The Hanon-Lee Company, which toured England and the United States, used twelve different kinds of trap doors, allowing them to perform such tricks as walking upside down.[7] Eventually, a set formula for pantomime developed:

There must be songs, there must be a ballet; there should be some sufficient reproduction of a fairy tale to be recognizable to the children, there should be scope for the impossible, the absurd, the grotesque and there should be a full stage and plenty of spectacle. The songs should be tuneful, the dances should be exhibitions of grace and skill, the ballet should be a harmony of movement. The transformation scene should be as beautiful as it can be made. Above all, the drollery should be droll and the fun should be funny.[8]

Often playwrights would feel obligated to make the pantomime "educational," but the emphasis was always on good fun. Producers usually hired large theatres, and held children enthralled with "elaborate scenery, pretty girls, striking costumes, and bright catchy music."[9]

By the beginning of the twentieth century, pantomime in the United States generally went by the new name of "extravaganza" or "spectacle." *Sleeping Beauty and the Beast,* a "fairy extravaganza," opened in November 1901 and ran through May 1902.[10] The play was revived in September 1904, and again in September 1905.[11] A production of the favorite, *Humpty Dumpty*, came from Drury Lane, London, on November 14, 1904, with a cast of two hundred, fifty of whom were children.[12] It was revived again in March 1906, just in time for Easter.[13] The popular *Mr. Blue Beard*, a 1903 English import, was called a "joy for children of all ages," with colored lights and many girls in tights.[14] Other spectacles presented during the decade were *Mother Goose* and *The Pearl and the Pumpkin*.

A second popular form of entertainment for children was a further development of the extravaganza called a "musical." These shows played in large theatres such as the Majestic. They opened in time for the holiday crowds and offered special matinees for children. Seven major Broadway hits during the decade fall into this classification: *The Wizard of Oz*, *Babes in Toyland*, *Buster Brown*, *Little Nemo*, *The Pied Piper*, *The Top o' th' World* and *The Red Mill*.

The Wizard of Oz was a typical example of this new family musical. L. Frank Baum wrote the book and lyrics with the music by Paul Tietjens and A. B. Sloane. It opened on June 16, 1902, at the Grand Opera House, Chicago, and played to an audience of 185,000 people in fourteen weeks, grossing $160,000.[15] The producers' aim was to devise an entertainment which would appeal to playgoers of all ages and all degrees of intellect, "to precocious juveniles and senile cynics as well."[16] The play opened in New York on January 20, 1903, at the Majestic. It played there to full houses for the season and returned in 1904. Attendance was as good as it had been the year before, and, because hundreds had to be turned away even then, the producers ran it the whole summer at the New York Theatre. Seats sold at the high price of $1.50.[17] In October 1904 the play reopened at the Academy of Music in Brooklyn [18] and was revived again in 1905 at the West End Theatre.[19]

Although producers made changes in the Baum story to amuse the "tired businessmen," a 1903 advertisement urged parents to "Bring your children."[20] The adaptation emphasized romantic comedy, making Dorothy a young woman, old enough to be the object of romance. The tin woodman fell in love with a lady lunatic, and a fetching chorus of girls in tights played the Wizard's army in Oz. But farce did not totally give way to romance, for a pet cow replaced Dorothy's familiar dog, Toto. In addition to the lovely chorus, the interesting music and flashy costumes, *The Wizard of Oz* depended upon the same sort of transformations as the pantomimes of old:

> The vivisection of the Scarecrow and his piecing together again constitutes one of the most diverting features of "The Wizard of Oz," at the new Majestic Theatre. This occurs in the last act of the play. . . . This illusion which, of course, emanated from the fecund stage manager, Julian Mitchell, evokes alternate gasps of astonishment and shrieks of laughter from young and old alike. The trick of the thing antedated . . . all necromancers of the last score of years. But the simplicity of the whole illusion doubtless enhances its effectiveness.[21]

The *New York Times* review of January 21 spoke of the pink and red settings, cyclones and snowstorms. Stone and Montgomery, as the scarecrow and the tin man, "cleverly made musical nonsense," while the rest of the musical, the writer claimed, was "brilliant and snappy."[22] There can be no doubt, diversion was the primary object of those who put this show together.

Throughout the decade, a variety of producers tried to match the success of *The Wizard of Oz*. *The Red Mill* of 1906 was one such copy. It too starred the vaudeville team, Montgomery and Stone, with music by Victor Herbert, composer of *Babes in Toyland*.[23] On May 15, 1907, its success assured, *The Red Mill* celebrated its three hundredth performance by presenting women and children in the audience with colored photos of the Dutch Kiddies at play.[24]

Another musical venture, *The Top o' th' World,* opened in October 1907 at the Majestic. The producer hailed this extravaganza as a new *Wizard of Oz.* Although less successful at the box office than earlier musicals, the very existence of *The Top o' th' World* illustrates the persistence of the professional theatre to satisfy the American passion for merrymaking.

The 1908 musical version of *The Pied Piper* was a resounding hit. It opened to an enthusiastic audience on December 3, just in time for the holiday season. The holiday performances of *The Pied Piper* provided a party atmosphere. On Christmas day about four hundred children, including one hundred from the Hebrew Orphan Asylum, attended a free performance at the theatre, where there was a Christmas tree with presents for all. Each child received a plaster figurine of DeWolf Hopper as the piper, either an apple or an orange and a toy. Produced especially for the holiday audience, this performance began with a scene from the musical and continued with a skit by composer Manuel Klein, entitled "An Afternoon with the Fairies." It featured such characters as Puss-in-Boots, the genie from *Aladdin*, Snow Drop, Jack Horner, Cinderella and others. Much of the play's appeal derived from the star, DeWolf Hopper, who wished to have all children, whatever their circumstance, see plays which they could enjoy. Hopper not only played the piper for children in New York, but later toured his zany character to theatres, hospitals and orphanages across the United States.[25]

Contemporary critical reviews were mixed. The *New York Times* critic recommended the show, but the reviewer for *Theatre Magazine* lamented the emphasis on empty fun:

> The thoughtful spectator doubtless felt, as he heard and saw the well-conceived and poetic prologue and the delightful first scene, that he was about to behold a rarely dainty version of the delightful legend. But with the appearance of the airship's owner and crew he gave himself up with a sigh to the same hackneyed devices, the same noisy vaudeville that seems so inevitable a part of the so-called comedy nowadays.[26]

The plot alone exemplifies the frivolity and plain silliness of the production. The story takes place in fabled Hamelin, scene of the original. It is 1908, but the village has changed very little in the 365 years since the children were piped away. The children have been returned by Father Time who, as a condition of returning them, strikes a bargain with the piper, the adults and the children of Hamelin: if they all remain pure and innocent, Father Time will allow them eternal life. The play opens on "marriage day," but one young woman in the village has no mate to marry. The piper solves that problem by piping a young American aviator and his cook and mechanic out of the sky. This causes complications, as the cook teaches the village girls how to wiggle when they walk and encourages the piper to drink too much champagne.

Father Time finally appears, frightening the bold cook, Lizzie, into confessing that it is she who has caused trouble in paradise. Good naturedly, Father Time agrees that the piper is an innocent victim of Lizzie's tricks. The town will be spared. The hero, with his pipes in working order, plays everyone, even the modern intruders, back to innocence; and the young people fall in love as they should have done in the first place. The theatre has rarely seen a more poorly written plot, with its emphasis on pure distraction; but in its time, *The Pied Piper* was considered quite suitable for the younger set.

In their search for fun, playwrights also adapted comic strips for the stage. The first of these, *Foxy Grandpa* (1901), was based on the popular comic of the same name:

That "Foxy Grandpa," who long since endeared himself to every youngster would eventually find his way from the newspaper comic supplements to the stage was a foregone conclusion. Mr. R. Melville Baker, taking the cartoons for his ground material, has made an amusing hodge-podge, which goes with snap and furnishes an evening of capital entertainment. Indeed it is a long time since the old Fourteenth Street Theatre has housed such a popular sucess.[27]

Buster Brown, also based on a popular comic strip, appeared in 1905. The *New York Times* reviewer noted that this production included "many spectacular features calculated to please the children."[28]

Tony Pastor, the showman credited with inventing vaudeville, devised that form specifically for the family audience. It is not surprising to see him continue to advertise his productions for young audiences well into the twentieth century. Children seemed mesmerized by vaudeville's charms, and many of them attended vaudeville unaccompanied by an adult. This was such a common practice that a *New York Times* reporter thought it amusing when an eleven-year-old boy went alone to see trained animals, but mistakenly got into a theatre where a serious play was housed. The newspaper captured the boy's disappointment through the headline, "Real Tragedy for the Boy."[29]

Pastor's vaudeville Christmas parties for stage children were a holiday tradition dating back to 1887. Pastor invited the public to these events, which always included a "Christmas tree"[30] and performances by his actors' children—a kind of try-out for future thespians. Not to be outdone by Pastor, other theatres followed suit, providing gifts to young patrons at their special Christmas matinees. For example, in 1905, actors at Proctor's theatre distributed one thousand presents to children—tops to boys and doll furniture to girls.[31]

The most popular and influential children's play in this decade was James Barrie's *Peter Pan*. Americans had been hearing about this play since it opened in 1904, and anxiously awaited the New York production. When the play opened in October 1905, in Washington, D.C., the *New York Times* reviewer wrote that he thought that the play was not for children.[32] But when it finally did open in New York, on November 6, 1905, children and youth had different ideas. The play's popularity was astonishing. And Maude Adams went on to appear in this play every year from 1905 to 1916, either in New York or on the road. This popular play, about which much has been written, has been performed repeatedly throughout this century. But its well-documented success during this decade did little to change the prevailing practices, and producers continued to explore a variety of frivolous theatre activities for young people.

The management of the Hippodrome, a gigantic vaudeville theatre, developed special matinees at 3:00 P.M. to encourage after-school attendance.[33] The *New York Times* described the kind of shows the Hippodrome offered to children at its opening in 1905:

The Hippodrome's popularity knows no diminution. Twice daily the crowds flock to the big playhouse to witness "The Romance of the Hindu Princess," and "A Yankee Circus on Mars." The climax of the East Indian spectacle, when the elephants plunge and the rout of the abduction of a Princess is complete, is a startling piece of stage realism. [34]

That the circus has always emphasized entertainment needs no documentation, and children loved the delights of the circus then as now. During the early part of this century, circuses had many characteristics in common with the drama: pantomimes, dances, singing, and something called "Melodrama" (skits with music); and most of these characteristics persisted well into the twentieth century. Buffalo Bill's Wild West Show had the same visual appeal as the circus; and although crude as drama, the action had a loose story line. Daily newspapers praised the content of the show and recommended it heartily for children, saying that it was as decorous as a Sunday school and more interesting than any circus. Adults saw it as an important attempt to preserve a unique time in American history. [35] Children thrilled to the sight of William Cody, their real-live hero:

[T]he small boys turned out in the 100's to do him honor. . . . No hero returning from war ever got more adulation from the youth of the city than this famous scout received yesterday. . . . Throughout the line of march, crowds of small boys clustered around Col. Cody like bees around a watermelon.[36]

This parade took place on a Monday morning, when children are usually in school studying. Obviously some adults thought the Wild West Show had as important a lesson to teach as an instructor in a classroom.

At this time, all manner of silly shows appeared for young people's delight. Promoters, social workers and ethnic organizations sponsored baby parades; and dime museums and the ocean boardwalk theatres presented pastimes for children in the summers on an irregular basis. One boardwalk production in 1903 offered the following:

Youngsters were in complete possession last night at Pain's Amphitheatre, Manhattan Beach, on the occasion of the first "children's night" of the season. A new feature was a high dive similar to one last season. A cock fight and a "Punch and Judy" show were among the funny stunts especially prepared for the children.[37]

Festivals of all kinds also developed, as pageantry and amateur theatricals for children became more frequent. Costume fetes for settlement children gained popularity, as did the annual Brooklyn children's Sunday school parade, which, in 1908, included an estimated 150,000 children.[38]

Even politicians provided frivolity for New York's children in hopes of winning votes. In 1905, Matthew F. Donahue treated 4,500 men, women and children from his district to a variety show at the Hippodrome. [39] That same year, Mrs. Clarence MacKay of Roslyn, Long Island, a candidate for trustee of the school board, treated five hundred children to a Punch and Judy show, food and games.[40] The following summer she gave a party with "exercises" and a moving picture.[41]

Theatre managers, actors and civic leaders cited the beauty, laughter and excitement of theatre as a balm for the pains of the world. Thus, wherever sick, sad or poor children gathered, actors appeared to cheer them up.[42] In 1900 alone, the Buffalo Bill Wild West Show played to 4,000 New York orphans.[43]

This was the age of the flowering of philanthropy, and society women developed many amusements to ease the burden of poverty among New York's poor. One organization that they founded was called "The Little Mothers," a club for young girls who stayed home from school to care for their younger brothers and sisters while their parents worked. At Easter, the socialites gave new bonnets to the girls. During other times of the year they offered the girls classes, parties and trips to the country. They also provided an annual theatrical event for the children. On Saturday, June 16, 1900, they treated the girls to an amusing performance by some young people from Brooklyn at the Little Mother's camp, a few miles from New York City:

> It was a most exciting play, all about a poet . . . who had only one chop for dinner for himself and his pretty young wife. . . . But the best part of it was where the young wife became jealous at this, and, putting her head down on the table, cried as if her heart would break. To cry because some one went off to leave her all of the chop! The children thought that was the funniest thing they had ever heard, and they laughed heartily all through the crying scene, and the little Armenian girl [to whom the reporter spoke] laughed harder than all the rest, and said that was the best part of the day.[44]

Although the women in charge of The Little Mothers may not have intended to provide merriment in the pork chop scene, the children certainly seemed trained to look for the comic, and to use it for recreation and restoration.

Occasionally actors themselves organized a special performance to tour to underprivileged, handicapped or sick children. A group of Cohen and Harris' talents planned a show for the children of the Hebrew orphanages in 1908.[45] On April 22 of the same year, the Plaza Theatre actors arranged a special performance and a "chocolate party for little consumptives."[46]

Settlement houses, designed to integrate the great masses of immigrants into the mainstream of American life, and run by a growing population of educated women, looked to theatre as a painless and witty way of presenting the lessons they needed to teach. Settlement houses sponsored semiprofessional theatre companies and developed drama programs for young people. Pageants also became a part of their programming. A typical performance occurred in 1909 on Jones Street in New York, where the Greenwich House sponsored a May festival. It was based on the Robin Hood myth and featured sixty of the neighborhood children. The performance followed months of rehearsing dances, tumbling, play fighting and winding the Maypole. Settlement house musicians played a piano and violin on the sidewalk, while the crowd on the street watched. The celebration went beyond the performance, as the tiny actors retired to the garden behind Greenwich House for ice cream.[47]

Theatre captured the imagination of children of the era, so much so that New York urchins passionately, and sometimes illegally, made their own theatre. In 1907 a group of newsboys set up an impromptu minstrel show while waiting for their papers to come off the press. Since this violated a city ordinance forbidding street performance, police broke up the show. [48] Two years later a boy entered a temporarily closed theatre and invited his friends to a great show of amateur acts. The police closed this performance, also.[49]

Critics concurred with parents and youth: theatre for children had to be jolly and not too complex. The entertainment value of a piece was the ultimate criterion for judging a production for children: the sillier the piece, the more the children would like it. In recommending Charles Klein's *Stepsister* for children, the *New York Times* critic said it was an ''agreeable little entertainment for people willing to overlook all sorts of implausibility.''[50] A columnist in *Theatre Magazine* wrote that *Top' 'o th' World* was especially appropriate for youth because it was ''well acted, novel, amusing, fun making, and free from vulgarity''; plus, it ''took place in Santa-Claus land.''[51]

Throughout the first decade of the century the entertainments devised for young people in New York City were fashioned to enliven and delight, whether spectacle, musical, vaudeville, pageant or show. Whether for the rich or the needy, the theatre provided charming escapism. Be it blessing or curse, this is part of the heritage of theatre for children in the United States.

NOTES

1. ''To Have a Stage Birthday Party,'' *New York Times*, March 23, 1908, p. 7, col. 4; and ''Had a Stage Birthday Party,'' *New York Times*, April 5, 1908, pt. 2, p. 11, col. 3.

2. ''Little Miss Astor Gives Birthday Party,'' *New York Times*, March 20, 1908, p. 7, col. 1.

3. ''Birthday Party for Little Miss Claflin,'' *New York Times*, April 4, 1908, p. 9, col. 1.

4. David Grimsted, *Melodrama Unveiled: American Theatre and Culture 1800 to 1850* (Chicago: University of Chicago Press, 1968), p. 81.

5. Maurice Wilson Disher, *Blood and Thunder: Mid-Victorian Melodrama and Its Origins* (London: Frederick Muller, 1949), pp. 291–92.

6. An entortilationist is a performer of such physical agility that his movements seem to be self-torture. The term, as well as the practice, is now out of use.

7. Richard Southern, *The Victorian Theatre: A Picture Survey* (Newton Abbot: David & Charles, 1970), pp. 104–5. Although Southern is British, it should be remembered that American and English theatre had as much exchange of genre, companies and stars then as they do now.

8. A. E. Wilson, *The Story of Pantomime* (1949; rpt. London: E. P. Publishing, 1974), p. 134.

9. "Little Red Riding Hood," *New York Times,* January 9, 1900, p. 5, col. 2.

10. " 'The Sleeping Beauty.' Fairy Extravaganza Produced at the Broadway Theatre," *New York Times,* November 5, 1901, p. 7, col. 1. The closing date can be found in an advertisement in the *New York Times,* May 26, 1902, pt. 2, p. 17, col. 5.

11. "Amusements Last Night," *New York Times*, September 20, 1904, p. 9, col. 3. "At the Theatres Yesterday," *New York Times,* September 5, 1905, p. 7, col. 2.

12. "New 'Humpty Dumpty' Is a Riot of Color," *New York Times*, November 15, 1904, p. 6, col. 2.

13. "Humpty Dumpty Revived," *New York Times*, March 13, 1906, p. 9, col. 1.

14. " 'Mr. Blue Beard' on Broadway," *New York Times,* January 22, 1903, p. 9, col. 1. This was the play showing on the day of the infamous Iroquois Theatre fire in Chicago, 1906, in which over five hundred died. One of the most shocking things about the disaster was that it took place during the Christmas season, and the victims were families seeking amusement and holiday fun.

15. David L. Green and Dick Martin, *The Oz Scrapbook* (New York: Random House, 1977), pp. 124, 178.

16. Souvenir Program of *The Wizard of Oz*, from Townsend Walsh Collection, New York Public Library.

17. " 'Wizard of Oz' to Broadway," *New York Times*, April 17, 1904, p. 9, col. 1.

18. "Notes of the Theatre," *New York Times*, October 30, 1904, p. 20, col. 6. There seems to be some discrepancy as to whether Stone or Montgomery got top billing, as the *New York Times* lists both names first on different occasions.

19. "Combination Houses," *New York Times*, September 17, 1905, pt. 3, p. 10, col. 3.

20. "Wizard of Oz" Advertisement, *New York Times*, January 25, 1903, p. 14, col. 5.

21. "Stageland Odds and Ends," *New York Times*, May 31, 1903, p. 10, col. 2.

22. "The Wizard of Oz," *New York Times*, January 21, 1903, p. 9, col. 1.

23. "This Week's Offerings," *New York Times*, September 23, 1906, pt. 3, p. 8, col. 3.

24. "Amusement Notes," *New York Times,* May 16, 1907, p. 7, col. 3.

25. "Hopper at the Majestic," *New York Times*, December 4, 1908, p. 11, col. 4.

26. "New Plays of the Month," *Theatre Magazine,* 9, No. 95 (1909), p. xiii.

27. Unidentified Clipping, Clipping File for *Foxy Grandpa*, Museum of the City of New York.

28. "This Week on the New York Stage," *New York Times*, January 22, 1905, Sunday magazine, p. 3, col. 1.

29. "Real Tragedy for the Boy," *New York Times*, December 28, 1902, Sunday supplement, p. 2, col. 3.

30. To "have a Christmas tree" at the turn of the century included the act of presenting gifts.

31. "Santa Claus in a Theatre," *New York Times*, December 25, 1905, p. 7, col. 2.

32. "For Believers in Fairies," *New York Times*, October 18, 1905, p. 11, col. 1.

33. "Theatrical Notes," *New York Times*, April 15, 1905, p. 11, col. 3.

34. "The Hippodrome," *New York Times*, November 5, 1905, pt. 4, p. 4, col. 3.

35. William Deahl, "A History of Buffalo Bill's Wild West Shows, 1883 to 1913," Ph. D. diss., Southern Illinois University, 1974.

36. "Buffalo Bill's Parade," *New York Times*, April 2, 1901, p. 9, col. 1.

37. "Gossip of the Player Folk," *New York Times*, July 21, 1903, p. 9, col. 3.

38. "150,000 Children March in Parade," *New York Times*, June 5, 1908, p. 3, col. 1.

39. "4500 in Theatre Party," *New York Times*, June 3, 1905, p. 9, col. 5.

40. "Mrs. Mackay Entertains Over 500 Children," *New York Times*, June 18, 1905, pt. 1, p. 7, col. 3.

41. In all likelihood these "exercises" consisted of an orator, scene or poetry reading. "For Good Children Only," *New York Times*, February 21, 1906, p. 3, col. 4.

42. DeWolf Hopper delighted in his ability to make unfortunates laugh. When he played for five hundred children at a Jewish Orphan Asylum in Cleveland in 1909, he noted that people who cannot pay deserve good amusement too. William E. Sage, "Making Little Children Laugh," *Cleveland Leader*, March 13, 1909, n. pag. DeWolf Hopper Scrapbook, Theatre Collection, New York Public Library.

43. "Orphans at Wild West," *New York Times*, May 2, 1900, p. 9, col. 3.

44. "Little Mothers Waiters," *New York Times*, June 17, 1900, p. 4, col. 3.

45. "Actors to Play for Hebrew Orphans," *New York Times*, March 10, 1908, p. 8, col. 4.

46. "Chocolate Party for Little Invalids," *New York Times*, April 10, 1908, p. 9, col. 1.

47. Zona Gale, "Robin Hood on Jones Street," *Outlook*, 92 (June 26, 1909), pp. 439–46. For more information on this movement see Percival Chubb, *Festivals and Plays in Schools and Elsewhere* (New York: Harper Brothers, 1912).

48. "The Sidewalk Minstrels," *New York Times*, September 13, 1907, Sunday supplement, p. 11, col. 2.

49. "Boy Opens Up a Theatre," *New York Times*, April 2, 1909, p. 1, col. 6.

50. "Modern Variant of Cinderella Story," *New York Times*, October 15, 1907, p. 9, col. 5.

51. "At the Playhouse," *Theatre Magazine*, 7, No. 82 (1907), p. xxiii.

4

Junior League Children's Theatre: Debutantes Take the Stage

ROGER L. BEDARD

The growth and development of American children's theatre can be attributed to the work of many notable individuals and groups. Yet only one organization, the Association of Junior Leagues, can boast a children's theatre tradition that extends from the beginning of this century to the present time, a tradition of producing children's theatre that has influenced virtually every aspect of the field.

The Junior League was founded in 1901 by Mary Harriman, then a young New York socialite, who was looking for a way to organize her fellow debutantes for work in the area settlement houses. Initially known as the Junior League for the Promotion of Settlement Movements, this group began with approximately eighty members, all of whom were local debutantes. The organization grew steadily in the following years, and by 1912 there were also Junior League organizations in Brooklyn, Boston, Baltimore, Philadelphia, Chicago, Cleveland, San Francisco, Montreal and Portland (Oregon). In 1921, the Association of Junior Leagues of America, Inc. (AJLA) was formed to unite the thirty leagues then in existence.[1] By 1984 there were 258 Junior Leagues in 45 states, Canada and Mexico, with approximately 160,000 members, constituting a large and geographically widespread volunteer service and social organization.[2]

From the very beginning, each league required its members to perform volunteer social work activities, and over the years Junior Leagues have made a significant contribution in many areas of community service, including virtually all aspects of social work. Although the work required varied from group to group, many leagues elected children's theatre as an important element of community service.

The work of the first league set the tone for the activities of those that followed. This was an organization designed to provide meaningful activities for wealthy young women, who, unencumbered by professions or families, wanted to serve their community. When thrust into the settlement house world, these young women quickly learned that they had few social work skills, so they capitalized on what they believed they could do well. They used their social connections to raise money through the performance of an ''entertainment,'' and they relied upon their artistic training—required of all well-bred young women of the time— to conduct music and art classes and to provide entertainment for the kindergarten. From these simple beginnings, leagues gradually moved into virtually every facet of social service activity, and most of them also conducted elaborate training sessions to equip the new league members for this work.

Early records are scarce, but by the association's own accounts, it was a small step from musical presentations and storytelling to writing and performing plays for settlement house children. Informal children's theatre was produced by some leagues at least as early as 1912, at which time the Boston league presented seventeen performances of *Aladdin*.[3] As early as 1913 the Chicago league performed a Christmas play at a children's hospital and a settlement house.[4] The Chicago group apparently continued this tradition for several years, although, by their own account, their work was not as sophisticated as that being done by the New York league.[5] By this time the New York league had also introduced children's drama classes and drama clubs into their settlement house work.[6]

These early, sometimes tentative, ventures in children's theatre production and drama classes were a natural outgrowth of the league activities and philosophies; and they complemented the other, more traditional social work activities that the leagues also pursued. The young women were accustomed to performing—as virtually every league used a gala variety show as its major fund raiser—and, as they immersed themselves in the world of the poor, they came to see children's theatre as an alternative to the vaudeville and burlesque entertainments prevalent at the time. Also, the women working with immigrants quickly recognized the value of drama classes in helping young people learn the language and the customs of their new land.

The first major change from this rather casual approach to producing plays for children came in 1921 when the Chicago League, with the help of noted playwright and league member, Alice Gerstenberg, tackled a major children's theatre project. Gerstenberg's play, *Alice in Wonderland*, had been presented on Broadway in 1915. Although this production had been designed for adult audiences, Gerstenberg was struck by the number of young people in the audiences. Thus, in 1921, when her theatre talents were in demand by the Chicago League, she enthusiastically focused her attention on the child audience.

The newly reorganized Dramatic Committee of the Chicago League chose to produce two fully staged children's theatre productions in a regular theatre. The committee's own report suggests the importance of this new method of operation:

The Dramatic Committee, organized . . . for the production of children's plays, was a success from the start. About thirty girls signed up for it and rehearsals [sic] were immediately begun of "Alice in Wonderland" which was presented at the Playhouse Theatre for eight Saturday mornings and one matinee, the latter performance being taken over by the Radcliffe Endowment Fund.

The first play was followed by "Sara Crewe" which ran for three weeks and was taken off to give time for the filming of "Alice" by the Junior League cast.

The Dramatic Committee plunged into the precarious producing sea equipped only with the strength of courage and vision, which equipment, since the committee was without funds, without backing, without "pull," and without experience, has been proved sufficient for success. The idea of a children's theatre was made a success by the girls who signed up to see it through for they responded to the demand of frequent, long, and trying rehearsals with promptness, patience and with intelligent ability. . . .

Its work will go on . . . and will be better work since the committee now has experience, scenery and costumes, a modest bank account, and what is more important, the serious interest of the city of Chicago.[7]

This same report quotes a Chicago newspaper account that states that the Junior League "has done a bigger thing than it has any idea of."

In 1924 the members of the Chicago League voted to make theatre their "main work."[8] Within a short period of time the Chicago League progressed from an organization that occasionally presented "a little fairy play, requiring the simplest of scenic arrangements,"[9] to a group that set as the major focus of its social work activities the production of a season of plays for young audiences. No longer concerned with informal settlement-house productions, the Chicago League now focused on budgets for the design and construction of elaborate scenery and costumes, salaries for professional directors, negotiations with union stagehands, theatre rental, ticket sales and the sales of advertisements in souvenir programs.

This emphasis on large-scale productions reflected similar transitions in other leagues. While virtually no other league embraced children's theatre as completely as the Chicago League, according to an account in one history of the Junior League, "children's theatre in one form or another was the pet project of nearly every 1920's Junior League."[10]

Many leagues subsequently patterned their activities on those of the Chicago League. This included elevating children's theatre to an important place in the overall scheme of social work activities as well as emphasizing the artistic goals of theatre production. Commenting on this several years later, Gerstenberg noted:

From its inception the theatre for children was intended to rank creditably with those many Little Art Theatres which have become a significant and vital part of the dramatic life of all countries today. The young and uninformed members entering the League must not look upon it as just a show for children for fun and charity. Those executive few chosen as leaders must inform themselves as to what has been going on in the world in the history of drama for the last quarter of a century and link their theatre creditably to the best of the day. . . .

The Junior League Children's Theatre must stand for more than charity, for more than the fun of play and self-expression; it has a spiritual obligation toward the grown-up audience of the future.[11]

This heightened seriousness of purpose brought an awareness of the lack of information available about literature and techniques appropriate for children's theatre; and it was left to the Chicago League to attempt to answer this need.

At the spring 1926 AJLA conference, the Chicago League invited all leagues with a children's theatre to attend a meeting to be held the following winter. The first national children's theatre meeting was held on December 3, 1926. Representatives from leagues in Detroit, Cincinnati, Buffalo, Brooklyn, Colum-bus, St. Louis and Kansas City met to discuss common problems and concerns. These included the need for a national "headquarters of children's plays," the possibility of an interchange of scenery and costumes and the problem of locating new plays. As a result of this conference, the Chicago League established a Bureau of Information to compile statistics and to facilitate communication about children's theatre among the leagues.[12]

In 1927, in response to the growth of children's theatre activities among the leagues throughout the country, a children's theatre column, entitled "Playbox," was introduced in the *Junior League Magazine*, the major publication of the Association of Junior Leagues of America. In addition, AJLA officials decided that the work of the individual leagues would be enhanced if the national as-sociation assumed the responsibility for, and expanded upon, the work of the Chicago Bureau of Information. What emerged as an idea from the 1926 meeting thus quickly brought about the creation of an important national children's theatre agency. In June 1928 the AJLA Play Bureau had become so well established that it advertised the following services to the leagues:

having original plays read and published when they merit publication; recommending plays by Junior League girls to our Leagues and other organizations inquiring about them; giving advice on all phases of production such as stage setting, scenic development, costuming, advertising, price of tickets; purchase of costuming at wholesale prices; telling Leagues how others have produced the plays they contemplate using; handling play contests with prizes offered by the Samuel French Company; managing annual theatre arts exhibit with prizes.[13]

The creation of this bureau was the beginning of a major commitment on the part of AJLA in supporting and encouraging children's theatre on a national scope. This is reflected particularly in the staff of the association, which, at that time, consisted of only two stenographers, a telephone operator, a part-time clerical staff person and Mrs. Howard, the director of the bureau.[14]

The most pressing concern of the bureau at that time was the identification and dissemination of "suitable" scripts, a need felt from the very beginning of league involvement with children's theatre. In the fall of 1928, the library of the bureau held "over a hundred children's plays, six books on direction and production and twenty volumes of adult plays."[15] Some of these plays were products of various play-writing contests; others were copies of plays published by Samuel French, Inc., that were given to the bureau so that league members might become more familiar with the available literature.[16]

At about that time AJLA hired Helenka Adamowska as a full-time director of the Play Bureau, and she, in turn, initiated several important projects. The first of these was the National Children's Theatre Conference, which was held in Chicago in 1929. Under the umbrella of the national association, this conference attracted over 150 delegates, including representatives from seventy-three of the ninety leagues then operating children's theatres. At the conference, delegates saw a production of *The Patchwork Girl of Oz*, produced by the Chicago League; they participated in discussion groups focused on production problems; and, more important, they heard talks given by noted scenic designer, Robert Edmond Jones, and drama critic, Barret H. Clark.[17] According to Adamowska, the 1929 conference was a milestone affair:

We began to grow up. From each other's presence we realized that we were a powerful organization with a variety of methods but a unity of purpose. We saw how deeply we could draw on our neighbors for inspiration, for new zest and vitality, for practical assistance, for influence on our future policies.[18]

The Chicago conference apparently did give the leagues a sense of unity as the delegates voted to adopt a plan for an ambitious "national production" for the following year—a production which, they hoped, would become the nucleus of a proposed National Junior League Theatre for Children. Noting the significant duplication of effort in theatre production from league to league, the delegates created a plan to produce one major production that would travel throughout the country. The original plan included provisions for a scenic and costume design competition; the play to be produced in the city where the scenery was built; the costumes, scenery, plus a business manager and a coach (director) to travel to the league cities that booked the production; and the leagues themselves to supply a cast for each location.[19]

Several months later Adamowska reported to the AJLA board that work was proceeding in Chicago with a production of *The Blue Bird*, which was to be financed by fifteen leagues. She noted that a business manager and publicity coordinator had been hired, that carpenters were working to make the scenery "adjustable," and that the costumes were to be "elastic." She also noted that the labor unions almost upset everything by insisting upon sending a professional stagehand along, until they were convinced that it was not a traveling theatre company, but merely traveling scenery.[20]

Billed as the "world premiere of America's National Children's Theatre," *The Blue Bird* opened on November 1, 1930, at the Selwyn Theatre in Chicago.[21]

With what was apparently a very elaborate production—with a costume and scenery budget alone of $4000—the Chicago League launched a project designed to offer all interested leagues a full-scale theatre production. However, the project met with mixed artistic, logistic and monetary success. In a report to the AJLA board after the production closed, Adamowska noted:

> A ban is put on the play in Louisville by one of the . . . churches; reason, that all Maeterlinck's works are on the index for dissemination of so-called heretical ideas. We battle with bishop. We point out that same play was banned in Soviet Russia because it drew people back to religion. We win.
>
> In Pittsburgh, blue-bird flying effect causes a child to exclaim, "Oh. Look at the fish."
>
> Financial depression seriously affects theatrical plans. In Louisville, three banks suspend, one containing League funds.[22]

In another report, Adamowska also cited problems with labor unions, noting that the project "got all mixed up with costumers' strikes, . . . and high officials of the International Alliance of Theatrical Stage Employees (and Moving Picture Machine Operators) who had had their heads cut open by gangsters."[23]

The association had obviously ventured into areas for which they were ill prepared. Although some of these difficulties may have been foreseen, economic considerations, brought about by the then deepening Depression, caught everyone by surprise. Yet, the project continued, and the AJLA ultimately brought *The Blue Bird* to thirteen different league cities, playing to audiences of thousands of young people. In addition, some of these leagues made substantial profits from this production for use on other charity projects.

Bruised, but undaunted, the association persisted in its attempt to create a National Children's Theatre. The following year the association mounted *Treasure Island* as the "national production." There is little information available about this production, except reports that indicate that the play "was not a happy choice."[24] By this time the Depression had caused leagues to curtail expenditures, and this production traveled to only eight cities. Although it is not clear where this production originated, the Chicago League apparently had no involvement with what was, by all accounts, an unsuccessful project. The idea of a "national production" was subsequently discontinued, reportedly "because they were too great an expense for the Association."[25]

During this period league children's theatre activity was expanding rapidly. In the spring of 1932, 109 leagues—out of the total 114 leagues in the association—were involved in some form of children's theatre activity.[26] Larger leagues, such as Chicago, were operating entire seasons of children's plays that not only provided theatre entertainment to paying and charity audiences, but also earned significant income for use on other projects. For example, for the 1930–1931 season, a time of financial restraint, the Chicago League sold $10,500 worth of advertising in the children's theatre program.[27]

In response to this growth, the association organized a second national children's theatre conference, which was held in Cleveland in January 1933. This conference, like the first conference in Chicago, pointed toward yet another direction for league children's theatre. The conference featured such noted theatre professionals as Hallie Flanagan and Montrose Moses; and speakers "called attention to the fact that League plays had been given to an audience limited to those who could provide high-priced tickets and to groups of children from institutions." The delegates were urged to explore their communities to discover the "proper niche for the children's theatre" to reach a larger and broader audience.[28]

Once more the leagues assessed their work and, in some cases, redirected their priorities, as they realized that the trend toward larger, centralized productions might not be the best approach for each group. In response to this assessment, the association hired Gloria Chandler as a field worker to "tour the country and assist the Leagues in solving their problems and raising the standards of production."[29] Chandler, long active in the Chicago League children's theatre (and director of *The Blue Bird,* the first "national production") was well qualified for this position: she possessed both an extensive background in theatre and years of experience working within the Junior League. The concept of the field worker was not new to the leagues, in that by this time the association also employed several people as consultants in various areas of social work. Chandler, however, was hired to work only with children's theatre.

For this field work, Chandler and Adamowska offered "Children's Theatre Institutes" to the individual leagues, as Adamowska explained:

All this really means is that Miss Chandler or I come to your city for five days in order to help you with production problems and to put on, very informally, a difficult scene from some play, using no scenery or costumes and relying upon the inner conviction of your actresses to make the scene real to a specially invited audience. The greatest function of these institutes is, I believe, to unite and coordinate all organizations interested in child welfare, in order to work out a permanent program of plays, marionettes and other entertainment for children.[30]

Reports show that Chandler held such institutes in virtually every part of the country over the next several years. During her visits with the various leagues, she worked specifically to help them broaden the community base for their children's theatres. For example, when she met with the Fairmont League in 1934, she convened a meeting of league children's theatre officials together with heads of the local school system, the Rotary Club and the Central Council of Social and Civic Organizations.[31] As a direct result of this work, many league children's theatres created community advisory boards and worked to integrate their children's theatre activities into the work of the local schools.

Children's theatre activity thus varied from community to community. The Grand Rapids and Cincinnati Leagues were, reportedly, the first to troupe plays to the schools; but many leagues quickly followed their example.[32] The Chicago

League worked on a large-scale children's theatre project in conjunction with the 1933 World's Fair, while, at the same time, they presented plays at major downtown department stores and continued with the regular subscription season. The year 1934 also saw the creation of the Children's Theatre Association of San Francisco. This community group, which served as a model for others, was brought together by the league to coordinate a sixteen-week program of "splendid entertainment for children."[33] These community children's theatres—as well as some league children's theatres—also began to hire professional groups, such as Junior Programs, Inc., and Clare Tree Major Children's Theatre, to supplement their production programs.

In 1936, this diverse, community-based activity was brought into focus on a national level at the Third Technical Conference on Children's Theatre. In discussing plans for that conference, Adamowska noted:

[W]e are trying to prove to our Children's Theatres that they should assume the leadership in their community, in working out this continuous program of children's entertainment, or where such leadership already exists, to coordinate our efforts with the existing leadership, and to justify that attitude by continually raising the standards of our own productions.[34]

This conference, held in Baltimore, generally followed the pattern of previous conferences, with the exception that there was an even greater emphasis on demonstrations and workshops conducted by leading theatre professionals. Sara Spencer (a league member who had, by then, established the Children's Theatre Press), Alexander Dean and Stanley McCandless were among the list of workshop leaders.

The Baltimore conference underscored the need for specific, skills-oriented training courses for league members; and the association was quick to answer that need. In 1936, Virginia Lee Comer was hired as a "technician" to supplement Chandler's institutes with those more directly concerned with theatre production techniques. Comer came to the league after having completed the professional theatre training program at Yale University. She was to spend almost fifteen years with AJLA, and her tenure essentially marked the last great era of AJLA direction and material support of league children's theatre.

While Chandler continued her work with community development, Comer quickly moved to bring the latest information about theatre production to the leagues. In addition to workshops held with individual leagues, Comer saw to the creation of "technical sheets," publications focusing on theatre production. Between 1937 and 1940 AJLA published at least ten of these sheets, with titles ranging from "Plan for the Organization of a Children's Theatre Group" to "Scenery." The latter publication was complete with sample drawings.[35]

In 1940, Comer initiated "The Children's Theatre Bulletin," which was sent several times each year to the chair of every league children's theatre. The bulletin contained information about new scripts and relevant new books, announcements about the sale or rental of scenery and costumes and a production calendar of league children's theatres.[36] Comer also oversaw the publication of *A Handbook for Children's Theatre,* a comprehensive guide to all aspects of children's theatre production.

These specialized publications helped the leagues with their production problems, but also began to segregate the children's theatre activity more from the other activities of the leagues. By this time, few if any leagues concentrated solely on theatre production, as league activity included virtually every aspect of community and social work.

In 1945, Comer created a League Council on Children's Theatre to "assist the children's theatre staff by giving suggestions and direct reactions from Leagues as to theatre programs and services of the children's theatre staff."[37] This group included representatives from all of the various league programs then in operation, including series programs, trouping programs, marionette productions and radio work.

As an increasing number of leagues relied upon professional groups to augment their programs, Comer turned more attention to the professional theatre scene. Junior League publications had long included information about the professional companies, but Comer used the council to help formulate specific recommendations about booking various companies. The council even requested review performances from groups such as Junior Programs and the Edwin Strawbridge Ballet. Minutes from various council meetings show that Comer and others were rigorous in their evaluations of the professional companies; and they did not hesitate to share their evaluations with the groups themselves. When a specific company did not meet council standards, this was communicated to the leagues through various publications. Such publicity surely had an effect on the professional companies since the leagues, as a ready-made touring network, represented much potential income for the few groups operating at that time.

In 1940–1941, Junior League children's theatres presented 1,679 performances to audiences totalling 592,814.[38] But the leagues could not sustain this production pace in the years immediately following, as the onset of World War II caused most league theatres to change their operations. The league children's theatres faced, in Comer's words, their "greatest challenge," and the children's theatre staff at the national office turned their attention to helping the theatres through these difficult times.[39]

In 1942, Comer reported that the war situation had reached a point where the problems confronted by the children's theatres were more obvious. According to Comer, these included a loss of volunteers—due to members moving from the city, losing domestic help or becoming involved with war work—and the technical problems caused by the rationing of gas and tires and the shortages of other materials.[40]

In 1942–1943 the leagues presented only 653 performances to an audience of 291,754.[41] The issues of the "Children's Theatre Bulletin" during the war years included many accounts of how the various leagues coped with the war situation.

For example, the Philadelphia group, then conducting the largest of the league touring programs, confronted the problem by using public transportation:

No private cars could be used as members are scattered far and wide through the gas-rationed suburbs. . . . All costumes, make-up, props will be stored at the League club rooms and transported by taxi for each performance. This leaves each member to get only herself by train, bus or street car to the appointed place. Plans are afoot to capitalize on the lack of scenery through a special art project. This will test the projection powers of the actors, as well as the children's imaginations.[42]

In contrast, this same bulletin notes that another league would not be able to perform for the duration of the war because it served only rural schools.

The Chicago League was forced to adopt yet another solution. Confronted with "rationed tires, gasoline and shortages, babies unborn and newborn," and "war jobs" the once robust children's theatre group "faced the opening of the 1943 season minus actresses." After consulting Comer at the AJLA office, they hired a professional company to tour the schools under the auspices of the Junior League.[43] They continued this practice throughout the war years.

During the previous year Comer had met with five professional companies to assess their ability to function under war-time conditions. She reported that they would probably be able to meet any booking commitments that they made.[44]

Because of the war, AJLA did not convene another national children's theatre conference. However, in 1944, when noted children's theatre practitioner Winifred Ward called together children's theatre workers from throughout the country, Comer, as well as representatives from many leagues, participated enthusiastically. Comer underscores the importance with which she greeted this meeting:

Children's theatre got a terrific boost this summer in the form of a Children's Theatre Conference at Northwestern University. Directors and teachers gathered together from all over the country for the first time to talk nothing but Children's Theatre for three days. As most people in Children's Theatre work along in a fairly isolated way the conference proved to be a welcome stimulus. The upshot was that those attending decided to join the American Educational Theatre Association—and form a strong Children's Theatre section. A conference is planned for Christmas week in Chicago and regional meetings on Children's Theatre will be arranged later. Committees are already at work combing the country for new, good plays which the A.J.L.A. Library will handle and on compiling a Roster of Children's Theatres in the United States so that we will know for the first time just what the true scope is. . . .

It seems logical that Leagues working actively in the theatre for and with children become A.E.T.A. members—both for their own benefit and to further strengthen the Children's Theatre section.[45]

Comer became actively involved in the administration of the new Children's Theatre Committee of the American Educational Theatre Association (AETA), and, because of this, a large number of league members also joined the organization. In one issue of the "Bulletin" Comer not only talked of the benefits of such membership, but she also offered to send membership forms to interested league members.[46] Comer planned three sessions on children's theatre for the 1945 AETA conference, and by 1947 she was chairman of the AETA Children's Theatre Committee.

The growth and development of the AETA Children's Theatre Committee coincided with the end of the war, which, in turn, brought an increase in children's theatre activity in the leagues. In 1946–1947, leagues almost equaled their production statistics of 1940–1941, by presenting 1,596 productions to an audience of 639,793.[47] But things had changed: many league children's theatres, in part because of the war, had ventured into puppetry and radio drama; professional theatre groups were an important part of many league programs; some communities now had children's theatre organizations independent of league sponsorship; and the American Educational Theatre Association was providing national leadership in the field.

After the war, a "Plan of Action for Children's Theatre," probably written by Comer, was presented to the AJLA Children's Theatre Council. This document acknowledges some of these changes:

[I]t is no longer possible, nor has it ever been desirable, for a League alone to provide all the children's theatre for a community. The war has broadened the base of Children's Theatre in many communities and we must capitalize on this to see that all drama groups, dance and music organizations are used as resources.[48]

This "plan" reinforces the often cited need for high-quality performances, but it also lists several specific objectives, including the need to work with publishing companies to get worthy scripts published and to encourage league productions of these scripts prior to publication so that they can be polished. This document also suggests a new area of investigation: the need to interest colleges, universities and teacher-training institutions in offering courses in children's theatre.

By the end of the war, AJLA was also placing a greater emphasis on a wide variety of arts experiences for children. A report published in 1947 lists 252 children's arts programs and projects sponsored by Junior Leagues. These ranged from children's theatre to film programs, from arts and crafts classes to Junior Museums. They also included many musical programs, such as glee clubs, youth orchestras and music appreciation programs.[49] This wider scope was also reflected in a new job title for Comer: "Consultant on Community Arts." Meanwhile, Chandler had been named "Consultant on Radio," and she was working with the new "League Council on Radio."[50] Also, by this time, the title of the children's theatre newsletter had been changed to "Community Arts Bulletin."

Subsequently, Chandler became a part-time field consultant, and, by the spring of 1949, she was no longer listed as an AJLA staff member. Comer resigned her position with AJLA at some time during 1949–1950.[51]

Thus, by 1950 great changes had been made in the organization of AJLA in terms of children's theatre. Mary Eleanor Weisgerber (Ciaccio), who was hired sometime during 1948–1949, was the last person to serve as full-time Children's Theatre Consultant. During her tenure with AJLA, Ciaccio maintained most of the services developed by Comer and Chandler, and also saw to the publication of an up-dated children's theatre handbook, *Prologue to Production*. At the time of her resignation in 1954, the leadership of the association questioned the need to replace her on a full-time basis; and from that time on AJLA hired only part-time consultants in the arts, including specialists in children's theatre, creative drama, puppetry, radio and television. By 1972 there were no arts consultants on the association staff.

These changes were not caused by the decline in interest in children's theatre in the leagues, since, in 1955–1956, leagues presented over five thousand per-formances, including league productions, and sponsored professional produc-tions.[52] Rather, these changes apparently came about from the association's assessment of needs in the field. A 1954 memo to the Association Program Service Committee discussing this change notes that there were then more people trained in the field, and that there was a growth of children's theatre activities within AETA, thereby lessening the need for AJLA children's theatre services.[53]

League children's theatre continued even after the national association ceased its organizational and consultant services. Even today many leagues produce children's plays, work with puppetry or support series programs of professional children's theatre. But this activity is at the discretion of the individual leagues, and the national association no longer provides support. In 1961, the Children's Theatre Conference (an outgrowth of the AETA children's theatre committee) presented the Association of Junior Leagues a citation for its pioneering efforts in children's theatre.

Although many leagues are still active in children's theatre, the Junior League, either as a total organization or through its individual leagues, does not exert the influence that it once did on the children's theatre field; but it has left a legacy that reaches into virtually every aspect of children's theatre in this country. The Junior League has affected the development of the literature and production styles and techniques as well as the development of scores of community and professional children's theatre organizations.

The most consistent and, perhaps, far-reaching influence of the league can be found in the development of children's plays. As early as 1924, well before the association established the Play Bureau, leagues were holding contests for new plays.[54] Beginning in 1928 the association publicized annual contests, in con-junction with Samuel French, Inc., wherein that company agreed to publish the winning plays. This program was dropped in 1939, reportedly because French was losing money on the publications. The association itself sponsored play contests occasionally in the years following. In 1946, Dramatic Publishing Com-pany published eight plays from the Junior League library. Beginning in 1947, AJLA began its own publishing operation by issuing some of its manuscript plays in mimeographed form.[55] AJLA continued the practice of licensing children's theatre productions until 1971.[56]

Throughout the years, AJLA strove to be a resource of high-quality children's plays for the leagues and an agent for the writers of these works. The association carefully evaluated and screened their library holdings and insisted upon the payment of royalties for the production of their plays. This group thus nurtured playwrights and disseminated plays at a time when there were few other avenues available. However, as the association sought plays appropriate for league productions, their library holdings and their contests reflected a narrow view of children's plays. AJLA generally handled only plays with familiar titles and plays that used small casts and minimal technical requirements. And, in most cases, they favored plays that could easily be presented by all-women casts. Thus, while the association greatly increased the number of plays available, and—within their often narrow definitions of appropriate plays—sought the application of rigorous play-writing standards, AJLA essentially perpetuated the need for the familiar fairy tale as the subject of children's plays.

Along the same line, much of the theatre presented by the leagues was produced by untrained and relatively inexperienced actors, directors and technicians; and it thus varied greatly in quality from production to production and from league to league. The leagues reportedly approached theatre with the best artistic intentions, and, with some of the larger and more expensive productions, they were able to hire professionals for the acting, directing and the scenic design and construction. But, the trend toward trouping productions placed even greater strains on the artistic values of the productions, since the leagues had even more technical hurdles to overcome. Some leagues, such as Chicago, advanced the children's theatre field by producing polished, and in some cases, innovative children's theatre; other leagues did not move much beyond the 1915 idea of "putting on a simple fairy play with the simplest of scenic requirements."

Yet, in spite of varying levels of quality, the leagues brought children's theatre to virtually every part of this country during the first half of this century. By doing so, they sowed the seeds for the continuation of children's theatre in their communities even after the leagues themselves were not involved. For example, many of the prominent professional children's theatre organizations in operation today grew from Junior League operations. Notable among these theatres are Stage One: The Louisville Children's Theatre, Omaha's Emmy Gifford Children's Theatre, the Birmingham Children's Theatre and the Nashville Academy Theatre.

The Junior League has also had an impact on the development of many college children's theatre training programs. The most prominent example of this was the noted child drama training program at the University of Washington. This formal university program, which offered work on the undergraduate and graduate levels, grew directly from the Seattle Children's Recreation Project, a project of the Seattle Junior League.[57]

Through serving as sponsors, the leagues have also, over the years, been important for the growth and development of touring professional children's theatre companies. And this practice has carried over into the contemporary scene, as community children's theatre organizations—many of which are sponsored by, or were created by, Junior Leagues—provide many of the necessary bookings for professional companies. A notable example of this can be seen in the Southern Children's Theatre Circuit, which unites community children's theatres in several southern states. This network provides enough work for professional children's theatre companies that the circuit annually hosts its own showcase where professional children's theatres present their plays for prospective buyers from community organizations.

When Mary Harriman organized her fellow debutantes for work in the New York settlement houses in 1901, she certainly did not envision that the Junior League would have such a significant impact on the growth and development of American children's theatre. The contemporary children's theatre field has grown well beyond the original social work orientation of the leagues, but the role of the Junior Leagues in this growth and development can still be seen in virtually every aspect of the field.

NOTES

1. Janet Gordon and Diana Reische, *The Volunteer Powerhouse* (New York: Rutledge Press, 1982), pp. 33, 50, 61. In 1971 the Association of Junior Leagues of America, Inc. (AJLA) changed its name to the Association of Junior Leagues, Inc. (AJL).

2. *1984–85 Annual Directory*, Association of Junior Leagues, Inc., p. 1.

3. *A Handbook for Children's Theatre* (New York: Association of Junior Leagues of America, 1942), p. 7.

4. *1913–14 Annual Report,* Chicago Junior League, pp. 7–8.

5. *1916–17 Annual Report,* Chicago Junior League, p. 5.

6. Mary Eleanor Ciaccio, *Prologue to Production* (New York: Association of Junior Leagues of America, n.d.), p. 6. This book was published sometime after 1949 and before 1954.

7. Catherine Rowland Cooke, "Report of the Dramatic Committee," *1921–22 Annual Report*, Chicago Junior League, p. 8.

8. "The President's Report of 1923–1924," *1923–24 Annual Report*, Chicago Junior League, p. 4.

9. *Handbook for Children's Theatre*, p. 7.

10. Gordon and Reische, *Volunteer Powerhouse*, p. 75.

11. "Children's Theatres," *Junior League Bulletin*, 13, No. 5 (March 1927), p. 29.

12. "Report of Children's Theatre Conference," *1926–27 Annual Report*, Chicago Junior League, p. 9.

13. "Financing of Play Bureau," *Junior League Magazine*, 14, No. 9 (June 1928), p. 107.

14. "Executive Secretary Report," minutes of AJLA board meeting, October 16, 1928. AJL Archives.

15. "Report from the Play Bureau," minutes of AJLA board meeting, October 17, 1928. AJL Archives.

16. "Play Bureau Will Have Reference Library," *Junior League Magazine*, 14, No. 8 (May 1928), p. 109.

17. C. Osborne, "Report of the Chicago Junior League Conference," *1929–30 Annual Report,* Chicago Junior League, pp. 18–21.

18. "Children's Theatre," *Junior League Magazine,* 19, No. 3 (December 1932), p. 86.

19. "Report of the Play Bureau," minutes of the AJLA board meeting, March 1930, p. 3. AJL Archives.

20. "Children's Theatre Report," minutes of the AJLA board meeting, October 1930. AJL Archives.

21. H. Adamowska, "The Children's Theatre," *Junior League Magazine*, 17, No. 3 (December 1930), p. 98.

22. Minutes of the AJLA board, March 2, 1931, as quoted in *Volunteer Powerhouse*, p. 79.

23. "The Children's Theatres," *Junior League Magazine,* 17, No. 8 (May 1931), p. 84.

24. "League Program Institute—Children's Theatre," TS, 1940, p. 2. AJL Archives.

25. Ibid.

26. *1931–32 Yearbook*, Association of Junior Leagues of America, Inc., p. 17.

27. "Report on Advertising 1930–31," *1930–31 Annual Report,* Chicago Junior League, p. 25.

28. Ciaccio, *Prologue to Production*, p. 6.

29. H. Adamowska, "National Scope for Junior League Plays," TS, n.d. AJL Archives.

30. "Address on the Children's Theatre," a speech delivered July 1935, TS. AJL Archives.

31. H. Adamowska, "Children's Theatre," *Junior League Magazine,* 20, No. 4 (January 1934), p. 50.

32. Ciaccio, *Prologue to Production*, p. 7.

33. Adamowska, "Address on the Children's Theatre."

34. Ibid.

35. Copies of "Technical Sheets" found in AJL Archives.

36. Copies in the files of the researcher.

37. "First Meeting of League Council on Children's Theatre," TS minutes from meeting held June 19, 1940. AJL Archives.

38. Gertrude L. Elliot, AJLA Secretary on Community Arts, letter to Sara Spencer, June 11, 1948. Found in Spencer Papers, Special Collections, Arizona State University Library.

39. Minutes from "First Meeting of League Council."

40. "Children's Theatre Bulletin," February 27, 1942, p. 1.

41. Gertrude L. Elliot, letter to Sara Spencer.

42. "Children's Theatre Bulletin," June 25, 1942, p. 1.

43. "Report of the Children's Theatre," *1943–44 Annual Report*, Chicago Junior League, p. 12.

44. "Children's Theatre Bulletin," June 2, 1942, p. 2.

45. "Children's Theatre Bulletin," September 30, 1944, p. 1.

46. "Children's Theatre Bulletin," November 17, 1945, p. 1.

47. Gertrude L. Elliot, letter to Sara Spencer.

48. "Plan for Action for Children's Theatre," TS, March 29, 1946, p. 2. AJL Archives.

49. "Community Arts Bulletin," February 17, 1947.

50. Information taken from AJLA *1944–45 Annual Directory*

51. Information taken from AJLA *Annual Directory* from the years 1947–1948, 1948–1949 and 1949–1950.

52. Uncatalogued lists and statistics found in AJL Archives.

53. Marge Twyman, memo to Bonnie Lee Inman and Program Service Committee, November 3, 1954.

54. *Junior League Bulletin*, 10, No. 9 (June 1924), p. 43.

55. "League Council on Community Arts," minutes from meeting held September 8, 1947, p. 3. AJL Archives.

56. George Latshaw, letter to "All Junior League Children's Theatre Chairmen," February 26, 1971. AJL Archives.

57. Mrs. Charles S. Monroe, "Junior League Projects in the Children's Field," TS copy of speech delivered at National Conference of Social Work, April 22, 1948, p. 4. AJL Archives.

5

Edith King and Dorothy Coit and the King-Coit School and Children's Theatre

ELLEN RODMAN

Edith King, an artist, and Dorothy Coit, a drama teacher, operated the King-Coit School and Children's Theatre in New York City from 1923 to 1958. At this unique part-time school, nonprofessional children, ages three to fifteen, studied art, drama and dance and performed plays based on classical stories from other cultures. The theatre attracted discriminating audiences, was an integral part of the New York theatre scene, was favorably reviewed by first-string drama critics from major publications, and was praised by important people in the worlds of music, dance, art and theatre.

Throughout their association Edith was responsible for painting and drawing classes, scenery, lighting and costumes; and Dorothy supervised the diction, storytelling, pantomime and acting classes as well as the adaptation of scripts and the direction of plays. If they decided to work on "Nala and Damayanti," a Hindu love story from the *Mahabharata*, for instance, they researched the literature, history, art and music of the period and designed the script and sets accordingly. The children visited museums to see the Rajput miniatures and painted their own versions in Edith's art classes, listened to authentic Indian music, and learned symbolic gestures from *The Mirror of Gesture*, the handbook for Hindu actors, in Dorothy's acting classes. The elaborate production which evolved from their studies resembled a Rajput miniature brought to life.

On the evening of May 1, 1979, twenty-one years after the lights went out in the King-Coit's last theatre, the Library and Museum of the Performing Arts at Lincoln Center in New York City was bristling with excitement. Food and drink were abundant as well-dressed men and women, including Lillian Gish and Anne Baxter, chatted incessantly and reminisced. The occasion was the opening of the King-Coit Children's Theatre Exhibition in Lincoln Center's Vincent Astor Gallery.

Preparations had been underway for months. Almost $17,000 had been raised from King-Coit admirers to cover the cost of the invitations, food, musicians, mannequins and other details. Total costs amounted to $12,000, and the remaining $5,000 benefited the New York Public Library, of which the Library and Museum of the Performing Arts at Lincoln Center is a part. In many ways, mounting the exhibit was a microcosm of mounting a King-Coit production: the same social dynamics and "perfection-at-all-costs" attitude prevailed. The results were beautiful and, to some, a sentimental reminder of a magical time gone by.

What the 1979 exhibit tried to evoke three-dimensionally, a thirty-year commemorative booklet, published in 1953, evoked verbally and pictorially:

"The best actors in the world, either for tragedy, comedy, history, pastoral, pastoral-comical, historical-pastoral, scene and individible, or poem unlimited," so wrote Shakespeare once upon a time, thus kindly providing the motto which ran in gold letters around the King-Coit Theatre at Fortieth Street.

For thirty years in a dozen different theatres in New York, the poem unlimited has been carried on—through wars and rumors of wars, and depressions which have been indeed depressing. Through the kindness of friends, the appreciation of audiences, the enthusiastic attitude of critics, the plays have appeared one by one and over and over.

The pictures [and text] on these pages bring memories of a few moments in the children's theatre and will perhaps suggest to the retentive mind the scarlet and the gold of Aucassin, the white silence of Blake's Morning Stars, or an Ariel, visible or indivisible above a magic island.

From the brighter side of the footlights the actors, now older, but not forgetful, will have their memories also—of high adventures in India, or Persia—in Ancient Greece or in medieaval Provence. For those children have lived for a while "richly in a palace of rare grace, Like a prince born heir to treasures of a thousand, thousand kings."[1]

For thirty-five years the King-Coit School and Children's Theatre educated and entertained in New York, but Edith and Dorothy's partnership and techniques had been formed years earlier at The Buckingham School, a private school for girls in grades kindergarten through ninth, in Cambridge, Massachusetts.

BEFORE 1923

Probably only their New England heritage, against which they were in partial revolt, could have spawned these wise and witty women. Certainly only the most fortuitous circumstances could have facilitated their joining forces. Edith Lawrence King and Dorothy Coit were strikingly different, equally talented and gifted teachers who believed the arts were an essential part of a child's education.

Edith King was twenty-five when she arrived at The Buckingham School in 1909 to teach drawing and painting:

My aunt told my mother I was no good in the world, just sitting around drawing pictures, so I sadly set out to earn my living. I got a job in a boys' school for $50 a year, $100 the second year. I was to earn $25 more the next year, but a friend was leaving The Buckingham School and through her I got a job there.[2]

Twenty-two-year-old Dorothy Coit arrived in 1911 to teach history and English for a yearly salary of $700.[3] Katharine M. Thompson was headmistress, and every year she produced a Shakespeare play with the ninth-grade girls. In 1914 she was away for a few months, however, and impressed with Dorothy—an unassuming, gentle, tactful, energetic and witty person according to those who knew her—named her acting headmistress.

"She had told me what I had to teach," Dorothy recalled later. "I had to read *Comus* with the oldest class—high-powered little thirteen-year-old girls who just played horse with me—and I realized it was inappropriate."[4] John Milton's *Comus*, a masque which was first produced in 1634, is a moral allegory set in the Kingdom of Neptune and stars Comus, the son of Bacchus and Circe; it is a rather tedious book for ninth graders.

Many experiences in Dorothy's background prepared her for coping with the crisis. Born in Salem, Massachusetts, on September 25, 1889, the oldest of four children, she grew up in a Congregationalist family (she became an Episcopalian after college) in Winchester, an affluent Boston suburb, with her sisters, Elisabeth and Mary, and a younger brother, Robert.

Her father, Robert, was an architect who had been educated at Harvard and at the Massachusetts Institute of Technology (MIT) and who, in between, had traveled to Persia as secretary to the consul.[5] His tales of an exotic land stimulated Dorothy's later interest not only in Persia but also in the cultures of other lands. "By great good luck," she exclaimed, "my father had gone to Persia as a young man."[6] Her mother, Eliza Richmond Atwood (usually referred to as "Lilla"), died young.

While attending the public schools, Dorothy enjoyed the "prop" room in the family's attic and used the old clothes and other objects there to put on plays for neighborhood children. She never had formal theatre training but trained herself while at the same time cultivating a love for music and poetry. After graduating from Winchester High School, she went on to Radcliffe College in 1907 and graduated *cum laude* in 1911.

Her Radcliffe days overflowed with experiences on which she would draw later at the Buckingham and King-Coit schools. She was active in a host of extracurricular activities, serving as class treasurer and holding offices, including the presidency of the Emmanuel Club, a social and philanthropic society which, among other things, produced one show each year for the benefit of the Emmanuel Scholarship Fund. The club also held debates designed to train students in the techniques of public speaking.[7]

Dorothy was also recording secretary of the Christian Association which, in 1911, merged with the Emmanuel Club and the College Settlement Chapter to form the Radcliffe Guild. Dorothy became the guild's first president and thus an important force behind the serious side of college life.[8] The guild continued the Emmanuel Club's tradition of mounting a theatrical production each year.

More interesting, perhaps, was Dorothy's involvement with the English Club, of which she was treasurer. The group met twice each month to discuss original papers written by students, and the members invited English professors, including George Pierce Baker, to speak at open meetings. Baker, who founded the Yale drama department in 1925, began teaching playwriting at Radcliffe in 1903. In 1912, his course, then open to Harvard students, included a workshop for play production. Eugene O'Neill, S. N. Behrman and Robert Edmond Jones were among the talented young people who studied with him and, sometime later, both Jones and Baker could be counted among the distinguished King-Coit fans.

A harbinger was the English Club's play selection in 1908 for their yearly production. They chose John Milton's *Comus*,[9] the play that a few years later at The Buckingham School would mark the beginning of the King-Coit collaboration.

Finally, Dorothy was active in the Idler Club, Radcliffe's oldest. It was a highly organized social and theatrical group that convened monthly and—like the King-Coit School and Children's Theatre—was known for its meticulous attention to details. To be sure, Dorothy's academic pursuits were also helping to form her philosophy regarding the arts in education. It is not clear whether any of her English courses included, or even emphasized, theatre and dramatic literature. She was not enrolled in any which were numbered "47," the designation for Baker's class. Her course work in English, history and literature served her well, nevertheless, as co-director of King-Coit, and she was convinced of the importance of participation in dramatic activities.

"I believe that our plays do us a great deal of good," she wrote, "and that they afford us valuable training in practical and executive work, that they develop our imaginations in a way nothing else could, and that they teach us the value of inconspicuous work."[10] In 1911, Dorothy wrote "A Defense of Dramatics" in *Radcliffe Magazine* in which she emphasized the value of theatre work in helping to teach students how to respond quickly to something unexpected, and she described its importance in strengthening the imagination:

The power to read a play, and to see it, as one reads, already upon the stage, the power to feel the difference between the colorless play, and the play alive with possibilities—such power means a growth of the imaginative and visualizing faculties which should not be underestimated. And when the play is once chosen, and one by one the characters grow from words and lines to clear-cut types, and from types to breathing personalities— . . . the wonderfully increased breadth and richness of thought and imagination can only be appreciated by those who have worked and lived in the heart of a play.[11]

As Dorothy's participation in college productions was more often behind the scenes than as an actress, she was quick to point out the value of working in any capacity to mount a successful production. "After all," she asked, "what training could be better" than working faithfully for the sake of the whole?[12]

Remembering the fun she had had with plays as a child and at college, Dorothy decided not to read *Comus* with the Buckingham girls but to act it instead. She cut it and edited it and made quite an interesting play out of it. She then realized they would need costumes if they were going to produce it. "I went to Miss King, who taught drawing and designing," Dorothy said. "She had good discipline and she had forty pupils in a room that would normally hold eight."[13]

Edith Lawrence King was born in Boston on October 9, 1884, into a Protestant family (she converted to Catholicism later in life), and she grew up in Chelsea, Massachusetts, a working-class Boston suburb, with her younger sister, Marian Elizabeth.[14] Their father, Edwin, who died when they were young, was an importer,[15] and their mother, Ellen Augusta Hough, was for many years a librarian at MIT in nearby Cambridge.[16]

When Edith was only two years old, she showed signs of artistic ability, so it was no surprise that, after graduating from Chelsea High School, she went to the Rhode Island School of Design (RISD) where she was one of the most talented students, despite her rebellious nature and disdainful attitude toward higher education. Under a cooperative program between RISD and Brown University, Edith was enrolled as a special student at the Women's College at Brown from 1903 to 1905.[17]

There was nothing in her background aimed directly at molding her into the great teacher she would become. She did not "practice-teach" or study the history of educational theories. Her class attendance at Brown was poor (she even missed a final exam or two) and, obviously, she did not attain honor grades. Her college course of study served as a foundation, nevertheless, for her work at the King-Coit School and Children's Theatre from 1923 to 1958. She was exposed to English literature; Jewish and early Christian history and literature; comparative literature; art history; ancient art and classical archaeology; and Roman, early Christian, Medieval, and Renaissance art history.

Edith's version of her education is somewhat different:

Radcliffe College threw me out after I told them I was an artist and would like to supplement my education with a little real knowledge. So from Radcliffe I went to Brown where I studied the "Book of Job" and had a good time while occasionally looking in on the Rhode Island School of Design.[18]

She had a way of making outrageous statements with casual irreverence, like boasting that she had been called up before the dean for bad behavior and that people used to rap on her walls to quell the noise!

Edith's pursuit of a college education led her to MIT where she had the dubious distinction of being the only female in a drawing and clay modeling class of forty men. "I was just too sensitive and miserable for words," she said.[19] But she managed to ingratiate herself with the professor, who played billiards with her occasionally and treated her to hot chocolate. There is no record that Edith was ever enrolled as a regular student at MIT and, frankly, no one seems less compatible with that institution. Her mother was employed there, however, so it is possible that she attended classes unofficially as a special student.

Always, painting and drawing took precedence over everything else in her life, and her friendship with Charles and Maurice Prendergast, both estimable artists, contributed to the shape and style of her life and work. The Prendergasts had a house in Capri, and around 1910 she, Marian and their mother traveled to Capri where Edith painted with the Prendergasts at the beach.[20] Maurice's portrait of her, entitled ''Portrait of a Girl with Flowers'' (ca. 1915), is owned by the Metropolitan Museum of Art in New York. Another Maurice Prendergast portrait of her, ''La Rouge,'' is part of the permanent collection at Lehigh University in Bethlehem, Pennsylvania. It was completed about 1913, the same year in which Edith exhibited her works in the historic Armory Show in New York.

Edith, who lacked Dorothy's cultural refinement and knowledge and who was known for her ruthlessness and brutally frank tongue, was humorous, vain, temperamental, tactless and demanding. When Dorothy asked her if she would make costumes and scenery for The Buckingham School's production of *Comus*, she replied, ''I have never heard of *Comus*. What is it?''[21] But soon after, she was on her hands and knees cutting a forest out of a piece of felt.

The entire school had never seemed more alive than during the preparations for *Comus* as everyone waited eagerly for the big day. Finally, the play opened with perfectly rehearsed children and Edith's dark purple felt trees against a light blue sky. Everyone was thoroughly entranced, the play was a huge success, and the women became fast friends and lifelong partners. Between 1915 and 1922, they produced and directed *The Tempest*, *Chansons de France* (known also as *Divertissement Français*), *The Story of Theseus* (known also as *The Sword of Attica*), *Ahmed the Cobbler*, *Aucassin and Nicolete* and *Nala and Damayanti* at The Buckingham School and other locations in Massachusetts.

In seeking a way to make Milton's *Comus* less dry and colorless, Edith and Dorothy devised an educational/theatrical mixture which was to become the foundation of the King-Coit School and Children's Theatre several years later.

Former Buckingham pupils, now in their seventies and eighties, offer vivid and poignant recollections of the women and their techniques. Jane Loring Noble Fiske recalls that Edith and Dorothy contributed tremendously to her appreciation of painting, history and theatre and that Dorothy directed her toward a lifelong interest in ancient history and mythology: ''I loved her history class. She inspired me to do my best work for her. Miss Coit was a teacher a child could love, always kind and gentle, but firm and serious too. She treated us as equals, never bullying or frightening us.''[22]

Fiske has similarly glowing memories of Edith, the first teacher ever to make her feel she was not utterly hopeless:

I must have been what they call dyslexic because I could neither spell nor do arithmetic, but her class was pure joy and relaxation from beginning to end. In Miss King's class I had my only real success. She taught me to flow on a watercolor wash, gave me the rudiments of perspective, light and shade, and a sense of form.[23]

Fiske recalls that Edith let the class draw and paint from imagination and does not recall her making suggestions to the class. Instead, the information simply passed from Edith to the students unnoticed, to be absorbed unconsciously. According to Fiske, "Miss King's class was not a formal drawing class with models and setups, it was designed to stimulate a child's creative ability, and long before I left Buckingham, I had chosen painting for my career. I truly loved Miss King."[24]

Carpenters were employed to execute Edith's carefully designed scenery, but Fiske said that Buckingham children were allowed to apply some of the paint. Scenery and costumes were not the only things painted, though. "Every bit of my skin that showed was painted," Fiske said.[25]

Dorothy taught every gesture by rote and under her, according to Fiske, "[t]he budding actor moved only as directed. There was no interpretation of a part by an incumbent. Every gesture, from the turn of my head to the bend of my finger, was studied."[26]

Elinor Hopkinson Barr echoes Fiske's recollections of the days at The Buckingham School and recalls, particularly, that Edith would stand for nothing that was not as right as she could possibly make it. She worked ceaselessly for as close to perfection of detail as could be achieved. "Miss Coit's genius was of another kind," Barr said. "While working with you individually, giving you gestures and attitudes, while teaching you the words by rote, what she was really giving you was an understanding and love of the period and work at hand." Barr said that the children did not imitate Dorothy exactly, but that her feeling became theirs. "She would give me the lines, phrase by phrase," Barr remembered, "while I repeated them with all the lovely feeling she conveyed, but with (I suppose) a change of intonation. I know I didn't imitate her pronunciation exactly, but her excitement, her poetry. . . ."[27]

Pleased as everyone who knew Edith and Dorothy's work in Massachusetts was, there came a point at which the teachers longed for a school of their own elsewhere. "Edith and Dorothy saw how much sense it made to center all the study of the arts around the term-long production of one play," a reporter, William Hawkins, wrote. With a simplistic view of their exodus from Cambridge, he continued: "The idea was so successful that they applied for assistance. Their only answer was that they were doing fine alone. They had given some benefits for French war relief in '21 and '22 in Manhattan, and when there was no further promise of growth in Cambridge, they uprooted and came to New York."[28]

The evidence suggests that lack of assistance was not the only reason Edith and Dorothy departed from The Buckingham School. Buckingham parents were alarmed by the cost of the productions the two women were producing.[29] Many were upset that Edith wanted to paint the children's entire bodies,[30] possibly even the insides of their mouths.[31] Although she settled for painting just the parts of the children's bodies that showed and allowed the youngsters to wear tunics, there were some complaints from those looking up at the stage from the front rows that they could see the children's "private parts."[32] In fact, the children were almost nude, because Edith had based the costume designs for the 1919 Buckingham production, *The Story of Theseus,* on the almost nude characters on Greek vases.

The feeling among many Buckingham parents was that Dorothy, and especially Edith, had gone too far. "All the Cambridge women wrote to the principal saying that they would not come to the play because the children were almost nude," Dorothy said. The principal said they could do the play, but that no boys could come. Edith accused everybody in Cambridge of having evil minds. Fortunately a woman who had seen the play and thought it was beautiful, intervened on their behalf, and the principal allowed boys to attend. "But Edith never got over it," according to Dorothy, "so we came to New York." "To New York," Edith added, "where it is all so progressive."[33]

Edith knew firsthand about New York's progressiveness. After all, she had participated in one of the most influential events in American art—the famous 1913 Armory Show in New York—which was the first full-scale introduction of modern art to Americans and fostered the acceptance of modern American artists as equal to the Europeans.

New York was the business, and financial, as well as the tourist mecca of the country, and throngs of American writers, musicians, actors and artists flocked to New York's Greenwich Village to celebrate life in New York, among other contemporary subjects, in their creations. The group of artists known as "The Eight" (including Maurice Prendergast) was there and, eventually, five of The Eight were associated in some way with King-Coit.[34] The Theatrical Syndicate and the Shubert brothers promoted the building of many theatres over which they exercised complete control, and first-rate performers and playwrights occupied center stage. Dorothy and Edith left Boston for New York at a propitious moment in New York's financial and cultural history.

In addition to the problems at The Buckingham School, it is possible that certain influential New Yorkers, who spent their summers in Massachusetts and saw their work, encouraged Edith and Dorothy to relocate permanently in New York. There is evidence of other links between New Yorkers and Edith and Dorothy's decision to teach, produce and direct there. Frederic Coudert, a well-known New York attorney, asked them to come to New York to do one of the benefit performances for French war orphans.[35]

Another link is that a member of J. P. Morgan's family may have arranged for them to come to New York.[36] Edith P. Morgan and Anne Morgan are names that appear on several programs for King-Coit productions. On the program for *Aucassin and Nicolete* (1921), for example, Anne Morgan is identified as First

Vice-President of the American Committee for Devastated France. Whether or not the Morgan family was instrumental in bringing Edith and Dorothy to New York, they were interested in the productions and secured access for Edith, and Dorothy and their students to the great Morgan collection of illuminated manuscripts from medieval France on which the scenery and costumes for *Aucassin and Nicolete* were based.

Then, too, Edith's artist friends, Charles and Maurice Prendergast, had already moved to New York and perhaps invited Edith and Dorothy, especially after their benefit performances in New York in 1920, 1921 and 1922 had been so well received. Anne Tonetti Gugler thinks that her mother's friend, Marie Russell, arranged for Edith and Dorothy to give the 1920 benefit performance for French war orphans of *Chansons de France* at New York's Punch and Judy Theatre.[37]

When Edith and Dorothy arrived, Mrs. Gugler's mother, who had arranged their sleeping accommodations and had gathered together several children to participate in the play for Marie Russell, happened to show them a riding school. Upon seeing that the riding school was a magnet for children from fine families, Edith and Dorothy decided that New York would be a good city in which to start their school.[38]

A letter from Dorothy sheds some light on the arrangements in 1920 for their first New York production:

They called from New York. "Will you and Edith bring your scenery and costumes and put on a play in the Punch and Judy Theatre?" "Yes," I said. Then I added, "We need about twenty-five good children."

"That will be all right—Mary Tonetti will get the children."

"We really have nowhere to stay in New York," I said.

"Don't think about it—Mary Tonetti has arranged for you to stay at the Cosmopolitan Club."

So we came. Mrs. Tonetti said, "I have twenty children from the Riding Ring." We wanted to import a child from Boston. . . .

This was only the beginning. When we came to New York the next year, and the next, and finally to stay, we were in the Tonetti studio.

I can't explain now why Mrs. Tonetti was so generous to us in the beginning, why she stood by us to the end. But I do know that she was the foundation on which we built our life, and our work in New York.[39]

In 1921, Edith and Dorothy mounted *Aucassin and Nicolete,* a medieval French romance, at the 39th Street Theatre (Jane Wyatt, who played "Mother" on the hit television series "Father Knows Best," was among the children in the cast) for the benefit of French war orphans and repeated it for a Radcliffe benefit. Alexander Woollcott, drama critic at the *New York Times*, commended this production. "It is pure gold, the more precious perhaps, because it was come upon unexpectedly," he wrote.[40] Dorothy wrote on a copy of this review, "This is what really launched us in New York."[41]

Edith and Dorothy returned to The Buckingham School and stayed to the end of the school year in 1923, although they did their last play, *Nala and Damayanti*, there in 1922. Discouraged at The Buckingham School and encouraged by friends, the warm receptions during their 1920, 1921 and 1922 forays to New York and Woollcott's review, they decided to return to New York where, in October 1923, they opened the school they would operate for the next thirty-five years. While painted bodies, elaborate productions and nudity would not prove too troublesome to the founders of the King-Coit School and Children's Theatre, they soon learned that other matters would.

1923–1958 FACILITIES

When Edith and Dorothy started in New York in 1923, classes were held in a variety of spaces, and performances were given in borrowed or rented theatres. About ten years later, they finally got a theatre of their own. Located at 135 East 40 Street, the theatre—which seated about two-hundred people—was designed and built by architect/artist Eric Gugler in collaboration with stage designer Cleon Throckmorton.[42] Critic John Mason Brown praised the "charming little auditorium" and concluded: "There is no theatre that I know of on Manhattan which can equal this diminutive one in either appropriateness or taste."[43] In 1940 the fire department intervened, and fire marshals, who had been bribed a few times before, closed the theatre.[44] For the next fourteen years, public performances took place in a variety of intimate spaces.

Finally in 1954, the King-Coit School and Children's Theatre acquired another theatre of its own. Scene designer Donald Oenslager, with money from the Mellon Foundation, converted an area of the Sutton Hotel.[45] Critic Richard Hayes described the result as a "most engaging of bandbox theatres: admirably proportioned and decorated, wholly winning in its assertion of color and liveliness and charm."[46]

After having taught and mounted productions in an assortment of places, Dorothy was able to formulate what she considered to be an ideal facility:

A very large rehearsal room must be had, a room which does not echo, a room high enough to house the set, and long enough to give the director a picture of the stage which will approximate its picture in the theatre. The transition from the rehearsal conditions to the performance conditions must be as slight as possible, because young children are totally unable to make artistic adjustments to material changes.[47]

STUDENTS

Throughout the years Edith and Dorothy intended to work with youngsters ages five to twelve, but often the children were as young as three or as old as fifteen; enrollment averaged about sixty each year and included children of Helen Hayes, Geraldine Fitzgerald, Herbert Brodkin, Maxwell Anderson, Mildred Dunnock, Lawrence Langner, George Bellows, Dorothy McGuire and Chandler Cowles; Tallulah Bankhead's godchildren (actress Eugenia Rawls's son and daughter); and the grandchildren of Mary Mowbray-Clarke, Arthur B. Davies, Walter P. Chrysler and Aline Bernstein. The children participated in drawing, painting, dancing and acting a few hours each week after school and on Saturdays and Sundays. There were more girls than boys, so boys with potential were always welcome. There were very few, if any, Jewish children; there were no black or Oriental children.

Weston Barclay, writing in the *New York World-Telegram,* offered one summation of the composition of the student body: "Town cars and limousines, of winter evenings, line up outside for young actors and actresses, but there are plenty of those who walk away, too. Wealthier parents and others have provided scholarships, and the final test is talent."[48] Writer Stella Block expressed a different view:

> The child actors were chosen with a keen wit: it was not always talent and never precocity that won for a child a place in this unique enterprise. In some it was a suitable physical presence, in others intelligence, now and then a peculiarity of gesture or speech to lend color and humor, and in others the aptitude for emotional expression. The need for talent was small because the performance was so minutely and clearly visualized by the director that the actors' ingenuity was superfluous: intelligent obedience, being all that was expected.[49]

It is most likely—based on other articles and interviews—that the children were selected for their pleasant appearances (features and build), talent, intelligence and social prominence. Tanaquil LeClercq, Jane Wyatt, Zina Bethune, Jacques D'Amboise, Madeleine L'Engle, Beatrice Straight, Anne Baxter and Lee Remick are some of the well-known adults who were part of the King-Coit circle when they were children.

FINANCES

Edith and Dorothy had several assistants over the years, including dancing teachers, musicians, craftsmen and other top professionals—with or without children at the King-Coit School—who gave of their talents freely and considered it an honor to be involved with the two women. Not all assistants received salaries; not all children paid tuition (around $200 for the October to May classes and rehearsals); and ticket sales (ticket prices ranged from $1 to $10 with $3 to $5 being the average) did not cover the cost of the school or productions. Since Edith and Dorothy spent money freely in the pursuit of achieving a specific style in costumes, makeup, scenery and properties, some productions ended up with hefty deficits. Socially prominent New Yorkers occasionally formed fund-raising committees, and grants from a few foundations helped. When the American Academy of Arts and Letters awarded King-Coit $1,000 in 1946–1947, Walter

Damrosch (Academy President), John Mason Brown, Katharine Cornell, Austin Strong, Rosamond Gilder, Guthrie McClintic, Donald Oenslager and Eric Gugler wrote a note expressing their happiness.[50] The list of faithful admirers who helped the King-Coit School and Children's Theatre in a variety of ways includes many of the most important people of the time.[51]

Both women would have liked to carry out their goals without worrying about money. Dorothy once quipped, "Life's too short for receipts."[52] They were wise, though, and when Dorothy's nephew, a teacher, was thinking about opening a school, Dorothy advised him to "figure out how much you need, then double it."[53] The women lived modestly and managed, and neither died penniless, much to Dorothy's brother's surprise.[54]

OTHER PROBLEMS

In addition to constant money problems and occasional problems with fire marshals, Edith and Dorothy had to contend with the theatrical unions (which led to unnecessary expenditures) and child labor laws. They had to pay a union curtain-puller even when there was no curtain, and they had to pay union makeup artists, carpenters and wardrobe mistresses even though they did not allow them to touch the children or the sets. One way they circumvented the child labor laws was to designate all the performers as "understudies," for understudies were somewhat exempt from the rules.[55] There were two or three casts for each production anyway, so, perhaps, it was fair to label everyone as an understudy. Another way was to stop advertising and to stop selling seats publicly, which made productions seem more like recitals than public performances and, therefore, child labor laws would be inapplicable.

METHODS AND PHILOSOPHIES

Although Edith and Dorothy often received requests from Broadway producers for child actors, the purpose of their school and theatre was not to train children for careers in the professional theatre. Rather, it was to afford children an opportunity to study history, literature, mythology, music, dance, art and drama after school and to show the fruition of their studies in a performance. Instead of the "three R's," Edith and Dorothy emphasized the "three D's": drama, dance and design. The "three D's," they believed, were fundamental in training taste, stimulating imagination and teaching manners. For Edith and Dorothy, culture as a process required careful and thorough work, plenty of time, first-class material and an environment that could be achieved best in a special school.

Edith and Dorothy spent months on research for each play. The plays had to be rich in imaginative content; their technical requirements had to be neither above nor below the children's abilities; the language had to be of a very high quality; the stories had to be appealing; and the subject had to be based on strong visual images. Everything pertinent to the culture and period of the play was presented to the children.

Before painting, the children drew for weeks in an atmosphere of quiet work rather than frivolous play. They were expected to stay within the lines and had a few paints and brushes they were expected to keep clean. They were expected to draw in the manner of the period of the play, and Edith provided the paints in the appropriate palette.

Edith and her assistants modeled the sets, costumes and makeup after figures in paintings, sculpture or pottery from the period on which the production was based. Material was often painted rather than dyed, and even the children's skin was painted. Edith paid scrupulous attention to every detail, including the children's hair and the lighting of the sets, some of which were designed in tiers. The children worked on props and on details within their capabilities, such as program covers or painting clouds on scenery. All other physical and visual aspects of the productions were designed by Edith (and implemented by Edith and professionals) based on available and relevant historical and artistic sources.

Dorothy believed five or six months with rehearsals two or three times a week were necessary in preparing a play with children. During this time Dorothy, a skillful storyteller, presented and explained the meaning of the chosen story, and other stories illustrative of the time and place, to the entire class. Slowly but surely the ideas of the story became familiar to the children. Sometimes she would ask the children to translate an idea into action by pantomiming with their hands only, and she would ask questions to ground the pantomime in reality. Then she would have the children act the story out, giving them words when they could not think of anything to say. Dorothy found that a few props could be helpful. For several sessions, the children acted the story out informally, invented dialogue or used pantomime, danced to appropriate snippets of music and drew, painted and modeled in clay the characters, incidents or objects that intrigued them. Dorothy eventually offered actual lines as the children pantomimed, and they became substitutes for the children's improvised lines. Eventually the lines were memorized from oral repetition. When children delivered lines without expression, Dorothy would interrupt and offer a hypothetical parallel from daily life. All of the children played each part before final casting took place.

There is contradictory evidence about whether the children's art work and acting were creative and spontaneous or copied and memorized. Some of the contradictory evidence comes from Edith and Dorothy themselves. The truth seems to be that sometimes the children's art work and acting were the result of copying and memorizing, and sometimes they were the result of creativity and improvisation.

Over the years Edith and Dorothy mounted productions of *Aucassin and Nicolete*, *Nala and Damayanti*, *The Tempest*, *Divertissement Français (Chansons de France)*, *The Golden Cage*, *The Rose and the Ring*, *Khai Khosru*, *Ahmed the Cobbler*, *The Story of Theseus* (possibly also called *The Sword of Attica*),

The Garden Wall—A Revue, The Image of Artemis and *A Midsummer Night's Dream*. Two hundred friends, relatives and discriminating people made up the audience at these twice-yearly "events."

King-Coit productions were reviewed by the well-known, first-string drama critics of important publications. The adjectives most often used to describe the productions were: heart-melting, remarkable, charming, refreshing, magical, perfect, professional, fresh, guileless, delightful, unusual, graceful, tender, enchanting, innocent, disarming, gem-like, irresistible, humorous, uninhibited, delicious, orderly, sincere, extraordinary, touching, beautiful and unique. In a letter (dated May 2, 1947) to Edith and Dorothy, Lynn Fontanne expressed succinctly the qualities of King-Coit productions which attracted the large and influential following:

Mr. Lunt and I went [to the play] and thought it such a rare and wonderful piece of art. The amazing direction of these tiny creatures, we know, is a job requiring as much patience as even Job never knew about. The costumes and decorations, which are the most beautiful we have ever seen on any stage whatsoever, were something you could sit and feast your eyes on for hours.[56]

Were it not for the outspoken support of influential critics and well-known theatre people, it is unlikely the King-Coit could have lasted for so many years. Rare criticism asserted that Edith and Dorothy's process was too rigid, that the children were manipulated and exploited and that their performances were too mechanical. Most believed, however, that the children gained so much that negative aspects were neutralized.

In 1958, financial problems and Edith's fatigue signaled the closing of the King-Coit School and Children's Theatre. Ten years later Dorothy wrote in *Radcliffe Quarterly*:

I live in Bethlehem, Conn. in summer—a long summer. I have a class in acting in New York, just two days a week for the winter months. My friend and colleague (Edith King) was not strong enough any longer and I could not carry on with any hope of keeping up our standard without her. I have done a less ambitious type of coaching the last few years, just simple drama with no costumes, scenery, etc., for various private schools who have wanted me.[57]

Edith and Dorothy's relationship has been described as similar to that between parent (Dorothy) and child (Edith). Ironically, Edith was not particularly fond of children, nor did she like to speak before groups, and she was not above using hysteria and migraine headaches to get her own way. Dorothy, on the other hand, spoke before groups quite comfortably, adored children, admired Edith's talent and devoted her whole life to making her pupils and Edith happy. Despite their differences they deeply loved one another, and, except for a few brief interludes, they lived together until Edith died on April 7, 1975, at the age of ninety-one. Eighteen months later, on October 20, 1976, Dorothy died at the age of eighty-seven. In Edith's obituary, the King-Coit Theatre was described as "an integral part of the New York theatre scene."[58] In Dorothy's obituary, the King-Coit Theatre was referred to as "a constituent part of New York Drama."[59]

The King-Coit School and Children's Theatre is unique in children's theatre history: it was an important part of the New York theatre scene; it was supported by many rich and famous people; it featured plays adapted from obscure literature; extraordinary attention to detail was a hallmark of the productions; and all phases of the school and theatre met high artistic standards.

It is unlikely that the King-Coit could survive in New York today, given contemporary family life and the economic realities of running a school or theatre. The King-Coit School and Children's Theatre, nevertheless, demonstrated the value of the arts in education and demonstrated that children's theatre—if it is well written, well produced, and appeals to adults—does not have to be the stepchild it often is now. Edith King and Dorothy Coit's accomplishments stand as an important model for the American theatre.

NOTES

1. Thirty-year Commemorative Booklet, King-Coit Scrapbooks, Billy Rose Theatre Collection, Lincoln Center Library and Museum of the Performing Arts, New York City.

2. Weston Barclay, "The Play's the Thing When It Comes to Progressive Education," *New York World-Telegram*, May 7, 1940, p. 19.

3. Radcliffe College Yearbook, 1911, p. 32.

4. Barclay, "The Play's the Thing," p. 19.

5. Personal interview with Elisabeth Coit, Dorothy's sister, New York City, June 13, 1978.

6. Barclay, "The Play's the Thing," p. 19.

7. Radcliffe College Yearbook, 1911, n. pag.

8. Letter from Jane S. Knowles, Radcliffe College Archivist, Cambridge, Massachusetts, January 29, 1979.

9. Ibid.

10. Dorothy Coit, "A Defense of Dramatics," *Radcliffe Magazine*, February 1911, 13:2, p. 93.

11. Ibid., p. 94.

12. Ibid.

13. Barclay, "The Play's the Thing," p. 19.

14. Personal interview with Marian (King) de Florez, Edith's sister, Cresskill, New Jersey, April 29, 1978.

15. Letter from Peter de Florez, Edith's nephew, Palisades, New York, March 8, 1979.

16. Letter from Peter de Florez, June 21, 1978.

17. Letters from Martha L. Mitchell, University Archivist, Brown University, Providence, Rhode Island, July 10 and October 3, 1978.

18. Barclay, "The Play's the Thing," p. 19.

19. Ibid.

20. Marian de Florez interview.

21. Barclay, "The Play's the Thing," p. 19.

22. Letter from Jane Loring Noble Fiske, Troy, New Hampshire, June 25, 1978.

23. Ibid.

24. Ibid.

25. Ibid.

26. Ibid.

27. Letter from Elinor Hopkinson Barr, Cornish, Maine, July 1, 1978.

28. William Hawkins, "Happy Birthday!" *New York World Telegram and the Sun*, Saturday feature magazine, April 25, 1953, p. 19.

29. Personal interview with Robert Coit, Dorothy's brother, and Robert Hawley, her nephew, Rockport, Massachusetts, July 26, 1978.

30. Marian de Florez interview.

31. Letter from Ira Glackens, son of William Glackens, the painter, Shepherdstown, West Virginia, April 10, 1978.

32. Personal interview with Charles Thompson, Katharine Thompson's nephew, New York City, November, 2, 1978.

33. Barclay, "The Play's the Thing," p. 19.

34. "The Eight" were: Robert Henri, George Luks, William Glackens, John Sloan, Maurice Prendergast, Ernest Lawson, Everett Shinn and Arthur B. Davies.

35. Marian de Florez interview. Paul Fuller, Jr., who was married to the sister of Edith's brother-in-law, had been very close to the Coudert family and later became a partner in the Coudert law firm. Through him Coudert may have known of the work Edith and Dorothy were doing in Boston and, liking what he heard, invited them to come to New York.

36. Personal interview with Helen Farr Sloan (among others), New York City, October 23, 1978. Sloan was a pupil and then taught painting and assisted King at the King-Coit School and Children's Theatre. She is the widow of John Sloan, the painter.

37. Mrs. Gugler, Edith and Dorothy's close friend, is a daughter of Mary Lawrence Tonetti and Francois Michel Louis Tonetti, both sculptors. Mary Tonetti was involved with the establishment and the continuation of the King-Coit School and Children's Theatre, and Mrs. Gugler's husband, Eric, an architect, designed the first King-Coit theatre in a building owned by the Tonettis on East 40 Street in New York City.

38. Personal interview with Anne Tonetti Gugler, New York City, May 16, 1978.

39. As quoted in Isabelle K. Savell, *The Tonetti Years at Snedens Landing* (New City, N.Y.: Historical Society of Rockland County, 1977), pp. 162–64.

40. Alexander Woollcott, "The Play: *Aucassin and Nicolete*," *New York Times* , April 9, 1921, p. 9.

41. King-Coit Scrapbooks, Lincoln Center.

42. Savell, *Tonetti Years*, p. 162.

43. John Mason Brown, "Two on the Aisle: Boutet de Monvel's Songbooks Charmingly Brought to Life at the King-Coit Children's Theatre," *New York Post*, April 30, 1934, p. 11.

44. Savell, *Tonetti Years*, p. 164.

45. Richard Hayes, "The Stage: The King-Coit Children's Theatre," *Commonweal*, May 21, 1954, p. 175.

46. Ibid.

47. Dorothy Coit, "Recipe for a Children's Theatre," unidentified magazine article,

from Jack Melanos, former business manager at the King-Coit School and Children's Theatre.

48. Barclay, "The Play's the Thing," p. 19.

49. Stella Bloch, "A Persian Play in New York," *New Orient,* 48, no other information available, King-Coit Scrapbooks, Lincoln Center.

50. Undated letter, King-Coit Scrapbooks, Lincoln Center.

51. John Singer Sargent, George F. Baker, Claude Bragdon, Edith J.R. Isaacs, Mrs. August Belmont, David Mannes, Paul Manship, Rosamond Gilder, Mrs. Otis Skinner, Hughes Mearns, Mrs. Gustave Shirmer, Robert Edmond Jones, Mr. and Mrs. Charles Scribner, Jr., Maria Ouspenskaya, Edith P. Morgan, Mrs. Philip Barry, Mrs. Irving Berlin, Richard Boleslavsky, Tallulah Bankhead, Mrs. George Bellows, Katharine Cornell, Lynn Fontanne, Alfred Lunt, Martha Graham, Walter Hampden, Beatrice Lillie, Beatrice Straight, Mr. and Mrs. Jo Mielziner, Mr. and Mrs. Donald Oenslager, George P. Baker, Ilka Chase, Anne Morgan, Alexander Woollcott, Stark Young, Mr. and Mrs. Jack F. Chrysler, Charles Prendergast, Georgia Eldred and Anne Hinchman. Also, Mr. and Mrs. Laurance S. Rockefeller, Mr. and Mrs. David Rockefeller, Mr. and Mrs. Harry Winston, Tamara Daykarhanova, Theresa Helburn, Hope Williams, Margalo Gillmore, Mrs. James West Roosevelt, Helen Keller, Van Dearing Perrine, Cecilia Beaux, Guthrie McClintic, Aline Bernstein, Mr. and Mrs. Paul Mellon, Mrs. Bela Blau, Rita Wallach Morganthau, Mildred Dunnock, Brooks Atkinson and Robert Henri.

52. Personal interview with Jack Melanos, New York City, September 22, 1978.

53. Robert Hawley interview.

54. Robert Coit interview.

55. Personal interview with Charles Thompson, New York City, November 2, 1978.

56. King-Coit Scrapbooks.

57. *Radcliffe Quarterly,* June 1968, 52:2, p. 30.

58. *New York Times,* April 9, 1975, p. 46.

59. *New York Times,* October 24, 1976, p. 36.

6

Children's Theatre Activities at Karamu House, 1915–1975

NOERENA ABOOKIRE AND JENNIFER SCOTT MCNAIR

In the first decades of the twentieth century, settlement houses were becoming increasingly important as social and artistic centers for adults and children living in inner-city neighborhoods. These settlement houses, usually located in crowded, poverty-stricken neighborhoods, provided a wide variety of social services. Settlement houses such as Hull House in Chicago, and the Henry Street Settlement in New York distinguished themselves with comprehensive social work activities. Like their many counterparts in cities throughout the country, such settlement houses utilized the arts in general, and theatre in particular, as an important element of their social work programs. And, these theatre activities often included theatre with and for young people.

Karamu House, founded in Cleveland, Ohio, in 1915, is a unique example of a settlement house that not only featured the arts, but, essentially, built its entire program around arts activities. At Karamu House children's theatre was the opening wedge that encouraged the thrust of art and theatre as the central function of the organization; and drama and the related arts eventually became the vehicle for all other settlement activity. Random storytelling and informal drama with children, that began in two small cottages next to a playground in inner-city Cleveland, developed into sophisticated theatre activity for children and adults that included full-scale theatre, dance and opera productions as well as art exhibits, drama classes, workshops in all of the arts and a continuing center for nursery care. From simple community support of the families of the children involved in play-making activities, the program at Karamu House grew to enjoy national and international acclaim as an arts center.

THE EARLY YEARS (1915–1925)

Karamu House got its start when the Neighborhood Association, sponsored by the Men's Club of the Second Presbyterian Church of Cleveland, commissioned Russell and Rowena Jelliffe to study the needs of the people in the area surrounding the church.[1] The Jelliffes were then recent graduates of the University of Chicago, with Masters degrees in social work. The area to be studied was, at that time, often referred to as "The Roaring Third," a poverty-stricken neighborhood heavily populated with families of black, Jewish, Syrian and Italian heritage.

As a result of recommendations made by the Jelliffes, the Men's Club purchased land in the area that contained two cottages that could be used for community activities. This property later became known as the Karamu House.

Russell and Rowena Jelliffe moved into the rear of one of the cottages and began working in the neighborhood to create a sense of community and racial harmony. Their task was a difficult one; the area was overcrowded, and the community was made up of unskilled workers, many of whom were migrants from rural areas. The residents felt isolated in the community because of the many cultural differences and prejudices prevalent in the diverse population.

The Jelliffes, determined to counter the community's prejudices and create an environment where the differences would be appreciated and respected, began their activities simply, by working with the children. Gaining the children's trust and friendship by acting as supervisors in an adjacent playground, the Jelliffes learned about the community's life-styles and family patterns; and this interaction gradually led into similar relationships with the parents of these children.

Games and outdoor activities were just the beginning of the relationship between the Jelliffes and the community surrounding Karamu House. In a short period of time a pattern of storytelling developed wherein the children began gathering around the Jelliffes' front porch every evening to hear Russell play the guitar and Rowena tell stories. These informal sessions were an important beginning, and they became the "seed for a total commitment to the use of theatre for and with children."[2]

The children of the neighborhood became increasingly interested in going to the Jelliffes' to play. Although the organization which the Jelliffes headed was initially called the Neighborhood Association, the children preferred, instead, to call it the "Jelliffes' Playhouse."[3]

The storytelling that had begun on the porch steps quickly developed into informal play-acting by the children. The Jelliffes encouraged the children to listen to one another, and stories were shared involving character interpretations colored by the different dialects and backgrounds present in the diverse group. As they shared their own stories before a respectful audience of peers, the children began to bond as a group. When both the children and their parents began requesting presentations of the stories for their families and friends, a transition began at Karamu House which, within a few years, was to take the group into a formal program of theatre for children.

The storytelling and play-making sessions brought children together from various backgrounds and races. The differences in the children created differences in the characters they were creating, which added life and believability to the informal dramas. No matter the background or life experiences of the children, the stories united the group, and all involved learned to respect one another's views.

As fall winds forced the children indoors, more space was needed for the drama sessions and the various classes that the Jelliffes were developing. In the fall of 1915, the Cleveland Board of Education arranged for the settlement house to use the Longwood School gymnasium, and this move ushered in an era of more formal children's theatre productions.

Records of these first few years at the settlement house are not available. But it is known that the Jelliffes built sets, sewed costumes and taught various theatre classes for the children, including creative drama, acting and production.

The Snow Queen, Alice in Wonderland and *Humpty Dumpty* were among the first productions. These plays, adaptations of children's stories about thirty minutes in length, were presented in an informal manner. The audience always learned something from these first productions, the major goals of which were group involvement. Not only did the children acquire speaking skills, but they also learned to discipline themselves by being at rehearsals and performances on time. And this need for responsibility, coupled with the experience of working with mixed-race casts provided important lessons for the young people that extended into their relationships with their families and the community. As the number of shows produced increased, Rowena also began making more artistic demands.

Rowena Jelliffe, who was to serve as executive director of Karamu and as director of Children's Theatre, supervised the children's activities from 1915 to 1949. The development of the children's programs—moving from storytelling to drama classes to rehearsed performances—was based on Rowena Jelliffe's philosophies that continued throughout her directorship at Karamu House. She was specific in her philosophies, and those assisting her adhered to the following:

1. The play was never more important than the preparation of the performance.
2. People of different cultures and races could work together toward the positive creative expression of a story.
3. The characters in a story would be acted out by several children in the group in an ensemble format; no one child ever "owned" a part.
4. There was a conscious effort to use the child, regardless of sex and race, who would best create the character.[4]

Rowena felt that children could realize their full potential as long as limits were not placed on them. And, seeing each child as a distinct individual, Rowena worked skillfully to achieve an environment of positive reinforcement:

These children came to me with great pressures from home and the neighborhood. I was familiar with the home life and the neighborhood. The particular needs of a family were discussed by Russell and myself, and I directed the experience toward the needs of the child. Sometimes they just needed to be a part of something—and they knew they could find it through children's theatre work.[5]

By 1917, some of the productions—particularly those that showcased inter-racial involvement—began to attract the attention of the community and beyond. Two such productions, *Cinderella* (1917) and *Fairies* (1921), were of special interest. Ormond Forte, publisher of the *Cleveland Advocate*, a black newspaper of that time said: "I beheld black children, brown children, white children—all mixed up in a glorious commonality—joyous, rollicking, delighted, care free—black mothers and white mothers, and a sprinkling of fathers 'polkadotting' the scene."[6]

Rowena also believed that each show should be cast according to who was best for the role, no matter the sex or race of the child.[7]

Beginning in 1919, with the opening of the nearby Grant Street Playground, "Circus Night" became a yearly happening. For this event, members of the settlement house's children's theatre formed a theatrical parade. In later years the parade became a celebration of the coming of summer.

Adult theatre activity grew out of the popularity and success of the children's theatre program. And, by 1920, the adults as well as the young people had a formal drama group, called the Dumas Players. This group later became known as the Gilpin Players, named in honor of the black actor, Charles Gilpin.[8] The Gilpin Players, while not an all-black company, was dedicated to supporting and creating a space and visibility for black actors and playwrights.

Traditional settlement house activities, including craft clubs, sewing clubs and standard welfare programs (such as assisting in job placement for adults), soon followed this thriving theatre program. Additional staff were added by 1921 to aid the Jelliffes with these activities.

At least six different children's plays were produced during the first decade of productions at Karamu. But not all children were ready for the intense group work necessary for a production; some preferred the storytelling and informal play-making, which the Jelliffes continued to nurture. And nonproduction activities for the children, such as creative dramatics classes, marionette workshops, and arts and crafts classes were continued even with the growth of formal productions.

A PERIOD OF EXPANSION (1925–1939)

As the activities grew, so did the need for space. The logistics of using Longwood School became a real problem, because the adults rehearsed every evening, the active children's theatre worked every afternoon, and the sets had to be mobile to accommodate rehearsal and performance schedules. This problem was exacerbated by the fact that the settlement house performers were only guests at the school, so nothing could be nailed or hung, even overnight, without difficulty. This all made it very difficult to continue the extensive theatre program in the available spaces.

In 1921, fund raising for a new building had produced enough to purchase a corner piece of property, adjoining the original settlement house. On this property stood the shells of two buildings. It was not until 1926 that volunteers began working to turn these two buildings into a nursery and a theatre. Members of the Gilpin Players, their friends and families gathered every evening, working long into the night renovating—and sporadically rehearsing—in the rubbish-filled space. This soon became the theatre home for the adults and the children.

Rowena reported fond memories of this time:

> Those are heavenly days and nights to remember. We did all our own work. We plastered it, papered it, wired it, installed new plumbing, put a furnace in it ourselves. Far into the night we worked, doing bits of rehearsing while we worked, singing, forgetting that we were tired, growing to love our little theatre in a way that one loves only those things which they have created.[9]

Throughout the twenties, as blacks from the South migrated to the North, the community surrounding the settlement evolved from the "Roaring Third" to the "Black Belt." Life was difficult in this underprivileged area, especially for the children moving from rural areas with little experience in large cities. Wanting them to feel at home, Rowena gave increased emphasis to the storytelling sessions. "Br'er Rabbit" tales, or tales of "Uncle Remus" offered refreshing contrasts to classics such as *Cinderella,* and were shared, complete with the deep-South dialects, during these sessions. Rowena encouraged all the children to appreciate the differences in dialects, which, in turn, helped the newcomers from the South gain acceptance in this unfamiliar city.

A few of these tales, such as *Shoes Fer De Feets, Sat'd'y Evenin'* and *How Come Br'er Rabbit Do No Work*, were adapted into scripts and performed in the theatre. The "Uncle Remus" tales, replete with exciting characters, were fun for the children; and the morals from the tales stimulated discussions. The positive qualities of the dialect brought a respect from the audience, and this encouragement "led many of the young people to write their own stories, their versions of the tales their parents told them."[10] The "Uncle Remus" plays became a permanent part of the repertoire from 1926 through 1939 and won first place for three consecutive years in the junior drama tournament of neighborhood centers.[11]

Rowena worked to make the theatre experience pleasant for both the participants and the audience. She would begin the productions by appearing in front of the curtain, meeting the audience and telling a short story. She would then go backstage to assist wherever needed when the curtain went up. She recalls this ritual fondly:

I had a great big pillow on which I sat in front of the curtain, told a seven to ten minute story and then after that, we would always do group singing. . . . All the building used to ring with singing—and not just the songs in the show. Then the play would follow.[12]

With the development and renovation of the settlement house and the changing demographics in the community, the settlement and the surrounding community began to manifest a new identity. Slowly, the two buildings, which were decorated with African art and motifs, became a dedication to the members' African heritage. By 1927, the new 120-seat theatre, home of the Gilpin Players and the Children's Theatre, was christened "Karamu House." The Swahili word, *Karamu*, meaning "a place of enjoyment, a feasting place, for ceremonials after a successful journey," was chosen because it expressed both the concept of the settlement house and its commitment to the black culture.[13]

Karamu was a haven for many inner-city children growing up in Cleveland. A former participant recalls:

As a child of eight, I was offered everything from the settlement. It was an enriching time of our lives—we had nine children in our family—and no family of nine or ten kids could afford to provide the wide range of cultural and artistic experiences to their children. Had it not been for the Jelliffes and the programs that they ran we never would have had the advantages of theatre and dance. My mother knew the blessing this house was—you learned to be a social being. We never had time to get into mischief—there was school, playhouse settlement, homework, and bed.[14]

The settlement theatre plays were presented in their home theatre, Karamu, and also toured area libraries, YMCA's and, on occasion, the Cleveland Museum of Art. The productions included the popular dialect shows and adaptations of popular children's stories. Between 1925 and 1939, ten puppet-marionette plays were also listed as productions by the Karamu Theatre. These included *Jack and the Beanstalk*, *The Magic Hat* and *The Three Wishes*.

The marionette classes were originally taught by Russell Jelliffe, but in 1925, one of the young members of the settlement, Rozell (Zell) Ingram, developed a touring troupe of young people. Carving and sculpturing led Ingram to create his own cast of marionettes, and he and a friend, along with other young people in their teens, began puppet tours that would thrive for the next ten years.[15]

"All marionette figures were designed, modeled and costumed by the puppeteers who also designed, built and equipped the stage."[16] "Theatre on Wheels," the name of the puppet-touring troupe, toured the area, performing at schools, in parks and at church fairs. The puppet troupe produced plays such as *The Gooseberry Mandarin*, *Circus Pantomime*, and *The Bee Man of Orn*. In 1939, when Ingram left Cleveland to become a sculptor and teacher in New York, "Theatre on Wheels" became a part of the settlement's history.[17]

In addition to the puppet troupe plays and the "Uncle Remus" tales, *Hansel and Gretel*, *The Brownie Bush* and *The Snow Witch* were dramatized during this period. Young members of the print-studio-workshop classes printed the programs for the Children's Theatre productions. Admission to the shows was ten cents for adults and three cents for children. Pennies were scarce at this time, and, sometimes, if a child did not have the admission price, he or she would pay what they could—or nothing—and pay the balance the next week.[18]

After working with children for over twenty years, the Jelliffes had learned how to handle children of various ages. The audiences, made up of friends and families who all knew one another, became more discerning as the children worked toward more artistic interpretations with each production. As one former participant recalls, healthy interchange between the children and adults working on productions at Karamu, helped to foster a sense of pride throughout the settlement community:

We were known as "slum kids." The Playhouse Settlement was like a gold mine—we would share our experiences with our friends at school and they would not believe it—until they came and saw the plays. It was a cultural clique. The whole community benefited from the activity, as did each individual and the family unit. It was an important part of all of our lives.[19]

These activities moved into the schools when the principal at the nearby Rutherford B. Hayes Elementary School began working with the Jelliffes on a special project for slow learners. This project began in the fall of 1939 and continued through 1941. The principal and the Jelliffes felt that the slow learners at the Rutherford School were handicapped more by limited background than by low mental capacity. They developed a program where a group of children were taken out of their regular school classes every afternoon and brought to the settlement for classes in play-making, modeling, drawing, model airplanes and ship-making. After five semesters of working afternoons at Karamu, all of the children needing special help improved not only in grades, but in attitude and attendance as well.[20]

By the late 1930s, the children's theatre at Karamu had gained wide recognition, and, in addition, the settlement offered classes in modern and tap dance, sewing, cooking, metal craft, astronomy, and creative dramatics, among others. By 1937, 1,500 people were registered as settlement members.[21] But this growth and success was threatened when, on October 22, 1939, fire destroyed the entire section of the settlement containing the theatre.

A PERIOD OF TRANSITION (1939–1949)

The 1939 fire was an unfortunate intermission to the theatre activity at Karamu, because theatre activities were the most visible aspect of Karamu House programs. According to one source, "that [theatre] is what everyone knew as the settlement."[22]

The fire began a ten-year period of transition for the Karamu Theatre. From

1939 to 1946 more energy was spent on searching for the right location and raising the funds for a new structure than was spent on theatre activities. In 1941, with the acceleration of World War II, fund raising slowed and by the end of 1942, ceased.

In 1942 "there was a membership explosion at Karamu House" as there were then 2,200 members—1,400 children and 800 adults—participating in various activities.[23] It had been difficult enough housing all the activities and members before the fire, and with the increased membership, finding the space to operate was almost impossible. The facilities now available included the two original cottages, the corner building, which housed a nursery school, and, next to the gutted structure that once housed the theatre, the Bokari, which was a shop that displayed and sold the craft products students made in the adjoining print shop and craft studios.

Many organizations offered Karamu stages on which to perform after the fire; but these possibilities represented much extra work, and the Jelliffes believed it was more important to concentrate on raising funds for new facilities and to work to manage the existing classes within the diminished space. The adults were able to tour with several productions, but to tour any Children's Theatre productions was considered too expensive. The Jelliffes thus turned their focus to social activities rather than productions for the young people.[24]

During this period, the adults in the community were caught up in war-time activities and were either in uniform or working long hours on the assembly lines at defense plants. Storytelling, art classes and creative dramatics became the activities for those children left at home while their parents worked. And social clubs, in areas such as metal crafts, card printing and journalism, became all-important to the children, who were bored because of the lack of productions. In addition, the Karamu House members continued to work with Hayes Elementary School, and other schools, to supplement classroom education for selected students.

In 1941, to ease the overcrowding, the board of trustees of Karamu purchased a plot of land, some distance from the original settlement house property, to build a multiunit facility. Plans were drawn to erect a youth and child care center.[25] By November 1946, the building was complete, with a nursery on the first floor and an arena stage at one end of a large room on the second floor. Productions could begin again and, depending on the size of the set, small audiences could gather around this space. The offices, still at the old location, continued to hold some of the classes, but with the new space, storytelling and creative dramatics classes had space and a ready audience in the nursery school. The new nursery school was the first of three structures that were to house the permanent facilities of Karamu House.

At the new facility, the students involved with storytelling and creative dramatics classes created the "Thimble Theatre." This group adapted favorite stories and tales into plays and presented them to the nursery school children on the premises.[26]

These new facilities and new activities caused renewed interest in the Karamu programs, and they also increased the work load for the Jelliffes. Dividing time between the work at two locations and fund raising was difficult, so, in 1946, the Jelliffes hired Gerald and Bernice Marans to help lead the adult and children's theatre activities.[27] Bernice, an experienced social worker, coordinated classes and productions with the children, while Gerald handled the Gilpin Players' productions.

Construction of a new Karamu Theatre building began on the new site in May 1948.[28] By the end of 1949, the facility, housing three theatres, was complete. The main part of the complex included a proscenium theatre seating over 200, an arena theatre seating up to 140, and an outdoor theatre with a concrete seating area for 1,000. The facility also included a Bokari shop for the sale of craft items made by the members; a large, mirrored dance studio; dressing rooms; showers and additional rehearsal rooms.[29] Thus, by the close of 1949, Karamu House had its first real home, thirty-four years after its inception.

With the expansion of Karamu House, Rowena began delegating the Children's Theatre responsibilities to full-time staff directors, but she continued to act as consultant and supervisor.

Between 1949 and 1952, there were several different directors of the children's theatre program. One of these directors, Olive Thurman, who worked with Karamu Children's Theatre from 1950 through 1952, assisted in starting a Junior Theatre group, comprised of teenagers working at Karamu. This group helped bridge the gap between the Gilpin Players and the Children's Theatre. With an increase in the number of productions, made possible by the three stages in the new facility, these young people were involved with some directing, and they occasionally led some of the children's creative drama classes. The teenagers also began playing adult roles in the Children's Theatre productions. In September 1951, the Karamu Junior Theatre changed its name to Karamu Student Theatre.[30]

Thurman directed productions, was responsible for costumes, set design and regularly scheduled children's nonproduction classes during her two seasons as director of the Children's Theatre at Karamu House.

CHILDREN'S THEATRE OF KARAMU HOUSE (1950–1962)

By 1951, Karamu House activities included plays, operas, concerts, dance recitals, classes in creative writing, photography and art, and the sales of crafts and art products in the settlement's craft shop. The Children's Theatre and the Karamu Student Theatre performed in their respective facilities as well as touring shows for Brownie Troops, local schools, and on occasion, the County Receiving Home for Children. Russell and Rowena Jelliffe were involved in coordinating the busy Karamu House, hosting foreign visitors, a staff of thirty full-time professionals and sixty volunteers, soliciting funds, supervising intern students from local universities and planning for the future. Karamu House was bustling

with activity when Ann Kathryn Flagg joined the staff as director of the Children's
Theatre in 1952.

Flagg, a native of Charleston, West Virginia, had received her B.A. from
West Virginia State University. Before joining the Karamu staff, she had directed
the drama activities at a high school in Fairmont, West Virginia.[31] Flagg would
remain at Karamu for nine seasons, training the two directors who would follow
her and raising the standards of the Children's Theatre work to its peak in Karamu
House history.[32]

Flagg supported the philosophy of teaching the children to concentrate on the
process of learning rather than the product, and she was committed to the challenge offered by the children at Karamu. A student of Flagg's, Gilbert Moses,
recalls fondly that "Ann was a great transmitter of love, and the power of self-
potential, self-discipline and self-control through the process of creating a character, or a prop, or a costume."[33]

During her first season at Karamu, Flagg was very busy. She taught storytelling
and creative dramatics and directed twelve productions. These included, among
others: *The Crowning of Arthur and Gareth, Lynette, Gareth and Lynette* (from
Legends in Action), *The Emperor's New Clothes* and *The Little Match Girl*. The
Children's Theatre productions were presented in the Arena Stage on Saturday
afternoons; the Student Theatre used the stage on Monday evenings for their
productions.

Flagg also initiated a program at Karamu that treated the audience, who came
to see the Children's Theatre productions, as students of theatre. This new
activity, "Story Hour," was a storytelling period that preceded the play and
acquainted the children with classical literature. If, for example, the play to be
presented was a Greek myth, Flagg would tell other Greek myths, thereby
introducing the theme or the historical perspective of the play before the actual
production.

With Flagg as director, the Children's Theatre at Karamu moved into its most
acclaimed period. A flyer promoting Karamu's Children's Theatre at that time
detailed some of the benefits of participating:

Karamu offers carefully selected entertainment for young people, a dramatic contrast to
the banalities and horrors to which they are subjected today through radio, movies and
T.V. And in the friendly, intimate Arena staging, audiences form a close unity of spirit
with the actors. Performances are Saturday afternoons at 2:30 p.m. in the Arena Theatre.
Each play runs for four consecutive Saturdays unless otherwise announced. Admission,
Adults 50 cents, Children 25 cents.[34]

Flagg carefully guided the children's activities by dividing the age groups.
The younger children worked on creative dramatics and puppet activities; the
nine to twelve year olds also worked on creative dramatics, but, in addition,
they learned the mechanics of stage sets; and the Karamu Student Theatre took
classes in improvisation, set design and technical theatre.

The classes were a combination of study and practice. In the "Play Production," for example, students met three times a week for creative dramatics activities and field trips as well as readings and rehearsals for the Saturday afternoon performances.[35] Members of the Student Theatre took classes in stagecraft, participated in crew work and visited other theatres, along with rehearsing regularly for their own productions.[36] The productions of both groups were thus a product of the classwork rather than isolated productions.

In July 1955, the Children's Theatre was asked to participate in the Tri-State Children's Theatre Conference held at Cain Park in Cleveland. A noted visitor at that conference, Winifred Ward, was particularly impressed with the performance by the Karamu group.[37]

By the mid–1950s, Ann Flagg was gaining recognition for her work with children's theatre activities. She was asked to give talks around the city on her work, and, in 1957, she was invited to chair a session at the National Children's Theatre Conference.[38] This type of recognition for Flagg and the Children's Theatre served to highlight Karamu more as a professional troupe than as a welfare agency.

During the 1957–1958 season, 1,290 young adults and children participated in the classes at Karamu, and twenty-four performances of four children's plays were given before an audience of 4,882.[39] It was also during this period that a community services building was opened. The building, which housed the administrative offices, music and band rehearsal rooms, a concert hall, the Magic Carpet Room (children's theatre and student theatre), along with various other rooms, was the third structure built for Karamu House activities.

Between 1956 and 1960, Karamu House Children's Theatre productions included such plays as *The Dreamy Kid*, *The Long Voyage Home*, *Old King Cole*, *The Magic Apple*, *The Dowry of Columbine* and *King Grog and His Grouch*. One account of the 1958–1959 season indicates that the Children's Theatre offered twenty-three performances of five different plays to an audience of 2,048.[40]

During the 1959–1960 season two musicals were staged, *The Blue Bird* and *The Magic Flute*, with the Children's Theatre collaborating with the Karamettes and the Karateens. (The Karamettes was a children's chorus made up of members ages nine to thirteen, and the Karateens was a chorus composed of those ages thirteen to sixteen.[41])

Continuing to expand activities for young people at Karamu, Flagg emphasized the teaching of the total production and ensemble work by frequent double-casting and requiring participants to share in all aspects of the production, such as costuming and set design. She also began a Youth Forum, designed to study and discuss the people and the problems of Africa. Occasionally, guest speakers would assist the forum, gathering with the group in the Magic Carpet Room.[42]

The Magic Carpet Room was designed for storytelling and creative dramatics. It had pillows all around for the children to sit on and flexible wood platform units for improvised stage settings. The children would read to one another and act out the stories in preparation for later participation in the productions.

In early 1961, Ann Flagg, encouraged by Rowena Jelliffe and Winifred Ward, left Karamu Children's Theatre to begin her graduate studies under Ward at Northwestern University. Ward was greatly impressed with Ann Flagg. Describing her as "the most remarkable teacher of creative drama" she had had in Evanston, Ward later noted about Flagg: "Ann felt deep pride in her race and taught it to her students. . . . Ann was interested in the children as individuals. When a child was lacking in confidence, she gave him parts to play to bolster his courage. And he never let her down."[43]

Ann Flagg brought the Karamu Children's Theatre to its zenith, and, stressing the importance of the process of creating a production, she championed and extended the goals articulated by the Jelliffes in their work at the settlement. Flagg not only brought national acclaim to the Karamu Children's Theatre, but this rare and, in the words of Winifred Ward, "exceptionally gifted"[44] teacher had a profound impact on the young people with whom she worked. According to Rowena, Flagg "as educator-director-actress had the combination of skills necessary to be the perfect staff person."[45] The future of Karamu Children's Theatre would demonstrate that Flagg truly was a remarkable teacher and director with skills that could not be duplicated.

CHILDREN'S THEATRE AT KARAMU HOUSE (1963–1975)

After nine years of stable growth and expansion of children's theatre activities under Flagg, the next twelve years saw six directors come and go. After Flagg left, the directors who replaced her attempted to maintain her goals and standards, but, for a number of reasons, they were unable to do so. With each new director came changes in the practice and the philosophy of the Karamu Children's Theatre, including the number and content of classes offered, meeting times, age groups served and production opportunities; the Children's Theatre at Karamu thus began a period of slow but steady decline.

Rowena and Russell Jelliffe stepped down from their forty-eight years of leadership at Karamu House in 1963. When they retired, there were 4,000 members of the settlement, and, that year, over 65,000 people attended adult and children's theatre, cultural arts programs, educational discussion groups and neighborhood activities sponsored by Karamu House.[46] The executive directorship would change six times between 1963 and 1975, and this administrative instability exacerbated the problems with the children's theatre activities.

In the early 1960s, Karamu House was known as one of the "most significant cultural and social centers in the country."[47] A week-long conference was held in November 1965, "The Role of the Arts in Human Relations: A Symposium," to celebrate the fiftieth anniversary of Karamu House. Guests from different areas in theatre participated in the celebration including Viola Spolin, demonstrating improvisation through theatre games; Dr. Charles McGaw, with a demonstration-lecture on "Acting Is Believing"; and Frederick O'Neal, founder of the American Negro Theatre and president of the Actor's Equity Association, who led a panel entitled "The Integrated Theatre of Tomorrow."[48]

In spite of the tradition and reputation of Karamu, the combination of the Jelliffes' retirement and the lack of continuity in the children's theatre staff resulted in an erosion of all children's theatre activities. Flagg had presented an average of eight shows per season during her nine-year tenure. Between 1961 and 1975, after Flagg's departure, the number of productions decreased. In 1975 only one children's play was produced.

The last full-time children's theatre director resigned from Karamu in 1972, and part-time staff continued the program for three years. By 1975, the position of director of children's theatre ceased to exist.

SUMMARY

Rowena and Russell Jelliffe nurtured children's theatre activities at Karamu for forty-eight years. During that time, the settlement house grew into a sophisticated arts center, complete with a three-building complex in inner-city Cleveland. Through a wide variety of children's theatre activities, including classes, workshops and productions, the Jelliffes—and later, Flagg—assisted children and their parents in coping with the multiracial, multicultural environment surrounding Karamu House.

Karamu was developed in response to particular community needs. But from the very beginning, the Jelliffes never thought of Karamu House strictly as a settlement house; their work was always directed toward fostering interracial appreciation through group work in arts projects. That Karamu built all of its programs around arts activities separates this social service organization from most other settlement houses of the time. It is even more significant that children's theatre was the seed from which Karamu House was born, as well as the inspiration and model for adult theatre, for diverse arts activities and for the more traditional settlement house programs.

A high standard of theatre work with and for children was maintained, cherished and honored for over forty years at Karamu House. While many settlement houses of the time boasted of active children's theatre programs, few such programs were on the same level as the Karamu Children's Theatre.

NOTES

1. Historical information about Karamu has been condensed from a more comprehensive study by Noerena Abookire, "Children's Theatre Activities at Karamu House in Cleveland, Ohio 1915–1975," Ph.D. diss., New York University, 1981.

2. Ruth Haydn Hitching, "Drama on the Corner," *Bystander,* December 9, 1933, p. 6.

3. Rueben Silver, "A History of the Karamu House, 1915–1960," Ph.D. diss., Ohio State University, 1961, pp. 53–54.

4. Rowena Jelliffe, interview, Cleveland, Ohio, October 17, 1978.

5. Ibid.

6. As quoted in Silver, "History of the Karamu House," p. 8.

7. Rowena Jelliffe, interview, Cleveland, Ohio, September 19, 1978.

8. Silver, "History of the Karamu House," pp. 106–12.

9. Ibid., pp. 166–67.

10. Rowena Jelliffe, interview, Cleveland, Ohio, September 18, 1978.

11. Cora Geiger Newald, "Karamu: 48 Years of Integration Through the Arts," TS, p. 157. This unpublished work is located in the Cleveland Public Library. See also Silver, "History of the Karamu House," p. 58.

12. Silver, "History of the Karamu House," p. 56, taken from an interview with Rowena Jelliffe, May 6, 1961.

13. "The Role of the Arts in Human Relations," Karamu House publication, 1965.

14. Roger Mae Johnson, interview, Cleveland, Ohio, November 14, 1978.

15. Silver, "History of the Karamu House," pp. 155–56.

16. *The Three Wishes* program, found in Rowena Jelliffe's personal scrapbook.

17. John Selby, *Beyond Civil Rights* (Cleveland and New York: World Publishing Company, 1966), p. 67.

18. Newald, "Karamu," pp. 156–57.

19. Roger Mae Johnson, interview, Cleveland, Ohio, September 18, 1978.

20. Rowena Jelliffe, interview, Cleveland, Ohio, September 18, 1978; and "Introduction to Final Report of Rutherford B. Hayes Study," TS, Fall, 1942.

21. *Playhouse Beacon*, published monthly by the Bokari Print Class of the Playhouse Settlement, February 5, 1937, p. 3.

22. Selby, *Beyond Civil Rights*, p. 111.

23. Newald, "Karamu" p. 182.

24. "Report to the Board," TS, Spring, 1941, p. 3, Karamu House Files.

25. Selby, *Beyond Civil Rights*, p. 129.

26. Newald, "Karamu," pp. 218–19.

27. Selby, *Beyond Civil Rights*, p. 135.

28. Silver, "History of the Karamu House," p. 341.

29. Press release in Karamu files, December 1949.

30. *Karamuse*, November 1951, p. 3.

31. *Karamuse*, July 1952, p. 3.

32. Selby, *Beyond Civil Rights*, p. 154.

33. Gilbert Moses, interview, Los Angeles, California, June 21, 1979.

34. 1951 information flyer in Karamu files.

35. "Karamu," information guide for children's programs for the 1952–1953 season.

36. Ibid.

37. Rowena Jelliffe, interview, Cleveland, Ohio, January 29, 1981.

38. "In Demand," *Karamuse*, April-May 1957, p. 4.

39. Silver, "History of the Karamu House," p. 422.

40. *Karamu House—A Statistical Picture of the Year: 1958/59*. Compiled by the Karamu staff; mimeographed copy in Karamu files, p. 8.

41. Silver, "History of the Karamu House," pp. 433–34.

42. Letter from Ann Flagg to Student Theatre members, February 29, 1960.

43. Winifred Ward, "A Retrospect," in Nellie McCaslin, ed., *Children and Drama* (New York: David McKay Co., 1975), p. xvii.

44. Ibid.

45. Rowena Jelliffe, interview, Cleveland, Ohio, January 29, 1981.

46. "Welcome to Karamu," a 1963 publicity hand-out, Karamu Files.

47. *Cleveland Plain Dealer,* January 1, 1956, p. 5.

48. "Who's Who at Symposium," insert in pamphlet, "The Role of the Arts in Human Relations: A Symposium," November 1965.

7

Charlotte B. Chorpenning: Playwright and Teacher

ROGER L. BEDARD

Throughout the history of American children's theatre, teachers, social workers and theatre artists have decried the lack of quality plays for young audiences. Until recently, few professional playwrights wrote for child audiences, and those who did offered only occasional works. For many decades the development of American children's theatre thus suffered demonstratively from this shortage. This situation began to change significantly, however, when Charlotte B. Chorpenning turned her attention to children's plays.

Chorpenning is best known for her work at the Goodman Theatre of the Chicago Art Institute, where, between 1932 and 1951, she directed an active children's theatre program. During this period, Chorpenning wrote and produced scores of children's plays, taught play writing and worked diligently with many national organizations and professional children's theatre groups to promote the development of dramatic literature for children. Because of her work as a playwright, theorist and teacher, one contemporary of Chorpenning called her "the most powerful influence in the children's theatre movement in this country."[1] While her reputation as a playwright has been eclipsed by contemporary writers, in her time, Chorpenning exerted significant influence on both the quantitative and qualitative development of the repertoire of plays for children.

In spite of the acknowledged importance of Chorpenning's work, few people realize that she did not become actively involved in formal theatre for children until she was sixty years old. Prior to that time she worked in adult theatre and pursued several other careers—careers that provided her with experiences upon which she built a unique sociological as well as aesthetic perspective of the role of theatre for children.

Charlotte L. Barrows Chorpenning was born in 1872 as the middle child in a family of four boys and five girls. Her childhood and family life were replete with artistic and intellectual stimulation in that her father was a scholar, poet, horticulturist and theologian; while her mother was an accomplished pianist.[2]

Chorpenning was educated at Iowa Agricultural College (where her father taught) and Cornell University. She graduated from Cornell in 1894 with a Bachelor of Letters degree. She then taught high school in Springfield, Ohio, a career which she interrupted for her marriage to John C. Chorpenning in 1896 and the subsequent birth of her daughter. When her husband's health necessitated that the family move to Colorado, Chorpenning took a job in 1901 teaching english and history at Wolfe Hall, an Episcopal girls school in Denver, Colorado.

There is no evidence available to suggest that Chorpenning was yet involved in drama or theatre in any way. It is known, however, that she was an avid writer throughout her life, and that she was particularly fond of writing poetry.

In 1904, Chorpenning accepted a position as an English teacher at the Normal School in Winona, Minnesota. This move was caused by the ill health of her daughter, whose condition was aggravated by the high altitude of Denver. Since Chorpenning's husband's health required such an altitude, the move meant that Chorpenning and her husband had to be separated. The couple never again lived together, though they maintained a surprisingly close relationship through correspondence and lengthy summer vacations together.

Chorpenning, reportedly, was never particularly happy either with her life in Winona or her position at the Normal School. She eased her unhappiness and loneliness, in part, by concentrating even more on her writing. This led to the publication of a short story in *Collier's* magazine in 1906.[3]

At that time Chorpenning was also using teaching techniques at the Normal School that would gradually move her into more formal theatre work. She was employed to teach, among other things, English Literature:

My students there turned the table on me. In my class on Shakespeare, I was so determined to keep them all creative as we studied the plays, that I assigned to special groups certain plays to interpret to the class. Always they discovered for themselves the famous scenes, and enthusiastically acted them out for the class, scenes which I would have been afraid to try to interpret through reading to them. This was the beginning of my absorbing interest in the relation between drama and life.[4]

Chorpenning, the developing writer, was thus introduced to the excitement and power of drama, but it was only through her husband's prodding that she applied her own talent to writing plays:

I suppose the acceptance of a story or two put it into my husband's head that I could write a play that he wanted to see written. My protests that the only plays that I knew were Shakespeare's made no difference.[5]

After writing her first play, *Between the Lines*, Chorpenning contemplated studying play-writing seriously.[6] To that end—and probably armed with just an early version of this one play—in 1912 she applied for admittance to George Pierce Baker's famous play-writing class at Radcliffe College in Cambridge, Massachusetts.

Chorpenning was accepted into Baker's program, took a leave of absence from Winona Normal School, and set out for this new adventure. This major transition in her professional life was, however, tempered by personal tragedy, when her husband, who decided he was by then well enough to join her, died en route to Cambridge.

By all accounts, the death of her husband had a lasting effect on both Chorpenning's personal and professional life, and according to her daughter, "when she finally came to an emotional adjustment of the death, work seemed to take the place of whatever satisfaction she could get out of family life."[7] From that point Chorpenning focused almost her entire attention on her professional life, a life which was to gradually, over the ensuing forty years, move into the forefront of American children's theatre.

Beginning in the fall of 1913, Chorpenning was caught up in the world of reading, writing and viewing plays, as a part of the stringent requirements of Baker's noted English 47 class. She passed this class with distinction and was one of six from the group invited to remain an additional year in an advanced play-writing class.[8] During the second year, Chorpenning also became involved in the 47 Workshop, a laboratory theatre connected with Baker's classes. Through this workshop she gained experience as an actress and director, as well as a playwright. During her last year at Radcliffe she was awarded the Craig Prize for the best play written in the workshop that year. As a part of the award, her play, *Between the Lines*, was subsequently given a professional production in the Castle Square Theatre in Boston.[9]

Chorpenning returned to Winona Normal School in the fall of 1915, but she was no longer content with her career as an English teacher. She was determined to become a professional playwright, writing plays for adult audiences. She never attained this goal, though she ultimately wrote at least nine adult plays, two of which were given professional productions.

When her dreams of becoming a professional playwright did not materialize as she had hoped, she began to work with community drama projects for various Winona organizations. Through this work she began to explore the benefits that a theatre experience could provide beyond mere aesthetic considerations. She noted that these included benefits both for the individuals directly involved in the group activity, as well as for the community as a whole.

Concentrating on this sociological perspective, Chorpenning developed an approach to community drama work that was to have national significance. She differentiated between product-oriented commercial theatre and participant-centered community drama, noting that the primary job of the community drama coach is to "first find your play in the people you are dealing with, then get it out of them.''[10] She would, in effect, become a playwright-in-residence for a given Winona community group. She would discern the major social and/or community concerns of the group and outline a play around these themes. Next, utilizing discussion and improvisation, she would create the necessary dialogue and guide the participants in realizing their production.

When her article, "Putting on a Community Play," was published in the *Quarterly Journal of Speech Education,* she received several requests to help with such projects at various places throughout the country.[11] Her influence in the field spread quickly, and, while continuing to support herself by teaching at the Normal School, she worked actively to promote this participant-centered approach to drama. By all accounts, Chorpenning attacked these projects with marked energy and enthusiasm. Her reputation was such that the 1919 senior class at the Normal School humorously bequeathed to Chorpenning "a year's rest, so that the students can catch up with her.''[12] This flurry of activity, and her resulting fame, in turn, led Chorpenning to yet another career shift.

In 1921, Neva Boyd, a leading theorist and proponent of the use of games and play activities for enriching the social, cultural and intellectual life of children, invited Chorpenning to present a workshop on community drama at the Recreation Training School of Chicago. After the session, Boyd offered Chorpenning a teaching position at the school, and Chorpenning wasted little time in accepting the offer.[13]

An account in the Winona newspaper, on the occasion of Chorpenning's departure from the city, provides a good picture of her activities at the time:

Mrs. Chorpenning will leave for California where she will spend five weeks in the San Francisco State Normal School training students in the use of dramatization in the elementary school, in coaching plays and pageants in the high school, and in co-operating with community work in drama. From August to October she will visit and study the noteworthy dramatic projects being done in various parts of California, where some of the most original and vital work in school and community drama in the country is being developed.

In October Mrs. Chorpenning will go to Chicago to begin work in the Recreation Training School, as head of the new department of dramatic art. Her work will consist of writing and producing plays for specific groups, and in training selected students to do the same, by associating them with her in the actual projects under way. The theatres and the neighborhood groups available for the work are many, including Hull House, several other settlements, the university, and two or three interested clubs. . . .

It is the expectation of the Recreation Training School eventually to train leaders for school and community drama of a much more valuable type than is now common, and to develop a supply of plays fitted for amateur productions.[14]

According to Boyd, Chorpenning "was engaged to experiment with unlimited freedom in making dramatic acting and directing educationally sound.''[15] Chorpenning's work in community drama complemented the play and game theory espoused by Boyd; and for the next few years Chorpenning worked closely with

Boyd in refining a group-work approach to social work, which was in marked contrast to the traditional case-worker approach then taught by other social work training schools.

Chorpenning participated in many facets of the training school program. She taught a variety of classes—both traditional audience-centered theatre classes and participant-centered recreational drama—and she supervised the field work of her students in the area settlement houses. This work, which allowed her to experiment with her own theories of recreational drama, had a direct influence on her later work with children's theatre:

It was at Hull House I first added group dramatics with children to my work with adults. . . . It was in overseeing an afternoon of free creative dramatics at Gads Hill Center that my first awed realization of the fateful intensity of a child's imagination as an educating force in children's growing personalities startled me. The children were story-playing Rumpelstiltskin, and had gone into a huddle to work out agreement on expression for what each high-creative actor was feeling at the exciting moment. The little queen stood curving her arms tenderly around her imaginary baby explaining her feelings to another actor. . . . She laid the imaginary baby carefully on a nearby sette [sic] and went into action. I tired of standing as I listened and dropped into the settee. A piercing shriek almost rent the roof. "You're sitting on my baby!"[16]

Although busy with her work at the training school, Chorpenning did not neglect her own writing, and during this period she initiated another attempt at a successful professional production of one of her plays.

In 1925, she contracted with a production team consisting of Earle Booth, James Gleason and Ernest Truex for a production of her play, *The Sheepman*. The play was cast with professional actors—including a then relatively unknown actor named Spencer Tracy—and presented in Stamford, New Haven and Hartford, Connecticut, with the promise of a New York opening.[17] The play closed permanently on October 21, 1925, in Hartford. A review of a Hartford performance suggests that Chorpenning's script was a major factor in the production's failure:

[I]t is at best a weak and futile effort, heavy and mechanical in its plot, confused in the working out. Yet there is at times good atmosphere, some excellent character portrayal, and the unmistakable suggestion of big drama lurking somewhere in the offing, but somehow never called into being. . . .

Dodson Mitchell . . . can hardly make real and human the rather clumsy lines that are given him. . . . Spencer Tracey [sic] and Miss Burroughs struggle in vain with lines that are well-nigh impossible.[18]

The failure of this production apparently finally extinguished whatever small hope Chorpenning might have had for gaining some fame as a professional playwright—at least with plays for adults. There is no record that she ever again initiated or encouraged a professional production of any of her adult plays.

Chorpenning worked with the Recreation Training School until 1927, when the school was merged with the sociology department at Northwestern University in Evanston, Illinois. While most of the training school teachers joined the faculty of the sociology department, Chorpenning joined the School of Speech as an instructor of dramatics.[19]

As a member of the School of Speech, Chorpenning worked both with recreational drama and with the university theatre production program. Although she taught only one class, designed for those "taking a major in Recreational Leadership,"[20] two other projects with which she was involved "laid a determining finger on all . . . her later life."[21]

The first of these was her work with the Playshop, a laboratory for a play-writing class. For a short time Chorpenning was in charge of directing "try-out" productions for this group;[22] years later she noted that that experience of "helping adjust halting plays to an audience" had given her a "deeper grasp of the basic necessities of an actable play which Baker had been trying to beat into . . . [their] heads."[23]

A second important activity that Chorpenning undertook as an instructor of dramatics was to serve as an advisor for Winifred Ward—with whom she shared an office—during the early years of Ward's Children's Theatre of Evanston. According to Chorpenning:

Winifred Ward . . . was working out organization of the University and P.T.A. and Public Schools for productions on the school stages, directed by herself and the students in her courses in creative dramatics. I attended committee meetings to contribute from my experience in community dramatics, and followed its eventual success with great interest.[24]

This work with Ward and the Children's Theatre of Evanston thrust Chorpenning into the middle of the children's theatre world. According to Ward, it was an almost natural progression for Chorpenning to move from being an advisor to the Children's Theatre of Evanston to her becoming a major author of plays for children:

Charlotte Chorpenning had been sharing my office . . . , and we had begun a kind of collaboration that was to last for some years. She was a remarkable woman, full of creative ideas and never-ending drive, and it was exciting to work with her. Though she . . . had had vast experience both with theatre and with sociology, she had been concerned chiefly with writing for adults. I had drawn her into writing for children when, in 1928, I had asked her to do some rewriting on *The Wizard of Oz*.

When I wanted a good script for Hans Christian Andersen's wonderful satire of *The Emperor's New Clothes*, it was natural that I should turn to Mrs. Chorpenning. And what fun we had talking over the plot, the characters, and the problem of the swindlers.[25]

The version of *The Wizard of Oz* that Chorpenning rewrote for Ward was produced by the Children's Theatre of Evanston in December 1928. Just two years later, the Children's Theatre of Evanston produced three Chorpenning plays. These included *The Emperor's New Clothes*, *The Princess and the Vagabond* and *The King's Ears*.[26]

Chorpenning had much early success with writing plays for children, and her fame spread quickly. In the spring of 1932, Maurice Gnesin, head of the Goodman Theatre of the Chicago Art Institute, directed a production of Chorpenning's *The Emperor's New Clothes* for the Goodman bill of children's plays. After working closely with Chorpenning on the production, Gnesin offered her the job of director of the Children's Theatre at the Goodman.[27] Chorpenning accepted this offer and, at the age of sixty, embarked upon that phase of her career for which she was to gain her greatest fame.

For several years after accepting the position at the Goodman, Chorpenning also taught part-time at Northwestern, including such classes as "Social Aspects of Dramatic Activity," "Dramatics and Personality Development" and "The Dramatic Group and the Social Process." In these classes, Chorpenning continued to advocate the then relatively new "process-centered" approach to drama.[28]

The majority of students in these classes were graduate students, and, through them, Chorpenning's theories were incorporated into most of the major social service organizations in the city. A former student recalls that, at one time Chorpenning's students were placed at Gads Hill Center, Hull House, Chicago Commons, Hyde Park Neighborhood Club, Howell Neighborhood House and others.[29]

While Chorpenning's work at Northwestern thrust her into the forefront as a theorist and practitioner of community drama, through her work at the Goodman Theatre from 1932–1952, Chorpenning found a successful outlet for her writing and gained a reputation as a leader in the children's theatre field.

Chorpenning was hired to direct children's plays for the Goodman children's theatre program. But Chorpenning found herself faced with a lack of shows she considered suitable for production. In addition, she considered it "both unethical and illegal to change the text of another author without permission."[30] Therefore, for the next twenty years she wrote as well as directed most of the children's plays produced at the Goodman.

During Chorpenning's tenure, the Goodman Children's Theatre presented eighty-one separate productions of fifty different plays. Chorpenning herself wrote twenty-eight and collaborated on eight others. While the records from this period are incomplete, it is also apparent that she directed at least sixty of these productions.[31] Through her work the Goodman Children's Theatre became one of the most important and respected children's theatres in this country.

Chorpenning quickly and easily moved into the new theatre world at the Goodman, and her work as a writer and as a director earned her the respect of both faculty and students. According to one observer:

Chorpenning was loved at the Goodman [emphasis hers]. . . . She observed, she listened, and was never afraid to adapt or correct or change things in her own scripts. . . . She was brilliant, energetic, persevering and never, never, never, satisfied with shoddy work.[32]

As Chorpenning continually sought to refine her work as a playwright and director, she developed systems to discern audience response. As she herself notes, this became an important part of her children's theatre work:

The observations relating to theatre for children, begun my first day in the Goodman, were confirmed over and over. Early in the check-up of my experiments, I found that it made a good deal of difference in my findings, from which part of the house I had been watching. While sitting front I would make an observation, walk to the back and find it did not apply; or sitting in the right section of the house I would cross the lobby to observe on the left side, and again disagree with myself. This led me to offer several students in my class at Northwestern University, free tickets to repeated attendance at a given play, on condition that they would observe and report to me on the points in audience reaction that I outlined for them. To this group of observers there were added several interested parents who reported to me on whatever caught their attention, each time they brought their children. This enlarged source of information became very valuable in testing and confirming conclusions.[33]

Playwright Martha Bennet King, one of the students Chorpenning recruited to work with this ongoing audience analysis project, recalls that Chorpenning was specifically interested in data that could be used to formulate theories of how to create, build and release suspense, and also, how to control excitement. To that end, she trained the observers to collect as much information as possible from many different vantage points in the theatre:

She especially wanted to know anything which could be surmised or proved about a child's physical, mental, emotional growth, and how his life might expand if he became a member of an audience. She kept us all reading madly. She assigned us to the study of audiences in every performance of a play. One time I would find myself at the back of the theatre, taking notes on the reaction to every scene. Again, I would be stationed in the very center of the crowd, at the left or right, close front. It might make a difference. We'd compare notes and impressions would be relayed to the actors at times.[34]

Chorpenning's plays remain the most visible facet of her contributions to children's theatre. During her lifetime she wrote at least fifty-five children's plays, thirty of which were ultimately published. Chorpenning herself virtually doubled the mid-century repertoire of American children's plays. The vast majority of these plays were written for production at the Goodman Theatre.

These plays, which include a wide range of styles and subject matter, represented a major step forward in the sophistication of dramatic literature for children. Unlike most playwrights who wrote for young audiences at that time, Chorpenning worked with a sophisticated theatre company, an organization capable of staging elaborate productions in well-equipped facilities, with mature and capable actors. Chorpenning thus had great freedom as a playwright to explore the dramatization of a wide range of stories and subjects with confidence that her plays could be staged, regardless of cast size or scenic requirements.

It was a challenging and, reportedly, satisfying job for Chorpenning. It was almost as if she had been training all of her life—as teacher, playwright, social worker and director—to combine her unique talents for her work at the Goodman. A friend of hers from that period attested to Chorpenning's excitement about this work:

How Chorpy loved it. I think I saw most of her plays . . . and some of them as many as nine or ten times plus rehearsals. And there was never a moment when she wasn't thrilled to be there. She made it a point, and made very few exceptions to be present for every performance. She felt she must know what her actors were experiencing, what the audience was experiencing, how different each audience was from the past one. Sometimes there were two performances in one day and she loved to contrast the response of the morning audience with the afternoon audience. . . . There was hardly a moment she didn't love.[35]

Chorpenning's work at the Goodman also extended into other areas, perhaps the most famous of which is a play-writing course that she taught sporadically in the late 1930s and the 1940s. Chorpenning supplies this account of the origins of the class:

That I organized a class in play-writing for children came about by request. A former student in my Northwestern University class in Social Aspects of the Drama, asked for private lessons. It seemed to me that to teach a class of one would involve too much influence by my creative individuality. So I told her to bring a group of at least six interested persons and we would start. . . . It was in preparation for and during my rich experience in the give and take of this class that I organized into outline what the children, through ten years of studying my Goodman audiences, had been teaching me.[36]

The membership of this ongoing and informal class apparently changed often, as many former participants report having attended the class during different years. Although it had no formal connection with the Goodman Theatre program, the class met on Saturday mornings in the rehearsal hall of the theatre. It would typically meet for three hours, after which the class members would sometimes view the current children's theatre production and assist Chorpenning with her audience analysis work.

At times, to motivate a new playwright, Chorpenning would collaborate with her or him on a play. According to King, "if an idea turned up which truly excited Chorpy, and if she wasn't sure which plays she would put on the calendar, she might collaborate with the new playwright, giving a chance to see a play from thought to evolvement on stage."[37] This process helped beginning playwrights gain confidence in their abilities, facilitated getting new plays for Chorpenning to produce at the Goodman and helped to increase Chorpenning's royalty income—the primary source of her support throughout the last twenty years of her life.

This class also had an impact on the development of the repertoire of children's plays available to other producers. According to Sara Spencer, founder of the Children's Theatre Press:

Mrs. Chorpenning's most noteworthy accomplishment has been the development of a nucleus of eminently successful plays, written by herself and her students, and tried out and perfected in the course of production at the Goodman Theatre. More than a third of the children's plays commonly presented in America today [1951] came from Mrs. Chorpenning's play writing classes at the Goodman, and new playwrights regard a Chorpenning play as a model to learn from.[38]

In 1943, Chorpenning took a one-year leave of absence from the Goodman and moved to New York to work with the United Service Agencies Inc. (USO) as their national coordinator of drama activities. At this time she resigned her part-time teaching position at Northwestern. Chorpenning was then seventy-one years old.

When Chorpenning returned to the Goodman in the summer of 1944, she no longer had to divide her time between her teaching at Northwestern and her writing and directing at the Goodman. But, she was soon busier than ever, becoming involved in all manner of national and international children's theatre projects. She was increasingly in demand as a writer, a speaker and a director. She worked with many organizations and individuals on everything from individual plays to the development of entire production programs. Prominent among the groups she worked with were: the Children's World Theatre, the Children's Theatre of Evanston, the Children's Theatre Press, the Children's Theatre Conference, the children's theatre program of the Association of Junior Leagues of America and the National Youth Theatre. She also worked, as a playwright, with several local and national radio and television projects.

Her letters from the period indicate that almost every day she received requests to collaborate on a play, speak at a conference, conduct a workshop, direct a new production, critique a script, adjudicate a play festival or lend her considerable children's theatre expertise in some manner. The requests came not just from friends and colleagues, but also from state and national government agencies and from foreign producers.

In 1949, at the age of seventy-seven, Chorpenning suffered a coronary occlusion, which resulted in a complete physical breakdown. Chorpenning's health recovered to the point where she could return to the Goodman for a short time.

At the end of the 1952 spring term, Chorpenning, at the age of eighty, retired from the Goodman. At commencement exercises that year she was awarded an Honorary Doctor of Fine Arts Degree by the School of the Art Institute of Chicago.

After her retirement, Chorpenning moved to New Milford, New York, to live near her daughter and son-in-law. And, for the next three years she continued her writing. Her immediate concern was completing a play entitled *Johnny*

Appleseed that had been requested by Sara Spencer and Campton Bell, who were looking for a play suitable for a European tour that following summer. Her progress on the play was slow, and when Spencer visited Chorpenning in the fall of 1952, she reported to Bell that Chorpenning was not well:

She has aged, Campton, and though her spirit is imperishable, and the glow of her genius still burns behind her tired eyes, she is not the keen old war horse we have been accustomed to. . . . She is constantly fatigued, and finds it difficult to find freshness and vigour in her writing.[39]

Spencer was also prodding Chorpenning to complete a book on her life and work. The result was *Twenty-One Years with Children's Theatre*, which was finished in September 1953 and published the following year by the Children's Theatre Press. When Spencer received the final manuscript she was enthusiastic in her praise to Chorpenning:

I read Twenty-One Years till 2:00 AM last night, utterly unable to put it down—and when I finally closed the manuscript I was too excited to go to sleep. . . . I regard it as quite as significant a book as *My Life in Art*—and truthfully feel a little reluctant to saddle it with a children's theatre title, which may prove a hurdle in adult circles. But the very fact that it is a children's theatre book will lend us stature, and pave the way for better understanding ahead.[40]

Chorpenning died on January 7, 1955. At the time of her death she was working on yet another children's play, *Humpty Dumpty*. The play was never finished.

CHORPENNING'S PUBLISHED PLAYS (Chronologically)

The Emperor's New Clothes. New York: Samuel French, 1932.
Rhodopsis—The First Cinderella. Chicago: Book House for Children, 1936.
Jack and the Beanstalk. Anchorage, Ky.: Children's Theatre Press, 1937.
The Indian Captive. Anchorage, Ky.: Children's Theatre Press, 1937.
Tom Sawyer's Treasure Hunt. New York: Samuel French, 1937.
Hans Brinker and the Silver Skates. Anchorage, Ky.: Children's Theatre Press, 1938.
Rama and the Tigers. Chicago: Coach House Press, 1954. Same as *Little Black Sambo and the Tigers*. Chicago: Dramatists, 1938.
Cinderella. Anchorage, Ky.: Children's Theatre Press, 1940.
Little Red Riding Hood or Grandmother Slyboots. Anchorage, Ky.: Children's Theatre Press, 1943.
Rumpelstiltskin. Anchorage, Ky.: Children's Theatre Press, 1944.
The Secret Weapon. Washington, D.C.: National Education Association, 1944.
Many Moons. Chicago: Dramatic Publishing Co., 1946.
The Sleeping Beauty. Anchorage, Ky.: Children's Theatre Press, 1949.
The Three Bears. Anchorage, Ky.: Children's Theatre Press, 1949.
King Midas and the Golden Touch. Anchorage, Ky.: Children's Theatre Press, 1950.

Robinson Crusoe. Anchorage, Ky.: Children's Theatre Press, 1952.
The Think Machine: A Play of the Future in *First Performance: Plays for the Junior High School Age*, eds. N. MacAlvay and V. Comer. New York: Harcourt & Brace, 1952.
Abe Lincoln—New Salem Days. Chicago: Coach House Press, 1954.
Radio Rescue. Anchorage, Ky.: Children's Theatre Press, 1954.
Rip Van Winkle. Chicago: Coach House Press, 1954.
The Prince and the Pauper. Anchorage, Ky.: Children's Theatre Press, 1954.
Lincoln's Secret Messenger. Chicago: Coach House Press, 1955.
Alice in Wonderland. Chicago: Coach House Press, 1956.
The Adventures of Tom Sawyer. Chicago: Coach House Press, 1956.
Hansel and Gretel. Chicago: Coach House Press, 1956.
A Letter to Santa Claus. In *Six Plays for Young People from the Federal Theatre Project*, ed. Lowell Swortzell. Westport, Conn.: Greenwood Press, 1986.

COLLABORATIONS (Chronologically)

The Elves and the Shoemaker, in collaboration with Nora MacAlvay. Anchorage, Ky.: Children's Theatre Press, 1946.
Little Lee Bobo, in collaboration with Rose Hum Lee. Anchorage, Ky.: Children's Theatre Press, 1948.
Flibbertygibbet, in collaboration with Nora MacAlvay. Anchorage, Ky.: Children's Theatre Press, 1952.
The Magic Horn, in collaboration with Ann Nicholson. Chicago: Coach House Press, 1955.
Juan and the Magic Fruit, in collaboration with Juan Edades. In *Short Plays of the Philippines*, ed. Juan Edades. Manila: J. Edades, 1958.

NOTES

1. Campton Bell, "Children's Theatre Conference Newsletter," 1952 convention edition, p. 1.
2. Biographical information condensed from a larger more comprehensive study: Roger L. Bedard, "The Life and Work of Charlotte B. Chorpenning," Ph.D. diss., University of Kansas, 1979.
3. Charlotte L. Barrows [her family name], "Elizabeth," *Collier's*, March 24, 1906, pp. 16–18.
4. Charlotte B. Chorpenning, *Twenty-One Years with Children's Theatre* (Anchorage, Ky.: Children's Theatre Press, 1954), p. 3.
5. Charlotte B. Chorpenning, untitled essay, TS, p. 4. Copy in files of researcher.
6. Although the play was produced professionally in 1916, no record of copyright or publication could be found. Chorpenning refers to this as her "first play" in the previously cited essay.
7. Personal interview with Ruth Chorpenning Norris and James Norris, June 21, 22 and 23, 1978.
8. "Mrs. Chorpenning Wins Prize for Dramatic Work," *Winona Republican-Herald*, May 11, 1915, p. 2.

9. The play opened February 7, 1916.

10. Charlotte B. Chorpenning, "Putting on a Community Play," *Quarterly Journal of Speech Education*, 5 (1919), p. 34.

11. Chorpenning specifically mentions two such projects in *Twenty-One Years*, p. 5. See also "Community Plays," *1919 Wenonah* (Winona, Minn.: Winona Normal School, 1919), p. 72.

12. *1919 Wenonah*, p. 92.

13. Chorpenning, essay, p. 4.

14. "Studio to Close," *Winona Republican-Herald*, May 28, 1921, p. 3.

15. "Development of the Chicago Training School for Playground Workers," assembled by Paul Simon from notes by Neva Boyd, in *Play and Game Theory in Group Work*, ed. Paul Simon (Chicago: University of Illinois, 1971).

16. Chorpenning, essay, pp. 4–5.

17. No record of publication found. Manuscript copy available at Copyright Office, Library of Congress.

18. "The Sheepman's Heavy Melodrama," *Hartford Daily Times,* October 20, 1925, p. 21.

19. *1927–1928 Northwestern University Faculty Directory*, Northwestern University Archives.

20. "The School of Speech Annual Announcement 1929–30," *Northwestern University Bulletin,* 30, 3 (1929), pp. 18–19.

21. Chorpenning, essay, p. 5.

22. "Plays," a bulletin of the School of Speech and Theatre Arts, Northwestern University, 1930. Northwestern University Archives.

23. Chorpenning, essay, p. 5.

24. Ibid.

25. Winifred Ward, "The Children's Theatre of Evanston: An Informal History," written for the Evanston Historical Society, TS, 1973, p. 21. Northwestern University Archives.

26. Ibid. *The Princess and the Vagabond* is an Irish version of *The Taming of the Shrew*. A manuscript copy is available at Northwestern University Archives. *The King's Ears* is, reportedly, an adaptation of the fable, "The Ass's Ears." Neither a copy of the play nor a record of production could be found.

27. Maurice Gnesin, foreword to Chorpenning, *Twenty-One Years,* p. xi.

28. "Announcement of the Courses for the College of Liberal Arts During the Year 1931–1932," p. 120, and "Announcement of the Courses for the College of Liberal Arts During the Year 1937–1938," p. 53.

29. Personal interview with Chester Bower, May 16, 1978.

30. Chorpenning, *Twenty-One Years*, p. 35.

31. Information gleaned from programs, publicity releases and other related materials located in the Goodman Theatre Archives, Chicago Public Library.

32. Letter received from Elinor R. Fuchs, September 27, 1978.

33. Chorpenning, *Twenty-One Years*, pp. 12–13.

34. Letter received from Martha King, March 20, 1978.

35. Tape-recorded information about Chorpenning received from Mary Dodge. Dodge recorded this information over several weeks during November–December 1978.

36. Chorpenning, *Twenty-One Years*, p. 41.

37. Letter received from Martha King, March 20, 1978.

38. Letter from Sara Spencer to Jay Gould, November 12, 1951, Anchorage Press Archives.

39. Letter from Sara Spencer to Campton Bell, October 14, 1952, Anchorage Press Archives.

40. Letter from Sara Spencer to Charlotte B. Chorpenning, September 27, 1953, Anchorage Press Archives.

8

Children's Theatre in the Federal Theatre Project

DOREEN B. HEARD

During the Great Depression of the 1930s, a nationwide theatre subsidized by the United States government was formed under the aegis of the Works Progress Administration (WPA). This was the Federal Theatre Project, organized to provide "free, adult, uncensored" theatre for people throughout the country.[1] Amid successes and controversies, from 1935 to 1939 the Federal Theatre provided a stimulus not only for adult theatre, but for children's theatre as well.

Some of the productions of the Federal Theatre are well known and remembered today. "Living Newspapers," such as *Triple-A Plowed Under* and *One-Third of a Nation*, dramatized in episodic documentary style urgent social problems of the day. *It Can't Happen Here*, a play based on the novel by Sinclair Lewis, warned against facism. The Orson Wells and John Houseman productions of the "voodoo" *Macbeth* and *Doctor Faustus* are still remembered for their innovations and excellence. The work of the children's theatres within the Federal Theatre Project, however, is not as well known, even though plays were performed in many cities throughout the United States.

What follows is an overview of the work done by the most active children's theatres under the Federal Theatre Project. With one exception, the discussion is limited to professional companies that performed in whole or in part for child audiences; Federal Theatre's marionette companies and amateur groups, which performed extensively for children, are not included. The exception is the Children's Federal Theatre of Gary, Indiana, which used child actors.

The Works Progress Administration was organized by Congress on April 8, 1935 to counteract the high unemployment of the Depression years.[2] The Federal Theatre Project was a part of Federal Project No. 1, a national program to employ people qualified in the arts who were then on relief. Under the sponsorship of WPA, Federal Project No. 1 included the Federal Art Project, Federal Music Project and Federal Writers Project, as well as the Federal Theatre Project.[3]

The Federal Theatre was formed in a climate of great discouragement for professional theatre people. During the Depression, theatre workers in the United States were among those affected most severely by the high rate of unemployment. Vaudeville had declined, and many playgoers considered legitimate theatre a luxury they could no longer afford. The motion picture industry, with the subsequent conversion of legitimate theatres to movie houses, deprived workers of their livelihood in the commercial theatre. As ticket prices to commercial productions remained high, the low admission prices to the movies became more attractive, thus depriving the theatre of a substantial segment of the population as potential audience. The Federal Theatre was conceived as a way to create jobs for professional theatre workers who were then on relief, and, through these workers, to provide performances for thousands of people who would not otherwise have the opportunity to see live theatre.[4]

In October 1935, the Federal Theatre national office announced plans for work to be undertaken by the various performing units. Organized independently from the adult theatres, children's theatres would be among the earliest units set up.[5] These children's theatre companies, to be formed all over the country, would use adult professional actors performing plays suitable for children. Not only would productions be free or at low cost, but the companies were urged to develop new material and techniques to supplant the traditional plays and methods that then dominated children's theatre.[6]

Federal Theatre officials dreamed of a nationwide network of children's theatres established in every large city and extending into every town and hamlet. Performances would reach thousands, perhaps millions, of children never touched before by live theatre. Entertainment and education would go hand-in-hand, as child audiences learned about various cultures and participated vicariously in problem solving. Flanagan and others believed that the Children's Theatre of the Federal Theatre Project, established on a permanent nationwide basis, could aid greatly in the development of future theatre audiences. With government subsidy, the Federal Children's Theatre would not be subject to the economic pitfalls of commercial children's theatre. The Federal Theatre, therefore, represented the first serious attempt by theatre professionals to create a theatre for young audiences on a scale large enough to reach the thousands of children who had never seen a play.[7]

Separate units for children's theatre, performed by adult professional actors, were established in New York City, Los Angeles and Cleveland, Ohio.[8] In addition to these separate units, adult professional Federal Theatre units performed children's plays on a regular basis in Chicago, Illinois; Boston, Massachusetts; Newark, New Jersey; New Haven, Hartford and Norwalk, Connecticut; Denver, Colorado; Tampa, Miami and Jacksonville, Florida; San

Francisco and San Diego, California; Portland, Oregon; and other cities. It was in New York, however, that the children's theatre of the Federal Theatre Project had the most extensive activity.[9]

The Gary, Indiana, Children's Federal Theatre was the only one in the country that used children as unpaid actors under the supervision of an adult professional staff. Flanagan enthusiastically endorsed this unusual arrangement: "It is probable that in terms of human value no money on Federal theatre was better spent than that which kept ten needy theatre people employed and at the same time gave . . . 179 performances before 66,980 children who had no other creative amusement."[10] The Gary theatre was based on a community project started in 1932 by Betty Kessler Lyman, who believed that children should have a creative outlet in the theatre. Lyman had turned part of her house into a workshop and theatre for children who wrote, produced and acted in their own plays. Economic conditions in Gary had caused the program to reach a point of dissolution by 1935 when the Federal Theatre started. Children had no money to buy tickets for plays, and the city and the schools were in no position to provide financial help.

Recognizing that this was a worthy enterprise, the Federal Theatre set up a project in Gary for ten workers: Lyman, a business manager, stage manager, set designer, musical director, dance director, wardrobe mistress and three assistants. The Federal Theatre helped remodel abandoned office facilities into a children's community center, including a small, well-equipped theatre, rehearsal hall, shop, sewing room, office and storage space.[11] All applicants between the ages of four and eighteen were accepted into the children's theatre, and each child was screened to determine placement which would maximize the child's abilities. Lyman and her associates divided the children into interest groups which presented plays, first in their own small theatre and then in locations such as schools, settlement houses, YMCAs and fairs. In 1936, after only a few months of operation, the Children's Federal Theatre had a membership of six hundred children, divided into fourteen theatre units, five music units, two "talent" groups and two puppet theatre groups.[12]

The musical units included a twelve-piece string ensemble, a guitar quartet and a band and variety unit. In addition, a professional puppeteer and woodcarver, Tud Kempf, worked with the children to produce puppet shows which toured the area.[13]

The productions by the Gary group were extremely varied. Some were based on classics, such as *Rip Van Winkle*, *The Shoemaker and the Elves*, *Robinson Crusoe*, *The Prince and the Pauper* and *The Connecticut Yankee*. Lyman adapted many of these stories for the stage, but in some instances the children themselves evolved the scripts by using creative drama techniques. Furthermore, original plays were developed from the ethnic culture of the participants. The Croatian folk play, *Reygoch*, and a Greek play using masks are examples of scripts drawn from the heritage of the child actors.[14]

New groups were organized whenever enough interested children were avail-

able. Lyman tells of visiting a school playground one day to see a member of
the theatre. She was "mobbed" by the children and heard a timid voice ask,
"May I have a group too?" The speaker was a "beautiful, red-haired hazel-
eyed" ten-year-old girl, who lived in a congested downtown area where the only
playground was a dirty street. Soon afterwards, this little girl became a leader
in one of the groups and subsequently played the role of the Korean Cinderella
in the play, *Pigling and Her Proud Sisters.*[15]

Lyman believed the theatre's program aided child development by encouraging
freedom of expression, by providing an emotional outlet and by giving opportunities for group cooperation. Although the objectives of the children's theatre
differed from the other Federal Theatre units, the Children's Federal Theatre in
Gary was able to weather administrative criticism and continue production until
August 1938, when Lyman's illness caused termination of the work.[16] From its
inception in April 1936 to June 1939, the Children's Federal Theatre presented
189 performances (all free admission) with a total attendance of 71,410.[17] Judging
from these figures, Lyman achieved her goal.

Among units with adult actors, the Los Angeles Children's Theatre, under
the guidance of Yasha Frank, was second in size and number of performances
only to the New York unit. Frank's creative energies as a writer and director of
plays for children provided the unit with three shows: *Hansel and Gretel*, *Pinocchio* and *Aladdin*. Each of these plays combined colorful costumes and sets
with special effects, music and dance.

Frank, who had a Ph.D. in philosophy, brought extensive theatre and motion
picture experience to his position as director. He worked at MGM, the Chaplin
Studios, Pathe and Paramount as a writer and production assistant before accepting the post as director of the Children's Unit in Los Angeles. Frank's
influence was felt far beyond the West Coast; in 1938 he was appointed national
consultant for the Children's Theatre division of the Federal Theatre.[18]

The production of *Hansel and Gretel*, adapted by Frank and incorporating
some of Humperdinck's music from the opera of the same story, opened on
February 18, 1937 at the Beaux Arts Theatre in Los Angeles. The show continued, including performances at the Greek Theatre, until February 5, 1938,
for a total of 113 performances.[19] Rehearsals for a New York production of
Hansel and Gretel were started in the spring of 1939, but the end of the Federal
Theatre Project in June 1939 stopped the production.

In his director's report for *Hansel and Gretel*, Frank mentions that he delib-
erately employed several devices in the production to "break the proscenium
line." One of these devices was a narrator, costumed as Father Goose, who told
the story and occasionally interrupted the play to clarify the plot. Another device
came near the end of the play when the cast threw lollipops to the children in
the audience. Frank declared that the ideas proved effective, and he continued
to use similar tactics in his later plays.[20]

Frank noted that a special problem in *Hansel and Gretel* was to eradicate any
possible fear of the witch that the child audience might have. He attempted to

solve this dilemma by transforming the witch into a "guardian angel in a 'Magic Book' " in the finale. Also, friendly animal characters in the forest helped soften the fearful aspects of Hansel and Gretel's plight.

Although the audiences apparently liked the show (many children came several times), the critic from the *Los Angeles Herald and Express* thought the story unfit for children. Calling the story the "Germanic legend of the forest witch who fattened, roasted and ate children," he commented that it was "encouraging to know that the government hasn't taken a leaf out of Jonathan Swift's old proposal to fatten Irish babies for English consumption." The critic did state that the show was staged with "playful informality," and that the costumes, settings, music and clowning were good. He also praised the acting of Virginia Murray as Hansel and John Merkyl as the witch.[21]

Frank's next show was *Pinocchio*, a more extravagant production than *Hansel and Gretel*. He conceded that the show depended very much on spectacle, with dialogue reduced to a minimum and with much use of mime. The circus scene was a good example of spectacle and also of Frank's desire to use as many unemployed vaudevillians as possible. He made the error of overloading the scene with vaudeville acts and, "for the good of the play," trimmed the scene down to five acts interspersed with several short bits by clowns. That, Frank observed, created a better balance in the show.[22] Sets for the nine scenes in the show were simplified by the use of set pieces against black velour drapes. Scenes set under the sea were performed behind a scrim upon which a water-ripple effect was projected.[23]

Pinocchio, with music by Eddison von Ottenfeld and Armando Loredo, opened on June 3, 1937, at the Beaux Arts Theatre in Los Angeles. By the time the show closed on December 3, 1938, a total of 173 performances had been presented. *Pinocchio* also had 197 performances in New York as well as productions in six other cities.[24]

The audience agreed with Frank's evaluation that the circus scenes were too long. One audience member commented that "too many circus acts detract from the theme of *Pinocchio,* which is beautiful in itself."[25] The critic from the *Los Angeles Evening News* complained that the play started out as an "agreeable fantasy" but changed to the "realism" of a vaudeville show. He doubted that young children would be interested in balancing acts and sharpshooters. He had special praise, however, for Bert Easley in the title role and John Merkyl as the ringmaster. On the other hand, the critic for the *Daily News* declared that *Pinocchio* was "genuine fun and first-class passage to Make Believe Land." He stated that Frank had "flavored the old-world" story with "modern and original musical novelties."[26]

Frank often used large casts in his plays (for instance, *Pinocchio* had a cast of sixty) in order to provide employment for as many actors as possible. By his own admission he overdid it. In his next production, *Aladdin*, the cast included over 150 people, and Frank declared that the "story line suffered somewhat from the emphasis on production numbers and effects."[27]

His approach to the play was purely "extravaganza," with every effort made to achieve mass effects, including bright colors in costumes and rich tones in sets. *Aladdin* also included an interesting solution to the problem of depicting a magic carpet flying through space. The carpet and the actors were on a large rocker platform, with a black cyclorama hung upstage. The illusion was created by the use of a front scrim with projections of clouds, passing cities and landscapes. The actors rocked gently as several spotlights illuminated only the actors and part of the carpet.[28]

Opening at the Mayan Theatre in Los Angeles on March 11, 1938, *Aladdin* received a generally favorable review from the *Daily News* critic. He stated that the production was "brilliantly costumed and well staged" and particularly commended the performances of Virginia Murray as Aladdin and Harper Roisman as the captain of the guards. The reviewer noted that the "biggest boost, and perhaps the most deserved" should go to the production staff, especially for the flying carpet sequence.[29] *Aladdin* closed on July 22, 1938, after forty-three performances.

At the highest point in employment, 125 people were assigned to the Los Angeles Children's Theatre unit. In addition to Frank's three shows, the unit also presented twelve performances of *Teller of Tales*, written and directed by Muriel Browne; a children's festival, which included performances from the regular season; and a dance program, *Music in Fairyland*, in collaboration with the Federal Music Project. After Frank's appointment as national consultant in December 1938, there is no evidence of further activity in the Los Angeles unit.[30]

Building upon previous children's theatre activity in the city, Elbert B. Sargent established the Cleveland, Ohio, Federal Theatre for Youth in April 1937. His professional company worked closely with the school systems in Cleveland and surrounding areas. Performances toured the schools and were received so well that Sargent was able to expand the repertory of the company. The group's first production, Chorpenning's *The Emperor's New Clothes*, played 195 performances, from May 1937 to June 1939. *Sir Frog Goes A-Travelin'*, by Isabel Anderson, received fifty-seven performances in the 1937–1938 school year, and an adaptation by Frank Shay of Dickens' *A Christmas Carol* was performed sixty times during the holiday seasons in 1937 and 1938. By June 1938, the company had played to 123,000 people, mostly children. The 1938–1939 season included productions of Shakespeare's *Twelfth Night*, A. A. Milne's *The Ivory Door,* and Collodi's *Pinocchio*, as adapted by E. V. Cooke, Jr.[31] When the Federal Theatre Project ended in June 1939, the Cleveland Theatre for Youth was thriving; the company had enough definite commitments for an additional year of touring. The program was sustained by a group of former Federal Theatre workers as a private enterprise retaining the same name.

The Chicago Federal Theatre Project, while not having a separate Children's Theatre unit, produced plays for young audiences on a regular basis. One of the most notable of these was Chorpenning's *Little Black Sambo*, which was presented intermittently from August 29, 1938, to June 30, 1939, by a cast of black actors. This play opened at the Great Northern Theatre, was directed by Shirley Graham, and starred nineteen-year-old Charles Johnson. Graham also wrote music intended to provide a "jungle" atmosphere for the play.[32]

In her director's report, Graham states that the overall production concept for *Little Black Sambo* was based on an attempt to catch "the whimsical, poetic and colorful" nature of the script. She wanted to create on the stage a fantasy land in which monkeys and tigers spoke to humans, a land of imagination where anything could happen. Brilliant colors were used in sets and costumes, and percussion instruments provided background rhythm.[33]

A reviewer for the *Chicago Herald and Examiner* wrote that the show was a "colorful, fast-moving fantasy, played in vivid and imaginative sets by a group of Negro actors who know the business of acting." She particularly liked the "splendid portrayal" of Sambo by Charles Johnson; and she also noted that *Little Black Sambo* was simply pleasant entertainment—a welcome relief from problem plays and propaganda pieces.[34]

The critic from the *Chicago Daily News* did not agree. He believed that the play missed an opportunity to develop deeper meanings in Sambo's journey alone into the forest. As examples of more fully developed similar themes, this critic cited Walt Disney's *Snow White* and the Maude Adams portrayal of *Peter Pan*. He declared that "*Little Black Sambo* misses its destination through vacillation of purpose, poverty of lines, overacting and unimaginative directing." Apparently his views were not shared by other reviewers and the audiences which kept the show in the repertory for ten months.[35]

Chorpenning's *Rip Van Winkle* was also produced by the Chicago unit. Kay Ewing, the director, cast seven "real little old men . . . only one over five feet two inches tall" to play Henrik Hudson's men. In rehearsal they were "spellbinding," but in costume and makeup their movements seemed somewhat clumsy and indefinite. Ewing was upset since she considered that scene her *pièce de résistance*. The child audience, however, responded well to the old men.[36]

Rip Van Winkle opened on November 8, 1938, and closed on January 19, 1939. The Chicago Federal Theatre Project also produced two other Chorpenning plays, *The Emperor's New Clothes* and *A Letter to Santa Claus*.[37]

In Seattle, Washington, the Federal Theatre Project had both white and black units, with personnel from defunct vaudeville companies. Hoping to build up larger audiences, Hallie Flanagan sent Esther Porter to Seattle as assistant to Edwin O'Connor. Porter had worked with the Federal Theatre in both New York and Washington. Under this combined direction the Seattle Children's Theatre improved greatly.[38]

For her first production, Porter combined various traditional nursery rhymes with vaudeville acts (previously done by members of the company) into a revue for child audiences called *Mother Goose Goes to Town*. In her director's report, Porter stated that a special effort was made when casting the nursery rhyme characters to find actors who resembled, as closely as possible, the traditional image of these characters. Moreover, audience participation was encouraged, and the children were led in singing by Mother Goose and Old King Cole. At other points during the show, the children were encouraged to call out for characters, such as Little Boy Blue and Little Jack Horner, to appear on stage. After the final curtain, children from the audience were invited to come on stage and recite Mother Goose rhymes or sing songs. The *Seattle Times* reviewer wrote that "the music, dancing, and comedy proved to be delightful entertainment."[39]

Mother Goose opened on December 23, 1937, and was performed twenty-three times, before closing on April 29, 1939. The Children's Theatre next produced *Radio Revue*, *Flight* (a Living Newspaper for young people, first performed in New York), *Alice in Wonderland* (a puppet show) and *The Dragon's Wishbone*. Before Porter's arrival, the company had produced *The Clown Prince*. Each of these shows had between three and eight performances each.[40]

In addition to these shows, the Negro Repertory Company of the Seattle Federal Theatre Project produced *Br'er Rabbit and the Tar Baby* for child audiences. Adapted from the Uncle Remus stories by Ruth Comfort Mitchell and Alfred Allen, with original music by Howard Biggs, the play was directed by Porter. The show was well received and played a total of fifteen performances between May 7, 1938 and March 25, 1939.[41]

The show began with a prologue in which a narrator came through the audience singing. She was joined on the side stage by several children, to whom she began telling the story of Br'er Rabbit and his adventures with Tar Baby. The children then joined Br'er Rabbit as the story continued in action. An epilogue brought the children back to the side stage. Again, the Federal Theatre had broken the proscenium "barrier" and involved the audience directly.[42]

The reviewer from the *Seattle Post-Intelligencer* commented on the versatility of the black unit. He noted that the play was a "riot of songs and dances as light and gay as spring itself."[43] The publicity director for the theatre stated in his report that audience reaction to the show was highly favorable. Children enjoyed the humor, and adults were appreciative of the music, dancing and lyrical quality of the production.[44]

Hallie Flanagan and other Federal Theatre officials wanted strong, active children's theatres all over the country. This goal was only partially achieved. The New York Children's Theatre unit, however, was the most active and was able to sustain production of high-quality plays over a period of three-and-one-half years.

The Federal Theatre project for New York City was established officially in November 1935, and the Children's Theatre was one of the first units organized. Originally a division of the Municipal Theatre unit, the Children's Theatre became a separate unit, under Managing Supervisor Jack Rennick, in August 1936.[45]

By December 20, 1935, rehearsals had begun on the first production for child audiences. *Federal Theatre Magazine* announced that the show would be a "telescoped dramatization of the adventures of Mark Twain's characters, Tom

Sawyer and Huckleberry Finn.'' Julias Evans, formerly with the Theatre Guild, and Elizabeth McCormick were named as co-directors. Irene Sharaff, costume designer for LeGallienne's production of *Alice in Wonderland,* was to create the costumes, and Nicholas Nabokoff, composer of *Union Pacific*, was to provide a special musical setting.[46]

The Children's Theatre seemed to be well under way; however, delays and frustrations were to postpone the first production for many months. The dramatization of Mark Twain's stories was never presented; the first production did not open until June 1936, when Chorpenning's *The Emperor's New Clothes* began a lengthy run.

The Children's Theatre unit had a large staff—directors, choreographers, musicians, composers, actors, designers, and technicians—to support the production program. The unit also had a repertory department which searched for children's play scripts that met the prescribed standards of the Children's Theatre. This department also worked with playwrights and coordinated the repertory of the unit. In addition, the Children's Theatre had its own research department which worked with both the repertory department and the production staff.[47]

The New York Children's Theatre unit produced nine plays and three festivals. Most of these plays were performed in midtown Manhattan theatres, and several also toured the five boroughs of New York City with the Federal Theatre's summer Caravan Theatre. The repertoire was varied and included: the old favorites, *The Emperor's New Clothes*, *Jack and the Beanstalk* and *Treasure Island*; a fifteenth-century French farce, *Pierre Patelin*; new, original scripts, *The Revolt of the Beavers*, *Flight* and *Horse Play*; modern comedy, *Mr Dooley, Jr.*; and a musical adaptation of *Pinocchio*. The festivals were produced in cooperation with the Federal Art and Music Projects and included musical groups, art exhibits and dance, as well as theatre.

The Emperor's New Clothes opened in New York at the Adelphi Theatre on June 2, 1936, and remained in the repertory of the Children's Theatre until its final performance on November 1, 1937, at the Children's Autumn Festival. This play also traveled on the Portable (Caravan) Theatre circuit, toured the New York area for spot bookings during the winter, and ran for two months at the Heckscher Theatre in Manhattan. The show achieved a total of 130 performances, to be surpassed in number only by the 1938–1939 production of *Pinocchio*. *The Emperor's New Clothes* played to a total audience of 284,365 persons; of this total, 16,936 were paid admissions and 267,429 were free admissions.[48]

The June 1936 production of *The Emperor's New Clothes* was directed by Turner Bullock and included in its company several people who later had distinguished theatre or film careers. The leading role of Zar was played by Jules Dassin, later the director of many films including *Never on Sunday* and *Topkapi*. During part of the run, the role of Han was played by noted actor John Randolph, whose most recent role was that of the grandfather in Neil Simon's New York success, *Broadway Bound*. The incidental music was written by A. Lehman

Engel, whose reputation was just becoming established at that time. Subsquently, Engel was composer, musical director, advisor or conductor for more than eighty shows produced throughout the world.

Visually, *The Emperor's New Clothes* was colorful and interesting. The costumes, designed by Andrei Hudiakoff, were not defined by any one stylistic period, but could be termed "fantastic" or "storybook." Costume elements from many periods were imaginatively put together. For example, the rogues Zar and Zan were dressed alike in pullover shirts randomly appliqued with large letters, *Z*, *A*, *R* and *N*. Their pants covered the knee, with the lower leg bare. Socks and suede leather dance sandals completed the outfits. On the other hand, the emperor and the empress were elaborately dressed in coordinated costumes with satin, velvet and white "fur." These costumes resembled eighteenth-century European court apparel. Hudiakoff's set was nonrealistic and unusual for the 1930s. It consisted of platforms and ramps with a colorful arrangement of rods, panels and streamers backed by black drapes.[49]

As an introduction to *The Emperor's New Clothes,* the Children's Theatre involved children in the production. After the house lights dimmed and came up again to signal the start of the play, the two rogues, Zar and Zan, appeared in the audience and proceeded to play ball. They threw the ball from one aisle to another, with children eagerly throwing the ball back to the actors. The audience was soon involved completely. Then Zar "accidentally" threw the ball on stage into the front curtain. Zan then ran up on stage to retrieve the ball, looked under the curtain and called Zar on stage to see what he had discovered. The curtain then rose to reveal the Street of the Royal Weavers; the play began, and the child audience was very much involved from the first moment of the performance.[50]

At another point in the production, the audience effected a revision of the script. Rennick tells of an incident that occurred during one of the first performances of the play in June 1936. In the play, the third act opens with Zar and Zan lost in the city and frantically trying to find the Street of the Royal Weavers. In the production, the sign designating this street stood in full view of the audience, but Zar and Zan did not see it. The child audience, from the first performance, shouted to the actors, jumped up and down, and pointed to the sign. The actors, however, stayed with the script and tried to continue the play as rehearsed, to the great frustration of the audience. At the second or third performance, an exasperated child ran up on the stage and grabbed Zar by the hand, pulled him over to the sign and shouted, "There it is, you dope!" After that episode, the two rogues took their instructions from the audience.[51]

Audience response to *The Emperor's New Clothes* was overwhelmingly positive, as seen by examination of the newspaper reviews and letters to the Children's Theatre from children and adults. The show became one of the most popular of the Children's Theatre productions.

Apparently, most of the professional New York theatre critics enjoyed the production. The critic from the *New York Herald* commented:

The Children's Theatre offers . . . a fairy-tale nicely fashioned for a young audience and staged with fitting illustration. Miss Chorpenning's story . . . is performed imaginatively by an adult cast which brings out proper light and shade for such a fragile piece and the Mother Goose costumes add a flavor of make believe in keeping with the fantasy.

The critic stated further that the story finishes with "a proper moral, which every good fairy-tale should have," and there is even "a hint of social equity, which every good W.P.A. play should have."[52]

The critic from the *New York Sun* wrote:

To be a member of an audience that is having a glorious time, and isn't in the least inhibited about showing it, is one of the most satisfactory experiences a playgoer can have. It awaits anyone who will drop into the Adelphi Theatre. . . .

The play has been mounted, costumed and directed with extraordinary wit and imagination. . . . [The child audience] scorned mere handclapping to express their approval, in favor of joyous whoops that must have been audible all the way to Times Square.[53]

As part of the ongoing effort to understand and fulfill the needs and desires of its child audiences, the Children's Theatre conducted a survey during the run of *The Emperor's New Clothes*. A questionnaire—prepared under the direction of Dr. Lois Hayden Meek and Christine Heinig, of the Child Development Institute at Teachers College, Columbia University—was distributed to the children after many of the performances at the Adelphi Theatre. Meek had designed the questionnaire to discover the children's reactions to the play and their preferences for future plays.

From thousands of answers, the results seemed to indicate that the majority of children were between eight and twelve years of age and were attending their first professionally produced play. Approximately half the children declared they liked seeing the live production better than seeing a movie, and most of the children were eager to see more plays. In general, the boys preferred adventure and historical stories, while the girls preferred fairy tales and plays which incorporated music and dancing. Familiar stories seemed to be popular, with "Cinderella" and "Robin Hood" leading the list of stories the children wanted to see dramatized.[54]

In addition to performances in theatres, *The Emperor's New Clothes* played to thousands of people in parks throughout the five boroughs of New York. Thus, the show helped to fulfill an objective of the Federal Theatre, that of providing live theatre for audiences not reached by commercial productions. Equally important, *The Emperor's New Clothes*, as the first production of the new Children's Theatre unit, demonstrated that the organization was serious in its intent to provide high-quality entertainment, coupled with educational values, for its audiences.

Even before *The Emperor's New Clothes* opened at the Adelphi in June 1936, the Children's Theatre started preparations for the second production, *Horse Play*. Written for children from five to eight years of age, *Horse Play* was an original script by Dorothy Hailparn, a young play-reader on the staff of the Children's Theatre. The story is a simple one about a farmer and his horse, Aggie, and the troubles they have with a greedy landlord. The show incorporated variety acts into a circus scene, thereby employing many vaudevillians. The play had a successful run on the Portable Theatre circuit in the summer of 1936 with a cast of white actors. It was revived in 1937, at the Lafayette Theatre in Harlem, with a cast of black actors. The Harlem production ran for four months and then toured with spot bookings in the boroughs.[55]

The third production of the Children's Theatre was very different from its predecessors. Recognizing that young people of junior-high age had very little theatre written specifically for them, the staff of the Children's Theatre determined that the Living Newspaper format would be appropriate to present a history of aviation for this group. The result was *Flight,* based on material compiled by the Living Newspaper staff and dramatized by Oscar Saul and Louis Lantz, of the Playwrights' Division of the Federal Theatre Project. The show was directed by Ira Silberstein, with production supervision by Rennick. *Flight* opened on December 26, 1936 and closed on February 13, 1937, after twenty-five performances.[56]

Flight used the 1927 transatlantic crossing by Charles Lindbergh as a framework for flashback scenes depicting some of the high points in aviation history. While Lindbergh was supposedly en route, various scenes told of Leonardo da Vinci and his early designs, Otto Lilienthal and his glider, the Wright brothers and their flight at Kitty Hawk and many other related stories. The play was long and didactic. The New York critics were not very enthusiastic but the production did represent an intelligent, if not totally successful, attempt to enliven factual material with dramatization and special effects.

None of the Federal Theatre officials anticipated the furor caused by the next play, *The Revolt of the Beavers.* Supposedly a harmless animal play about anthropomorphic beavers, the play was accused of being a lesson in Marxism for children and, subsequently, was cited by the House of Representatives Un-American Activities Committee as an example of radical activity in the Federal Theatre Project. Written by Oscar Saul and directed by Lewis Leverett from the Group Theatre, *The Revolt of the Beavers* opened in May 1937 at the Adelphi Theatre. The play opened amidst rumors of impending personnel and appropriations cuts and while the Federal Theatre union members were creating unfavorable publicity through strikes and demonstrations. At this time, the Federal Theatre Project, confronted by an increasingly hostile Congress, was struggling to maintain its very existence. *The Revolt of the Beavers* was greeted with mixed reviews from the critics and a storm of protest from various concerned citizens. So much controversy was engendered by the production that the Federal Theatre decided to close the show on June 17, 1937, after seventeen performances.[57]

The Revolt of the Beavers tells the story of two impoverished nine-year-olds, Paul and Mary, who are whisked off to Beaverland by Windy (Mr. Wind) on a dream-adventure. The worker beavers in this country must all work on the Busy

Busy Wheel, preparing bark for the use of the beaver chief. They get no bark for themselves and are kept in submission by the chief's henchmen. Into this unhappy situation come the two children and two beavers—the Professor and Oakleaf, a "union organizer"—both of whom have been exiled for their activities. After many confrontations with the chief and his henchmen, Oakleaf succeeds in rallying beaver forces to rout the chief. All the beavers can then share the bark and live "happily ever after."

Actors John Randolph and Perry Bruskin, reminiscing in 1976 about their roles in the play, had pleasant recollections of the production. Randolph recalled the children's delighted reactions to the throne used by Ben Ross as the chief. The throne was actually a barber chair with levers that moved it up, down and around. The chair "was connected with a slide so that when he wanted to get down and talk to anybody, he'd just press a lever and the front of his chair went down," causing the chief to slide to the floor. The children were fascinated with this.[58]

Bruskin played a roller-skating beaver in the chief's retinue. He commented that the show was "a lot of fun." He was dressed in a "large beaver costume" with a "tail connected to a little string" in his hand. When he was "happy" he would "pull the string and the tail would wag."[59]

Although they were in general agreement as to the social significance of the script, New York theatre critics had mixed opinions about the production. The critic from the *New York American* declared that the play was "comic strip as much as . . . fantasy" and that the youngsters in the audience "voted it a grand time, and the grownups found it passably amusing. . . . If there is any underlying significance to the story," the critic continued, "the children probably will not see it."[60]

Brooks Atkinson, theatre critic for the *New York Times*, called the play "Mother Goose Marx." He alleged that the Federal Theatre produced "a revolutionary bed-time story," and that it was "a primer lesson in the class struggle." While acknowledging that "unformed minds accustomed to innocent play in the streets may not grasp the Marxian dialectic," Atkinson declared that the WPA had produced for children's "entertainment and education" a play depicting class struggle in terms of oppressed beavers, in which "beavers of the world, unite!" is the message. Atkinson noted further that the play "ought to improve our diplomatic relations with Soviet Russia."[61]

On the other hand, with a headline declaring "*Revolt of the Beavers* Makes Theatre History," the critic from the Communist *Daily Worker*, offered a highly favorable review. The subheading to the review sums up her reactions: "WPA Children's Theatre Thrills Kiddies With Beaverland Fantasy Rich with Social Significance—Brilliant Production Staged with Enthusiasm." Declaring that the play was "the first, full length, social fantasy of any pretentions [sic] to be produced" by children's theatre in America, she wrote: "Let thanks and bouquets be delivered at the door of the WPA Children's Theatre."[62]

In the wake of the largely negative publicity, Children's Theatre officials were understandably concerned about the public reaction to *The Revolt of the Beavers*. In order to ascertain as accurately as possible what children really perceived in the performance, an extensive survey of audience members was undertaken, under the general supervison of Max Shohet, research director for the Children's Theatre. The survey was directed by Dr. Frances Holden of the department of psychology at New York University, with the aid of four students trained in analyzing the reactions of children.[63]

The survey consisted of two parts: first, a set of seven questions requiring written answers from parents, teachers and college students who queried the children; and second, informal interviews with some of the children, conducted by the psychology students. The interviews were designed specifically to determine if the children had sensed any "class angle" in the play.[64]

After hundreds of children were queried, the four psychology students affirmed that most children apparently saw a moral to the story, but no deeper significance. One group of eleven-year-olds from the Bronx offered typical replies. When asked what lesson they thought Paul and Mary had learned in Beaverland, they answered: "Don't be selfish," "Beavers really talk," "Do unto others as you would have them do unto you," "Not to boss someone else" and other similar replies. According to the study, with very few exceptions, the children who attended *The Revolt of the Beavers* failed to see any political or "class" implications in the play.[65]

The next production of the Children's Theatre provided a welcome relief from controversy. This play was Chorpenning's *Jack and the Beanstalk,* directed by Peter Hyun and presented on the Caravan Theatre (formerly known as the Portable Theatre) circuit during the summer of 1937. The play continued on spot bookings until March 1938, with a total of thirty-five performances.[66]

In comparison with previous years, the 1937–1938 season was a low point in production for the Children's Theatre. The Federal Theatre underwent drastic personnel cuts and administrative changes dictated by WPA officials in Washington. Morale among the employees was low, and the future of the Federal Theatre was uncertain. The Children's Theatre did continue, however, despite the worsening conditions. Three festivals for child audiences—Autumn, Holiday and Easter—included performances of plays already in production. The festivals also included contributions from the Federal Music and Art Projects.

In response to thousands of requests for "exciting adventure plays," the Children's Theatre decided to produce Jules Eckert Goodman's dramatization of Robert Louis Stevenson's *Treasure Island*. Opening on Saturday, May 14, 1938, at the Hippodrome Theatre in New York, the show was touted as a major production. Costumes were elaborate, and the promotional campaign harked back to the early, enthusiastic days of the project. Directed by William Rathburn, *Treasure Island* played for several weeks at the Hippodrome, then toured the Caravan Theatre circuit. In the fall, the show played spot bookings, and it eventually closed on December 21, 1938, after twenty-eight performances.[67]

In the fall of 1938, Yasha Frank came to New York from the Los Angeles unit to direct his *Pinocchio*. The show proved to be the most popular of all the productions of the New York Children's Theatre. *Pinocchio* opened on December 23, 1938, at the Ritz Theatre in Manhattan and closed on June 30, 1939, when the entire Federal Theatre Project was terminated. The show was performed 197 times in New York.[69]

Many people working on *Pinocchio* brought much experience to that production. Edwin Michaels, who was about twenty-nine when he appeared as Pinocchio, had started his career at the age of nine in a children's vaudeville act. He had appeared previously in Broadway shows and films. Gepetto was played by Allan Frank, a veteran of many Children's Theatre shows, including *The Emperor's New Clothes* and *The Revolt of the Beavers*. Set designer Perry Watkins had also designed the scenery for the Negro Theatre's production of *Horse Play,* among other shows. Costume designer James Cochrane had designed for several Federal Theatre plays. Lighting designer Abe Feder subsequently became one of the leading lighting designers of the Broadway stage.

Pinocchio, like some other shows produced by the Children's Theatre, included audience participation. In one scene of the play, a blind woman approaches Pinocchio and begs him to give her some pennies. Pinocchio, troubled, asks the audience directly for advice. The stage directions indicate that he crosses back and forth downstage, asking different sections of the audience the same question; and, with the children's aid, he decides to give all four of his pennies to the woman. According to a Federal Theatre press release, children at the California performances of *Pinocchio* encouraged the puppet to be generous, but New York children "caused no end of embarrassment with their sophisticated replies." One child yelled, "Hang onto yer pennies; tell the old woman to go on relief!"[70] Brooks Atkinson, in his review for the *New York Times*, wrote that "they screamed their opinions, some of which were distinctly on the covetous side."[71]

Technically, *Pinocchio* was a complex production with many special effects. One of the most effective, reportedly, was the whale used in act 3. It measured sixteen feet in length and nine feet in height and was mounted on a wagon which enabled the creature to glide onto the stage, thereby frightening Pinocchio. The whale presented a profile view to the audience, with a rear section cut away, so that spectators could view the next scene inside the whale. The mouth of the whale was designed to open and close by means of a flexible covering stretched over a series of movable frames, operating much like an accordian. The eye of the whale was a shuttered lamp which could be opened or closed on cue. For example, when Gepetto unwittingly sang the whale to sleep, the eyelid came down and the mouth opened. Lighting effects provided a red glow in the whale's mouth, a light for the eye, and red and green lights on the tail. This was viewed through a scrim, so that the audience was transported beneath the sea.[72]

The New York theatre critics were kind to *Pinocchio*. After initial grumbling that the press was not allowed to see the show for the first week of production (reporters were invited to a special matinee on January 2, 1939), Brooks Atkinson admitted that this resulted in "letting the spoiled brats of the press see a finished and fully equipped performance." He wrote that the "stupendous" equipment included "a regiment of actors, dancers, clowns, and musicians, a jungle of animals, seven seas full of fish and mermaids . . . and about everything else the good geniuses of the Federal Theatre were able to think of." He commented that the music was "lovely," particularly the "beautiful lullaby."[73]

Calling *Pinocchio* a "complex and intricate bit of stagecraft," the critic from the *Wall Street Journal* wrote that the Federal Theatre "brought off this ticklish bit of balancing between adult standards and juvenile appeal in excellent shape." The critic was particularly impressed by the work of former vaudevillians in the cast, and he commented that Frank, with the help of these artists, had turned the whole production into a "pyrotechnic display which is beautifully paced, full of wit and sheer belly laughs," but that he had not lost "sight of the fact that it is essentially the story of Pinocchio."[74]

In early 1939, the turmoil which had existed in Congress over continued appropriations for the Federal Theatre Project finally came to a head. Extended congressional committee hearings had succeeded in presenting the Federal Theatre in an unfavorable light, often through hearsay testimony from witnesses. These people declared, without hard evidence, that the Federal Theatre was a hotbed of communist activity. Hallie Flanagan and her staff fought with every weapon they could muster to counteract these impressions. Flanagan argued that the Federal Theatre, while admittedly containing some radical thinkers, was primarily a constructive project employing thousands of people who had formerly been on relief.

Flanagan believed that the Federal Theatre Project was being offered as a sacrifice to placate opponents of President Roosevelt's programs long enough to pass the New Deal relief appropriations bill. Though comparatively small, the Federal Theatre was significant enough that its demise would provide a victory for New Deal opponents.[75]

All efforts to save the project failed. On June 30, 1939, Congress passed the Emergency Relief Appropriation Act of 1939, which included a section forbidding the use of funds made available through the act for the operation of any theatre project. The Federal Theatre was dead.[76]

The work of the Children's Theatre in New York and other Federal Theatre groups throughout the country had a stimulating effect upon the field of theatre for young audiences. Heretofore, with some exceptions, children's theatre had been in the hands of amateurs and educators; the Federal Theatre brought professionals into an ongoing program for child audiences. Moreover, children's theatre was given a status equal to that of other divisions in the Federal Theatre hierarchy. Thus the impetus given the children's theatre movement was a welcome benefit, derived from what was conceived as a massive relief program. Though an indirect and immeasurable legacy, these benefits affected thousands of lives.

NOTES

1. Hallie Flanagan, *Arena: The History of the Federal Theatre* (1940; rpt. New York: Arno, 1980), p. 28.

2. Ibid., pp. 15–17.

3. William F. McDonald, *Federal Relief Administration and the Arts* (Columbus, Ohio: Ohio State University Press, 1969), p. 129.

4. Flanagan, *Arena*, pp. 12–14.

5. "Supplement No. 1 to Bulletin No. 29," September 30, 1935, Section 9, Works Progress Administration, as quoted in McDonald, *Federal Relief Administration*, p. 503.

6. McDonald, *Federal Relief Administration*, p. 510.

7. [Ethel Fagon?], "Children's Theatre," [1937], p. 1, File "Children's Festival," Ethel Fagon's File, Records of the Federal Theatre Project, Records of the Works Progress Administration, Record Group 69, the National Archives, Washington, D.C. Hereafter citations from this record group are indicated by the abbreviation RG 69, and records in the National Archives Building in Washington, D.C. are indicated by the symbol NA.

8. [Ethel Fagon?], Memorandum, [May 1937], p. 2, TS, File "Programs," Ethel Fagon's File, RG 69, NA.

9. Flanagan, *Arena*, pp. 387–88, 421–22.

10. Ibid., pp. 152–53.

11. Ibid.

12. Betty Kessler Lyman, Report, August 24, 1936, pp. 1–3, TS, File "Children's Theatre—Misc.," National Office Subject File Car-Com, RG 69, NA. Hereafter the National Office Subject File will be abbreviated NOSF.

13. "Indiana Children Create Own Theatre," *Federal Theatre Magazine,* 2, No. 2 [Fall 1936?], 21, 34.

14. Flanagan, *Arena*, p. 153.

15. Lyman, report, p. 3.

16. Ibid., p. 3; Flanagan, *Arena*, p. 153.

17. Mr. Snitzer, "The Children's Theatre Under WPA," June 9, 1938, TS, File "Children's Theatre—Misc.," NOSF Car-Com, RG 69, NA.

18. John O'Connor and Lorraine Brown, eds., *Free, Adult, Uncensored: The Living History of the Federal Theatre Project* (Washington, D.C.: New Republic Books, 1978), p. 126.

19. Production Chart, Los Angeles Children's Theatre Unit, n.d., n. pag., TS, Library of Congress Federal Theatre Project Collection at George Mason University Library, Fairfax, Va. Hereafter the above citation will be abbreviated FTP Collection, GMU.

20. Yasha Frank, "Director's Report," in Production Notebook for *Hansel and Gretel,* [1937], n. pag., TS, PNB—*Hansel and Gretel*—Los Angeles, FTP Collection, GMU. The next paragraph is from the same source.

21. Review of *Hansel and Gretel, Los Angeles Herald and Express,* February 26, 1937, as quoted in Production Notebook for *Hansel and Gretel,* n. pag.

22. Yasha Frank, "Director's Report," in Production Notebook for *Pinocchio,* [1937], n. pag., TS, PNB—*Pinocchio*—Los Angeles, FTP Collection, GMU.

23. "Technical Report," in Production Notebook for *Pinocchio,* n. pag.

24. Production Chart, Los Angeles Children's Theatre Unit, n. pag.

25. "Audience Reaction," as quoted in Production Notebook for *Pinocchio,* n. pag.

26. Review of *Pinocchio, Los Angeles Evening News,* June 4, 1937; review of *Pinocchio, Los Angeles Daily News,* June 4, 1937, as quoted in Production Notebook for *Pinocchio,* n. pag.

27. Yasha Frank, "Director's Report," in Production Notebook for *Aladdin,* [1938], n. pag., TS, PNB—*Aladdin*—Los Angeles, FTP Collection, GMU.

28. "Technical Report," in Production Notebook for *Aladdin,* n. pag.

29. Review of *Aladdin, Los Angeles Daily News*, March 14, 1938, as quoted in Production Notebook for *Aladdin*, n. pag.

30. Production Chart, Los Angeles Children's Theatre Unit, n. pag.; O'Connor and Brown, *Free, Adult, Uncensored*, p. 23.

31. Flanagan, *Arena*, pp. 169–70; Production Charts for Cleveland, Ohio, Federal Theatre for Youth, TS, FTP Collection, GMU.

32. Flanagan, *Arena*, p. 388; Shirley Graham, "Director's Notes," in Production Notebook for *Little Black Sambo,* Chicago, [1938], n. pag., TS, PNB—*Little Black Sambo*—Chicago, FTP Collection, GMU.

33. Graham, "Director's Notes," n. pag.

34. Dorothy Day, "Federal Theatre Scores with Its Children's Play," *Chicago Herald and Examiner,* August, 31, 1938, as quoted in Production Notebook for *Little Black Sambo*, Chicago, n. pag.

35. C. J. Bulliet, "Little Black Sambo Goes into Jungle at Great Northern," *Chicago Daily News*, August 30, 1938, as quoted in Production Notebook for *Little Black Sambo,* Chicago, n. pag.

36. Kay Ewing, "Director's Notes," in Production Notebook for *Rip Van Winkle*, Chicago, [1938], n. pag., TS PNB—*Rip Van Winkle*—Chicago, FTP Collection, GMU.

37. Flanagan, *Arena*, p. 149.

38. Ibid., p. 308.

39. Esther Porter, "Director's Report," in Production Notebook for *Mother Goose Goes to Town*, [1937], n. pag., TS, PNB—*Mother Goose Goes to Town*—Seattle, FTP Collection, GMU; "Press Reports," as quoted in Production Notebook for *Mother Goose*, n. pag.

40. Production Chart, Seattle Children's Theatre, n.d., n. pag., TS, FTP Collection, GMU.

41. Production Chart, Seattle Children's Theatre, n. pag.

42. Esther Porter, "Director's Report," in Production Notebook for *Br'er Rabbit and the Tar Baby*, [1938], n. pag., TS, PNB—*Br'er Rabbit and the Tar Baby*—Seattle, FTP Collection, GMU.

43. "Repertory Group in *Br'er Rabbit*," *Seattle Post-Intelligencer,* May 8, 1938, as quoted in Production Book for *Br'er Rabbit,* n. pag.

44. Burke Ormsby, "Audience Reaction," in Production Notebook for *Br'er Rabbit*. n. pag.

45. "WPA Municipal Theatre Reorganized into Six Divisions," Press Release, August 11, 1936, Dept. of Information, FTP 000 112, FTP Collection, GMU (mimeographed).

46. [Pierre de Rohan], "Twain for Children," *Federal Theatre Magazine*, December, 1935, n. pag., FTP Collection, GMU.

47. Jack Rennick, "Children's Theatre—New York," *Federal Theatre Magazine*, No. 3 [March 1937?], p. 24, FTP Collection, GMU.

48. "Attendance and Receipts, W.P.A. Federal Theatre Project, N.Y.C., Nov. 11, '35, thru July 4, '37 (By Production Units)," TS, File "Facts 1937," New York City Alphabetical Subject File R, RG 69, NA. Hereafter this subject file will be abbreviated NYCASF.

49. Photographs, *The Emperor's New Clothes,* Adelphi Theatre, New York, 1936, P 165—NYC, File *"The Emperor's New Clothes*—New York City: Reprints," FTP Collection, GMU.

50. John Randolph, transcript of personal interview conducted by Diane Bowers, May 28, 1976, TS, pp. 45–46, FTP Collection, GMU.

51. Rennick, "Children's Theatre—New York," p. 26.

52. Marguerite Tazelaar, "*Emperor's New Clothes*: WPA Play by Charlotte Chorpenning at the Adelphi," review, *New York Herald Tribune,* late city ed., June 10, 1936, p. 18, col. 4.

53. W.G.K., "Children's Theatre: *The Emperor's New Clothes* at the Adelphi," review, *New York Sun*, complete final ed., p. 8, col. 3.

54. FTP National Information Service, "Children's Lives Enriched by Theatre," October 17, 1938, pp. 4–5, FTP 000 337, FTP Collection, GMU (mimeographed).

55. "Summary of Attendance and Receipts, Federal Theatre Project, N.Y.C. Fiscal Year 1938 (July 5, '37-July 3, '38)," File "Facts 1938," NYCASF R, RG 69, NA (mimeographed).

56. Marguerite Tazelaar, "*Flight*: Drama by Oscar Saul and Lou Lantz at Heckscher," review, *New York Herald Tribune*, late city ed., January 9, 1937, p. 10, cols 6–7; "Summary of Attendance and Receipts, Federal Theatre Project, N.Y.C. Fiscal Year 1937 (July 6, '36-July 3, '37)," File "Facts 1937," NYCASF R, RG 69, NA (mimeographed).

57. Flanagan, *Arena*, p. 388.

58. Randolph, interview, p. 28.

59. Perry Bruskin, transcript of interview conducted by John O'Conner, October 22, 1976, TS, p. 22, FTP Collection, GMU.

60. John Harkins, " 'Beaver's Revolt' Pleasing Fantasy for Children," review of *The Revolt of the Beavers. New York American,* 6 A.M. final ed., May 21, 1937, sec. 1, p. 11, col. 1.

61. Brooks Atkinson, "*The Revolt of the Beavers,* or Mother Goose Marx, Under WPA Auspices," review, *New York Times*, May 21, 1937, p. 19, cols. 2–3.

62. Mary Morrow, " 'Revolt of the Beavers' Makes Theatre History," review, *Daily Worker*, late city ed., May 24, 1937, p. 9, cols. 7–8.

63. Max Shohet, comp., "Audience Analysis: *Revolt of the Beavers*," June 1937, n. pag., File *"Revolt of the Beavers* NYC," Audience Survey P-Z and Misc. Survey Reports, RG 69, NA (mimeographed).

64. Shohet, n. pag.

65. Ibid.

66. "Summary of Attendance . . . 1938," p. 1.

67. "Federal Theatre Productions: Since Inception of the Federal Theatre in Nov. 1935 to Jan. 1, 1939 and Beyond," TS, n. pag., File "Federal Theatre Productions 1935–39," FTP Statistical Summaries, RG 69, NA.

68. "Federal Theatre Productions: Since Inception," n. pag.

69. Flanagan, *Arena*, p. 346; Federal Theatre Project: Regional Production Charts, n.d., TS, n. pag., FTP Collection, GMU.

70. FTP Department of Information, Press Release, December 29, 1938, TS, File "Dec. 1938," Publicity—NYC, RG 69, NA.

71. Brooks Atkinson, "Uncle Sam Produces *Pinocchio* Primarily for the Citizens of Future Generations," review, *New York Times*, late city ed., January 3, 1939, sec. 1, p. 19, cols. 2–3.

72. Emmet Lavery, "The Flexible Stage," [1940?], TS, pp. 98–99, FTP 000 268, FTP Collection, GMU.

73. Atkinson, review of *Pinocchio*.

74. William T. Cobb, "Click," review of *Pinocchio*, *Wall Street Journal*, January 3, 1939, p. 59, cols. 5–6.

75. Flanagan, *Arena*, pp. 348–53.

76. Ibid., p. 362.

9

Winifred Ward: Catalyst and Synthesist

CHARLES E. COMBS

During Winifred Ward's active career, which spanned seven decades and extended almost twenty-five years beyond her official retirement, she compiled a remarkable legacy of achievements: she taught at Northwestern University for thirty-two years; she served as supervisor of dramatics in the Evanston Public School System for twenty-three years; she founded, then served as director of the Children's Theatre of Evanston for twenty-five years; she was instrumental in founding the Children's Theatre Conference (the forerunner of the current national children's theatre organization, the American Alliance for Theatre and Education); and she authored four books, two monographs, nine contributions to books, sixty-nine articles in journals, magazines and newspapers, and presented numerous speeches and special workshops.[1]

Her contributions to children's theatre and creative drama, both in the United States and worldwide, are well known and well documented.[2] However, in order to appreciate the remarkable significance and profound resonance of her work, it is important to review her life, her teaching, her artistic work, her organizational achievements, her philosophy and her writing as a whole from our present perspective. Gerald Tyler, a well-known British drama educator, writing a tribute to Ward, noted, ''She seemed to be of the theatre and of creative education at the same time.''[3] In that sense, one could see Ward as a synthesist, as a person who drew from disparate areas to educate the whole child in his or her thinking, feeling and physical complexity. Ward was a master at teaching, at reaching the child or adult student through the medium of theatre and drama, as well as at inspiring others to high levels of achievement through the force of her personality and the power of her enthusiasm. And through her work, Ward literally gave definition to the creative drama field.

In her book, *Playmaking with Children*, Ward discusses the "qualifications of a teacher of playmaking." She notes that "an ideal woman teacher of creative drama" will have "all the finest qualities of women in general, all the assets of the best teachers in any field, besides all the special qualifications needed for her work in creative dramatics." She states further that, "*Integrity* in character and art comes first. . . . " She then lists other necessary qualities such as sensitivity, emotional maturity, judgment, taste, a sense of humor and vitality.[4]

Earlier in the same chapter, Ward describes the ideal specialist teacher in creative drama, saying that this person should be a speech (theatre) major, trained with a broad liberal arts education and "courses in child psychology, children's literature, storytelling, creative dramatics, and probably children's theatre and dance. . . . " Ward continues:

A leader should be skilled enough so that she is an excellent example to the children in posture and grace, in pleasing voice and clean-cut diction. And she would not be a specialist in creative drama if she did not have a strong belief in the power it can be in the lives of children.[5]

Perhaps her vision of the ideal teacher of children and drama accounts for the high standards Ward set for herself and her profession. These, in turn, probably account for the remarkable effect she had on her profession in terms of substance, style, personnel and organizational structure.

THE PERSON

Winifred Louise Ward, the youngest of four children, was born on October 29, 1884, in Eldora, Iowa. Her father was a prominent local attorney, and her mother, whom Ward extolls highly, was active civically and socially, and gifted with cosmopolitan attitudes and energy. In a theme, written in 1918 for an English class at the University of Chicago, Ward states:

If it had not been for my mother and Washington, my childhood would have been commonplace. My mother differed radically from the rest of the mothers in the little Iowa town where I was born. She came from the east. . . . Her Eastern accent, her liberal views, and above all, the link which she made with great, beautiful Washington, my dream city, would have been enough to set her apart from all others. But she had other characteristics which made her the dominating force in my early life. She was large and capable, able to do well anything she undertook, but preferring always the big things. . . .

In bringing up her children . . . she insisted upon instant and absolute obedience. . . .

She played the piano exceedingly well, too, and it was from hearing her that I came to love so much of the best music.

I did not realize as a child, however, how really remarkable she was. Always a great reader, she was interested not only in the latest fiction and in the magazines and newspapers, but also in the most substantial literature. Her convictions were decided and her executive power unusual, and consequently she has always been a leader. . . .

My father looked on rather quizzically at the bringing up of his children. . . . I always wished that I could get better acquainted with him. . . .

It was very seldom that the vital things in life were discussed in our home, and I regret the fact that we lived so much of the time on the surface. Religion was never talked about; deep experiences, though we had them, were kept hidden. The reason we were silent about them was, I think, that we were not in the least demonstrative, and we feared sentimentalism. We children always stood a little in awe of our parents, and we all tended more or less toward stoicism. As a result, we did not know each other as well as many families do. We talked often of serious things—of world events, of education, of moral issues—but we were seldom intimate. It was well understood that the standards of the family were high and were to be kept so. . . .

I think my home life as a child would have been more enjoyable, and at the same time more helpful as a preparation for later life, if my parents had been more like companions to me—that is, if I had felt free to talk to them unrestrainedly, feeling sure of their understanding and sympathy. . . .

Naturally, there are many ways in which it seems as though I could have improved on my bringing up. I should have learned to swim and skate, to play the piano, to be more observant of the wonderful things in nature, to read with more discrimination. I should probably have made a self-satisfied little prude of myself if I had managed my own early life. My days would have been so crowded with preparations for grown up life that I should have missed half the fun of living. So, on the whole, I think it is just as well that the care of my youth was put into such capable charge as that of my parents.[6]

While the closing paragraph of her essay is characteristic of Ward, insofar as it is self-effacing and placating, there are some themes running through her comments which seem to permeate her life and work: the influence of her mother, her heritage of organizational expertise and responsibility, her love of cultural vitality, and her desire or need for intimate familial sharing of deeply felt feelings. The combination of these qualities seems to have created the dynamic personality who catalyzed a movement in creative education—in a form, it should be noted, which allowed the teacher to nurture the emotional growth of the students as well as to cultivate their intellectual and artistic abilities.

In a speech given at the University of Iowa in 1952, Ward commented on the personal motivations, arising from her childhood, which contributed to her desire to improve creative opportunities in education:

I am conscious in what I say this evening, that children's theatre and creative dramatics stem from certain deep interests and yearnings of my own childhood, the satisfaction of which would have counted immeasurably in my development and happiness. It is, therefore, something more than my general concern for the welfare of boys and girls that prompts me, for I should like to have some small influence in bringing to all Iowa children today something that was lacking in the education of this Iowa child many yesterdays ago.[7]

In a 1962 letter, Ward discussed the shortcomings of her own education: "I really think that for a formal, traditional school, it was good. But if experimentation was going on, it had not reached Eldora. I doubt if the word, 'creative' was ever used during my whole public school life."[8]

Ward devoted her career to formalizing, articulating, organizing and advocating a form of education which would offer more than she had received as a child, both in the home and in the school. The genesis of her career, however, was not a simple, straightforward progression, for Ward practically had to "invent" the field she was to make her life's work.

HER TEACHING

Ward graduated from high school in 1902, leaving Eldora the following year for college. Life away from home was relatively routine for a person of her status, because as a woman she was to prepare for a career in teaching. In 1903, she enrolled in a two-year course of study in the Cumnock School of Oratory, in Evanston, Illinois. (This was later to become the School of Speech at Northwestern University.) The curriculum in which Ward enrolled was geared to prepare her to teach English composition and literature as well as elocution. In addition to the course work in English, there was training in "physical culture," which was to "make the body responsive to the thought and emotion of literature and to gain 'freedom from awkwardness and self-consciousness in gestural expression.' "[9]

After completion of the two-year course in 1905, Ward returned to Eldora, where she coached declamation contests and directed plays.[10] In 1907, she returned for a post-graduate course at the Cumnock School; and in 1908 she took a job with the Adrian, Michigan public schools. There, she was paid $60 a month for "coaching public speaking contests; directing the senior play; teaching reading in the upper grades; coaching girls' basketball; and conducting calisthenics once a week for children in the primary grades."[11]

In a 1962 letter, reflecting on the experience, Ward writes:

It seems as if I am always faced with some task for which I have no precedent to follow. This has been more difficult (having to be a pioneer) because I have always been so critical of myself, so conscious of my own limitations. In my first teaching position in Adrian, Michigan: special teacher of dramatics and physical education, which I had accepted because jobs were so scarce in those days, I was prepared for the dramatics, but not for the physical education. I had to study out courses for the grades and take special work to fit myself to it.[12]

In 1916, after eight years of teaching at Adrian, Ward enrolled at the University of Chicago, majoring in English. Upon her graduation in 1918, she was asked to join the faculty of the Cumnock School of Oratory, which was at that time in a period of transition under its new director, Ralph Dennis. Ward arrived at the Cumnock School at a fortuitous moment, for until that time no drama courses were offered. Shortly thereafter (especially after 1923 when Alexander Dean was named associate professor of dramatic literature and production), there was a proliferation of drama courses, and by 1930 twelve of the twenty-six new courses were in the general area of speech education.

By 1923, Ward, seeing the educational benefits of enacting stories, began to have members of her advanced storytelling class engage in story dramatization. Subsequently, she was encouraged by Dennis, then a member of the Evanston Board of Education, to use the elementary schools as a laboratory where she and her students might practice this method of teaching. During the academic year 1923–1924, Ward was named supervisor of dramatics for the Evanston elementary schools, and, by 1929, thirty-eight drama classes were being taught in the public school program. Concurrently, Ward's classes at Northwestern were undergoing an evolution, having been called educational dramatics (1925), junior dramatics (1926), and finally creative dramatics (1928).[13] Notably, her creative dramatics course was the first university-level class so titled.[14]

Ward's first book, *Creative Dramatics: For the Upper Grades and Junior High School*, was published in 1930. This book grew out of her work in the Evanston public schools, and, according to one authority, it provided definition for the field:

The term "creative dramatics" is recognized as a specialized term in education and theatre, was invented for this specific use and popularized by Winifred Ward. Until 1930, no one had ever used "creative dramatics" consistently as the title of a specific activity. Various applications of "creative drama," "educative dramatics," "Junior Dramatics," "educational drama," "creative group activities," "auditorium," etc. had been used prior to 1930. Miss Ward, in searching for an apt description, had herself used several of these. But once she happened on "creative dramatics," she consistently used it in its specialized meaning, employing it as the title of her first book and as the name of her college course.[15]

At the same time as she was developing her course work in creative dramatics at Northwestern, Ward was involved in other curricular projects, especially in the area of children's theatre. Shortly after his arrival at Northwestern, Dean suggested that the School of Speech might sponsor a children's theatre. In 1925, the plan reached fruition, and with Ralph Dennis and Dean as advisors, Ward was named director of the Evanston Children's Theatre. Ward then carried three professional titles simultaneously: instructor in dramatic arts at Northwestern University, supervisor of dramatics in the Evanston public schools and director of the Evanston Children's Theatre.[16]

HER ARTISTIC WORK

In 1927, Dennis arranged a co-sponsorship of the children's theatre between Northwestern and the Evanston public schools—a sensible thing to do since Ward was supervisor of dramatics for the schools, and used her public school children as well as the Northwestern students in productions. Clearly, this was a fruitful arrangement, as the theatre flourished and attendance grew from approximately 3,500 for the first season, to 8,000 for the second and 16,000 twenty years later.[17] Ward remained director of the Evanston Children's Theatre until her retirement in 1950, producing four plays per season, many of them premieres. In all, during Ward's twenty-five year tenure as director (as well as for the following two years, 1950–1952), it is estimated that the theatre played to a total audience of 103,000, with 12,000 persons actively engaged in the productions, along with another estimated 3,000 audience members and participants coming from the productions which were added to the university theatre's summer schedule.[18]

From the outset, Ward's work with the children's theatre was guided by two primary objectives: "(1) to bring joy to the children in the audience, [and] (2) to give students in the School of Speech an opportunity to gain experience in a community project."[19]

Other values to be derived from theatre for children are articulated by Ward in two particularly apt statements. In the program for the 1940 production of *Marco Polo*, Ward notes:

The reasons for our Children's Theatre are obvious. First and foremost is the joy of our children. We do not care to provide bare amusement, nor do we want our plays to mean escape from reality. What we do care about is that they shall help to make life richer, more delightful; set true standards in artistic and human values; and help in the formation of a discriminating taste in recreation.[20]

In an article for a Northwestern University bulletin, Ward gives an even more detailed statement of this philosophy:

Whether one considers a children's theatre from the standpoint of the player, the backstage worker, or the audience, he discovers values which are unique.

Participation as a player or worker means a kind of creative self-expression which brings intense joy and satisfaction. When a child studies and portrays a character in relation to other characters, he is studying life itself. His horizon is broadened, his interest in people deepened, and his power of expressing himself grows stronger.

Whether he is in the cast or stage crew, he learns much from the experience of working closely with others toward a common end. Self-discipline in the subordination of self, democracy from working with children of other stations in life, other races and beliefs; responsibility, good sportsmanship, poise.

When he is a part of the audience he learns how to express his enjoyment without overstepping the bounds of good taste; how to respect the rights of others by allowing them to enjoy the play without interference, and how to appreciate good drama.[21]

This philosophy is manifested particularly in Ward's comments about her techniques of working with children:

I believe definitely that formal children's theatre should be geared to a high quality of performance. I think children's theatre should be for the audience first and the players second. Now, not nearly everybody agrees with me on that. Many people have the children's theatre to give the children experience in being in it, and of course, children do get a great deal out of it. But, I believe that you have such a responsibility to your audience in children's theatre that they ought to be placed foremost. . . .

And so, I choose the very best players I can find. They may happen to be children, but not little children, whose dramatic experience should be creative dramatics. If you must use children, it is better to use junior high school age; junior high people are so varied in size that you can usually find enough difference to give the audience an illusion of both child and adult characters.

So, starting with my philosophy of a children's theatre's being directed, first of all, for the benefit, the entertainment, the education and delight of the audience, I want to have it as good as possible, and so I want children with ability.[22]

HER ORGANIZATIONAL WORK

As if it were not enough to juggle her three professional responsibilities, in 1936 Ward took on another charge. With the founding of the American Educational Theatre Association (AETA), Ward was asked to head a new committee on children's theatre. Subsequently, children's theatre meetings became a regular component of AETA national conventions. However, there was not yet any coordination among creative drama and children's theatre practitioners throughout the country; thus, at the urging of Dennis, Ward began to organize her burgeoning field.

In 1944, she began plans for a conference at Northwestern, sending announcements to all the people she knew who were connected with children's theatre. These announcements were met with enthusiasm: "Eighty-three children's theatre directors, writers, producers, and other leaders from twenty states overcame the difficulties of wartime travel to attend the conference."[23]

Among those who attended the conference were such significant persons as Isabel Burger from the Children's Experimental Theatre (Johns Hopkins University), Gloria Chandler and Virginia Lee Comer representing the Association of Junior Leagues, Charlotte Chorpenning from the Goodman Children's Theatre, Rita Criste, Dina Rees Evans, Kenneth Graham, Rosemary Musil, Hazel Robertson of the Palo Alto Children's Theatre, Oleda Schrottkey (head of drama for the Girl Scouts of America), Geraldine Brain Siks, Sara Spencer, Julie Thompson, Mildred Harter Wirt of the Gary, Indiana Board of Education and, of course, Ward.[24]

After three days of meetings, the decision was made to affiliate with AETA, rather than to form a separate children's theatre organization. Consequently, Hazel G. Robertson, AETA Children's Theatre Committee Chairman, became the leader of the new group.[25] In a report of their first meeting, Sara Spencer, the editor of the Children's Theatre Press, wrote:

There were five or six men in the audience, but for the most part, they were women— privileged women, women of culture and education, women of taste and charm. There were more than a hundred of them, and they made a very stylish and attractive audience in their colorful summer frocks and gay, mad hats. It was a pleasure, Dean McBurney said, to welcome them to the Children's Theatre Conference that Northwestern University was sponsoring, and to introduce to them the one who had been responsible for bringing them all together.

When Miss Winifred Ward arose, many of the visitors saw her for the first time, though they had known her for long through her books, through her kind and tireless letters, through her fame in the profession she had helped to create. She was a slender little woman, and very pretty, her young vivacious face and bright brown eyes giving the lie at once to her snow-white hair. It was hard to believe that such a little wisp of smiling woman had, in a time of war, simply by her own personal magnetism, drawn together, from the farthest reaches of the country, such an audience.

She glowed with pride, as she greeted her guests. She gave them clearly to understand that this was not her meeting at all. She named and introduced the people to whom the credit should really go. But everybody sitting in that audience knew that the thing that had brought them from all their far places—from Waco, from Baltimore, from Cheyenne, from New York City, from Palo Alto, from Portland, Oregon, from places requiring full days and nights of travel under wartime conditions—what had brought them all together was Miss Winifred Ward herself. In every sense of the word, it was Miss Winifred Ward's Children's Theatre Conference, and as such, history would remember it.[26]

Clearly, Ward's vision was to shape the future of the children's theatre movement, for in *Theatre for Children,* she recounts some of the early meetings of the Children's Theatre group (at the University of Washington in 1946; and later at the University of Indiana; the University of Denver; in New York City, hosted by the American National Theatre and Academy; and the University of Minnesota). She notes:

The programs at these conferences include every aspect of theatre by and for children, from demonstrations of creative dramatics, of formally-produced plays, of technical manipulation, of puppetry, radio, and television; to speeches by acknowledged authorities on child psychology, sociology, and education; panel discussions on playwriting, on the choice of plays, on stage settings; evaluation of formal productions by experts....

The purpose of such conferences is chiefly to educate leaders in the field of child drama, whether they are directors, teachers, writers, or sponsors of children's theatres. To educate them, first of all, to believe in the intrinsic worth of children's theatre; to believe that it is infinitely important to choose plays of high standard; to produce them as beautifully as possible; to make each one a fine and lasting experience for every child, whether he is a player or audience. And along with the experience of beautiful formal productions, to give each child the fun, the creative and social development, and the therapeutic values which come from participation in creative dramatics.[27]

In 1950, the name of the Children's Theatre Committee was changed to the Children's Theatre Conference (CTC), and the annual conventions were renumbered, with the 1944 meeting at Northwestern designated as the first. In 1952, CTC became the first formal "division" of the AETA, with an organizational structure involving sixteen "regions" that were intended to provide grassroots support for the CTC.[28]

Subsequently, Ward was appointed Honorary Director for Life of CTC (1958); elected a Fellow of AETA (1967); and given the AETA Award of Merit, the highest honor awarded by that organization.[29]

THE CONTEXT FOR HER EDUCATIONAL PHILOSOPHY

In the last article Ward was to write, she noted that in her public school teaching at Adrian, the declamation contests were easy; the reading classes, especially when students read "parts," were successful; the senior play was a hit; and, though they rarely won games, her girls' basketball team members were always good friends.[30]

She goes on to say that she discovered that if she could add a dramatic element to the physical exercises of her elementary pupils, they enjoyed them more. Consequently, she employed imaginative games, never realizing just how popular they would be. "Creative dramatics!" Ward exclaims, "Why didn't I think of it then? The children and I could have had the joy of it several years sooner."[31]

Ward then notes that when she returned to teach at Northwestern she soon began to hear more of John Dewey, subsequently reading his works, visiting the Francis Parker School, and studying the works of Kilpatrick, Rugg and Shumaker, and Hughes Mearns. While she was influenced by all the proponents of "progressive education," she states that when she read Mearns' three books, *Creative Youth, Creative Power*, and *The Creative Adult*, she was particularly moved:

I knew that, for me, these were the best! . . . By this time, I was enthusiastic about creating a new course which I would call Creative Dramatics. It was based on the philosophy of Hughes Mearns and the 'new education' . . . I was to use *Creative Power* as required reading in my course.[32]

In fact, though Ward and Mearns met only once, each dedicated revised editions of their respective books, *Playmaking with Children* and *Creative Power,* to the other. Mearns' dedication reads:

To
Winifred Ward
who believes with the author that the natural creative interests of childhood and youth may be developed into superior personal powers.[33]

In addition to Mearns, Dewey (with his concept of experiential learning), Kilpatrick (with his project method of learning), and Rugg and Shumaker (with their child-centered curriculum) were all stimuli for Ward's process for creative dramatics; and clearly, they all prepared the way. However, two other educational pioneers also provided an atmosphere conducive to the development of creative dramatics at that time: Francis W. Parker and William Wirt.

The Parker School, founded in 1901, implemented the educational philosophies of Pestalozzi and Sheldon. In addition, Parker advocated oral expression as an excellent technique for teaching, and he emphasized correlated projects utilizing dramatization.[34] Fortuitously, Ward was able to visit this school at the beginning of her tenure at Northwestern. About this visit she wrote:

> One of the earliest schools I visited was the Francis Parker School in Chicago. I thoroughly liked what I saw. The attitude of both teachers and pupils was unlike any I had ever seen. There was no lifeless response to teachers' questions, no looking at the clock to see if it was almost time for the class to be over. There seemed to be a feeling of responsibility on the part of the young people. If this was the "new education," I approved most heartily.[35]

Another example of educational practice which was to prepare the way for Ward's pioneering work in creative dramatics was the Gary, Indiana, plan of William Wirt. Dissatisfied with the traditional educational practices of the nineteenth century, Wirt organized the Gary schools on three fundamental principles:

1. that they should provide opportunities for work, study, and supervised play for children in urban areas;
2. that school facilities should be used to their maximum efficiency; and
3. that children should come in contact with a varied and enriched curriculum.[36]

A significant aspect of this school organization was the notion of "auditorium," a concept which was strongly influenced by Mildred Harter. She contributed to the "work-study-play" model of education by insisting, early in her work in the Gary schools, that one of the principal objectives of "auditorium" be the "training of children in oral communication through related dramatic activities."[37] This "platoon" type of organization for schooling was significant in the development of creative dramatics, for it created an opportunity for it to be used and an atmosphere where it was valued.

With the existence of this educational ferment, it was important to train people to take advantage of the new situation, and a listing of the people Winifred Ward influenced reads like a "Who's Who" in American educational theatre.[38] Equally important, however, was Ward's contribution to the burgeoning field through her writing, because at that time, there existed no texts which dealt specifically with creative dramatics in education.[39]

HER WRITING

Ward's *Creative Dramatics: For the Upper Grades and Junior High School* (1930) was considered a landmark in the field of theatre and drama education.

This book was followed by *Theatre for Children* (1939; rev. 1950, 1958), which was designed to give the inexperienced director guidelines for "the production of artistic and beautiful plays for the joy of child audiences."[40]

Ward's third major work, *Playmaking with Children: From Kindergarten to High School*, was published in 1947. In 1957, it was revised and newly subtitled, "From Kindergarten through Junior High School." This book was based on ideas and experiences that Ward had developed since 1930, when her first book was published. *Stories to Dramatize* was published in 1952 to serve as a companion to *Playmaking with Children*.

In the preface to *Creative Dramatics*, Ward underscores the pioneering nature of the work:

> This book has grown out of the creative dramatic work in the public schools of Evanston, Illinois. . . . It was necessary to experiment, for there were no precedents to follow, no available plan for educational dramatic courses in the grades. . . . It has been fascinating, this pioneer work, and it will continue to be an absorbing study, for our courses will go on developing as long as we teach them.[41]

And, develop they did. Ward goes on to say that this book was written chiefly for directors of children's dramatics, but that it would also prove useful to "regular" teachers who wanted to make their teaching more effective by using the dramatic method in studying literature.

Because this book was the first in its field, it covered a vast amount of material, ranging from a definition and philosophy of creative dramatics to an extensive section (about half the book) on the production of the school play and the organization of a children's theatre. While much of the material on technical production is out-dated, and while there have been many advances in theories of acting, directing and pedagogy, this book remains a valuable asset because of its seminal nature.

Although Ward wrote her book almost sixty years ago, the sentiments she expresses seem to apply today. In her introduction she writes:

> The old education had no place for dramatics. It was a frill. . . . Mental discipline was the one important aim in the school of the last century. Facts must be stored in intellectual cupboards, rules must be learned, lessons must be memorized and recited.
>
> Along came such leaders as John Dewey, Francis Parker and William H. Kilpatrick, who declared that an education which recognized the mind alone . . . was not true education. The whole child must be developed if he was to reach his maximum growth. . . .
>
> Coincident with this shifting of emphasis in education has come a change in the manner of teaching dramatics. . . . In the place of stressing the finished production, modern teachers of children's dramatics stress the process of developing the production. . . . This change in emphasis from the exhibitional to the educational has made of dramatics a new subject— one that has a valuable contribution to give to education.[42]

Later in the introduction, Ward defines creative dramatics, delineates the material appropriate for drama, and discusses the value of drama to education as well as its place in the school curriculum. Finally, she uses her experience in the Evanston school system as an example of the place and function of drama in education. Succeeding chapters include a fusion of philosophical and practical advice, ranging from discussions on attitude to examples of course guides and scripts for dramatization. Significantly, throughout the work, one feels the passion of Ward as she seems to speak inspirationally and directly to the reader from her vast storehouse of experience, insight and sensitivity.

In her next book, *Theatre for Children*, Ward sets a different goal:

> The very gracious reception given my *Creative Dramatics* has encouraged me to write this sister volume, which has as its objective, not the development of children through the creating of original dramatizations, as did my former book, but rather the production of artistic and beautiful plays for the joy of child audiences.[43]

Ward goes on to say that this book is written primarily for the beginning director of children's plays, whether in a school, camp or community setting. The majority of the book is devoted to such specifics as organizing a theatre, choosing a season, playwriting, casting, designing and building settings and costumes, as well as the principles of house and business management. However, perhaps the most telling aspect of her work is the fact that Ward devotes the first two chapters to placing the practice of children's theatre within a historical and philosophical context.

While the facts included in Ward's swift overview of the history of children's theatre are of some value to the reader, her considered opinions are of equal or greater worth. In fact, it is this capacity to keep theory and practice in balance, the one informing the other, that makes Ward's contributions significant and applicable to current work in the field of creative drama and theatre for children. In addition, in her description of a children's theatre of the future, Ward suggests a vision which has yet to be realized.

In her third book, *Playmaking with Children*, Ward writes that "the only teaching which really counts is that which gets over into the lives of children to the extent of making them better people—people of finer sensitivities, attitudes, and appreciations. This is our great objective."[44]

Clearly, this is no simple task; however, in this book Ward attempts to delineate an approach to creative dramatics that will facilitate the achievement of such an objective. In the preface, Ward writes that since she realized that most creative dramatics in the schools was being led by elementary teachers without formal training in speech and drama, she would direct this book toward their needs. This book is, thus, readily accessible to the classroom teacher, yet it is also useful for the experienced drama leader.

Again, in this work, Ward's personality shines through her writing, particularly in her depth of feeling regarding children, drama and education. A brief examination of the objectives of playmaking, along with a discussion of its underlying principles, indicates the range of interests that concerned Ward.

Ward regards playmaking as a term which may be used interchangeably with creative dramatics to designate all forms of improvised drama, including "dramatic play, story dramatization, impromptu work in pantomime, shadow and puppet plays, and all other extemporaneous drama."[45] Its objectives are:

1. to provide for a controlled emotional outlet;
2. to provide each child with an avenue of self-expression in one of the arts;
3. to encourage and guide the child's creative imagination;
4. to give young people opportunities to grow in social understanding and cooperation; and
5. to give children experience in thinking on their feet and expressing ideas fearlessly.[46]

Subsequently, Ward articulates principles and objectives of creative dramatics. To paraphrase her lengthy descriptions, in brief, the principles are:

1. The whole child should be educated, not only for the future, but for the present, by participating in activities which challenge his deepest interest and highest powers.
2. The child's natural inclinations should be taken into account by curriculum developers so that the child may be encouraged to deepen his knowledge and expand his interests.
3. The child learns through experience; therefore, the school should provide carefully planned classroom experiences which are designed to relate subject matter to the child's ongoing life.
4. What children learn should have meaning for them, thus children should have an immediate use for what they learn. If they have a purpose for learning, then they will understand the reason for learning the material.
5. Children should be given the opportunity to help plan what they do.
6. Schools should help every child develop a sense of self-confidence and adequacy.
7. Attitudes are the "moving force of life"; therefore, their teaching should be valued above the teaching of skills and facts.
8. The best preparation for future life in a rapidly changing civilization is living democratically in the classroom where students are involved in creative thinking, problem solving, planning, and carrying out projects, thereby developing their ability to contribute to society and understand their work.
9. Our children should be educated for democracy; therefore schools must help them develop a sense of responsibility, a respect for the rights of others, and the courage to speak out for their convictions.[47]

Given these premises as a starting point, Ward utilized the remainder of her book to interweave a philosophy and a method of using drama in the schools, in religious education, in recreation and for therapy and speech improvement. Clearly, she set high standards for herself and her field, and in order to achieve them she not only maintained her teaching and organizational work, but she continued to publish in a field which was still in its infancy.

Ward's last major publication, *Stories to Dramatize*, was designed to be a companion volume to *Playmaking with Children*. It is considered by some as "the most ambitious of all Ward's books," especially since it was the first of its kind, enjoying remarkable popularity and critical acclaim.[48] In this work there are very few pages devoted to the ideas behind creative dramatics; rather, the bulk of the text consists of stories to be used as a basis for dramatization. These are arranged according to the age group for which they would be suitable, roughly paralleling the contents of *Playmaking with Children*.

SUMMARY

Winifred Ward built upon her strong organizational capabilities, while entering a career that would fulfill her needs for cultural vitality and emotional commitment and communication. She taught school as a "regular" teacher, yet was also involved in coaching basketball and directing theatre productions. As such, she was involved in the children's intellectual, emotional, aesthetic, social and physical education. After several years of experience as a teacher, she attended graduate school where she continued to integrate her seemingly disparate areas of interest. Then, while teaching at Northwestern University, she brought definition to her profession by drawing from educational theory and practice as well as from the theory and practice of theatre production and instruction. This fusion was to become the centerpiece of an entire subfield in education—creative dramatics.

Working at a time when the ideas of Dewey and others in the progressive education movement were fresh, and in an environment open to and ready for innovation (such as the Evanston school system and the Northwestern University School of Speech), Ward was the right person, in the right place, at the right time to synthesize her approach to theatre and education with the ideas of the time, to formalize them in her teaching, thinking and writing, and to spur her colleagues into action in the formation of a new professional organization and an emerging educational field.

Clearly, Ward fits Agnes Haaga's description of her as a person, "charged with energy and possessing the ability to charge others with like energy; to combine energies to set in action a positive and constructive chain reaction that goes on endlessly to affect a multitude of other beings."[49]

ACKNOWLEDGMENT

The author would like to thank Patrick M. Quinn, Northwestern University Archivist, and Kevin B. Leonard, Associate University Archivist, for their assistance.

NOTES

1. Winifred Ward was born October 29, 1884, and died August 16, 1975, after suffering a stroke in June 1974.

2. Ward's life and work are documented in several dissertations and theses, most notably: Charles Jones, "An Evaluation of the Educational Significance of the Children's Theatre of Evanston," Ph.D. diss., Northwestern, 1953; James E. Popovich, "A Study of Significant Contributions to the Development of Creative Dramatics in American Education," Ph.D. diss., Northwestern, 1955; Barbara Likens, "A Historical Study of Winifred Ward and Her Contribution to Education Through Creative Dramatics," Master's thesis, University of Washington, 1963; Mimmye Wilson Bradley, "The Contribution of Winifred Ward to the Children's Theatre Movement in the United States," Ph.D. diss., Memphis State University, 1969; Kenneth R. Hosie, "Theatre 65: Its Organization, Operation and Function as a Children's Theatre," Ph.D. diss., Pennsylvania State University, 1972; and Jan Guffin, "Winifred Ward: A Critical Biography," Ph.D. diss., Duke, 1975. The last work contains an extensive bibliography listing numerous books, scholarly works and articles by and about Ward. In addition to this material, there is a significant archival collection at Northwestern University, Evanston, Illinois.

3. Gerald Tyler, "Dr. Winifred Ward: An Appreciation," in *Go Adventuring*, ed. Ruth Beall Heinig (New Orleans: Anchorage Press, 1977), p. 80.

4. Winifred Ward, *Playmaking with Children*, 2d ed. (New York: Appleton-Century-Crofts, 1957), pp. 283–86.

5. Ibid., pp. 273–74.

6. Winifred Ward, "My Environment," in *Go Adventuring*, pp. 18–25.

7. Winifred Ward, speech and broadcast given at the University of Iowa, June 1, 1952, at a conference on child development, as quoted in Likens, "Historical Study," p. 27.

8. Winifred Ward, letter to Barbara Likens, September 11, 1962, as quoted in Likens, "Historical Study," p. 27.

9. James Lawrence Lardner, "A History of the School of Speech, Northwestern University," TS, 1951, p. 19. University Archives, Northwestern University, Evanston, Illinois.

10. Ruth Beall Heinig, "Winifred Ward: Her Life in Art," in *Go Adventuring*, p. 12.

11. Guffin, "Critical Biography," Ph.D. diss., p. 6.

12. Winifred Ward, letter to Barbara Likens, September 16, 1962, as quoted in Likens, "Historical Study," p. 39.

13. Guffin, "Critical Biography," Ph.D. diss., pp. 48–51.

14. Jan Guffin, "Winifred Ward: A Critical Biography," in *Go Adventuring*, p. 36.

15. Popovich, "Significant Contributions," p. 210.

16. Guffin, "Critical Biography," Ph.D. diss., p. 107.

17. Ibid., p. 109.

18. Jones, "Evaluation," pp. 85–86.

19. Winifred Ward, personal interview with Charles Jones, as quoted in Jones, "Evaluation," p. 69.

20. Winifred Ward, program note for a production of *Marco Polo*, March 1920, as quoted in Jones, "Evaluation," p. 69.

21. Winifred Ward, "Why a Children's Theatre?," unpublished article written for Northwestern University bulletin, as quoted in Jones, "Evaluation," p. 71.

22. Winifred Ward, personal interview with Mimmye Wilson Bradley, as quoted in Bradley, "Contribution of Winifred Ward," pp. 112–13.

23. Guffin, "Critical Biography," Ph.D. diss., p. 131.

24. Roster of names of participants in the conference, TS, Northwestern University Archives.

25. Winifred Ward, *Theatre for Children*, rev. ed. (Anchorage, Ky.: Children's Theatre Press, 1950), p. 28b.

26. Sara Spencer, "Children's Drama Newsletter," vol. 1, no.1 (December 1944), Northwestern University Archives.

27. Ward, *Theatre for Children,* pp. 28c–28d.

28. Guffin, "Critical Biography," Ph.D. diss., pp. 134–35.

29. Ibid., p. 139.

30. Winifred Ward, "A Retrospect," in *Children and Drama*, ed. Nellie McCaslin (New York: David McKay Co., 1985), p. ix.

31. Ibid., p. x.

32. Ibid., p. xi.

33. Hughes Mearns, *Creative Power: The Education of Youth in the Creative Arts,* 2d rev. ed. (New York: Dover Publications, 1958), p. v.

34. James E. Popovich, "Development of Creative Dramatics in the United States," in *Children's Theatre and Creative Dramatics,* ed. Geraldine Brain Siks and Hazel Brain Dunnington (Seattle: University of Washington Press, 1961), pp. 117–18.

35. Ward, "Retrospect," p. xi.

36. Popovich, "Development of Creative Dramatics," p. 120.

37. Ibid., p. 120.

38. For a thorough discussion of personnel influenced by Ward, see Guffin, "Critical Biography," Ph.D. diss., esp. pp. 116–21.

39. In 1929 *Creative Drama in the Lower School* was published. However, it had little impact on the field, and was considered to be influenced by Ward's work and writing. See Guffin, "Critical Biography," Ph.D. diss., pp. 52–54 for details.

40. Ward, *Theatre for Children*, p. v.

41. Winifred Ward, *Creative Dramatics: For the Upper Grades and Junior High School* (New York: D. Appleton & Co., 1930), p. vii.

42. Ibid., pp. 1–2.

43. Ward, *Theatre for Children*, p. v.

44. Ward, *Playmaking with Children*, p. 45.

45. Ibid., p. 3.

46. Ibid., pp. 3–8.

47. Ibid., pp. 17–19.

48. Guffin, "Critical Biography," Ph.D. diss., pp. 158–60.

49. Likens, "Historical Study," p. 91.

10

Sara Spencer: Publisher, Advocate and Visionary

KATHERINE KRZYS

Sara Spencer is perhaps most noted for her work as a publisher of children's plays and a friend and supporter of playwrights. But this work is only the most visible aspect of an important and influential career in children's theatre. Not only did Spencer establish Children's Theatre Press (later known as Anchorage Press) and remain editor there for over forty years, but she was also a major force in creating the Children's Theatre Foundation, national and international children's theatre associations, several community children's theatres, and, through her work as a publisher, a new style of American play writing for children's theatre.

But the extent of Spencer's contributions to American children's theatre is generally not well known. This can be attributed, in part, to Spencer's behind-the-scenes style. Orlin Corey, current publisher of Anchorage Press, attributes this method to much of her success:

It was . . . her style to work quietly—to steer unseen—to shape without public knowl-edge. . . . So much that is attributed to others, really turned on her insight, her influence, her encouragement, her contacts. Many took the credit and flew skyward for public recognition. Sara, who had no need for this to survive, never ridiculed or regretted. She felt this was the humanity of all. She used this, too, as a catalyst, to achieve her own larger idealisms. She did all with a quiet passion beyond the ability of many to appreciate, or even understand.[1]

Throughout her life, Spencer carefully saved much of her correspondence and memorabilia, plus copies of her many speeches and related professional presen-

tations. What follows is an overview of Spencer's major professional activities
as reflected in these materials.

Sara Katherine Spencer was born on February 18, 1908, in Louisville, Kentucky, to Joseph and Julia Vaughn Spencer. [2] Both parents were native Ken-
tuckians and her grandfather Harlow Spencer had owned a grist mill at Slickaway,
Kentucky. Her father was a Mayflower descendent, and Spencer was ninth in
descent from John Alden. (In her later years Spencer became very active in the
Commonwealth of Kentucky Society of Mayflower Descendents and served as
their governor in 1958.) Her family consisted of three girls and three boys.
Shortly after Spencer was born, she contracted polio, which forced her to wear
leg braces for her entire life.

A theatre production that Spencer saw during her early years in Louisville
was to remain with her vividly throughout her life, and it most certainly had an
effect on her approach to children's theatre:

One day, . . . matinee tickets were offered to school children at special rates. . . . My
family was good enough to buy me a ticket to THE MERCHANT OF VENICE. . . . There
was the gilded proscenium, . . . and the hushed atmosphere as the ushers bowed [sic]
people to their places and left them to read their programmes. And the orchestra began
to file in, and tune up with that wonderful, discordant melody of sound that seems to
promise a new world is coming, and then began to play with a depth and body I had
never heard before. . . . And a gray-haired lady, also alone, slipped into the seat beside
me.

The gray-haired lady must have sensed my bewitchment, for she took me kindly into
her care. . . . And by the time the court-room scene was played, I was wholly transported
to Venice. There was only one odd thing about her. After the first scene on the Rialto,
when anybody could see that Shylock was a very wicked man, she clapped for him—
and indeed the whole audience did—when he stepped before the curtain for a bow. To
me, there was no pretense on that stage, and Robert Mantell was not an actor. He was
really Shylock, and I could no more have applauded him than I could have applauded
the pictures of Satan in my Aunt's Jesus book. . . .

I left MacCaulay's that afternoon completely stage-struck. . . . From that time on, I
knew the difference between a real, live play and a film and the flimsy pictures at the
Aristo paled into insignificance, though they were better than no theatre at all. [3]

In the early 1920s Spencer's family moved to Charleston, West Virginia, and
purchased the Silver Dream Cake Company.

Spencer enrolled in Vassar in 1926. There she indulged her star-struck side
by studying theatre with Hallie Flanagan (who later became director of the Federal
Theatre Project). Upon graduation from Vassar in 1930 with a B.A. in English
and a minor in Botany, Spencer was unable to get a job, so she "stayed at home
in Charleston, twiddling [her] thumbs, burning with a desire to do something
perfectly world-shaking." [4]

To indulge her interest in theatre she began helping at the local community
theatre, the Kanawha Players. The Players had decided to produce several chil-

dren's plays to increase interest in their playhouse and, when Spencer "was at the point of suicide, the director of the Kanawha Players, . . . [wanting] nothing so much as to get [her] . . . out from under his feet," asked her why she "didn't direct a play for children."[5]

Spencer "volunteered her services as director, and undertook the post lightly, feeling that this was only a stepping stone to much higher things."[6] She was placed in charge of the Kanawha Players Children's Theatre Project.

But there were important changes taking place in Charleston that would lead to the growth of children's theatre there. According to Spencer:

Junior League Headquarters were urging their Leagues to take on such projects, and the native women of the Charleston League were interested. Moreover, it was a time when the two chemical plants had brought to Charleston a group of people of education and taste, who wanted such advantages for their children. [7]

In the spring of 1931, Spencer called a general meeting for all the children in Charleston who were interested in performing. When she asked this assembly what play they wanted to see produced, the children named mystery dramas of the ilk they had seen in the movies. Motivated by the desire to provide for the "enjoyment" of children, but wanting to "train that enjoyment . . . to establish standards of taste . . . [that could be] carried over into later life," Spencer seized the opportunity to develop an ongoing children's theatre program.[8]

That spring, Spencer directed a group of children in two separate programs of one-acts with prologues and musical interludes, and in one full-length play, *Helga and the White Peacock*. The plays paid for themselves through audience response, but Spencer was not pleased with what she had seen on the stage. She felt that she had "directed too much," "had imposed her own ideas upon" the actors, and thus her actors had "lacked fascination, and therefore credibility."[9]

In the summer of 1931 Spencer took a summer course at the American Academy of Dramatic Art in New York City. When she returned to Charleston in the fall, she found that the Kanawha Players had reorganized and cancelled their children's theatre productions. Spencer therefore relocated to the YWCA and offered classes in dramatic art to twelve of the children who had acted in her plays the previous spring. She taught them dramatic skills and, by her own account, she "learned a great deal more than she taught. . . . She learned something of the simple processes of a child's mind, and she learned to meet those minds in terms of the theatre."[10]

In 1932 Spencer became a member of the Charleston Junior League. She knew the importance of the Junior League affiliation for children's theatre. Not only did their endorsement offer prestige in the community, but it also offered a body of volunteers, a source for playscripts and a national support network through the Association of Junior Leagues of America (AJLA).

In the spring of 1932, Spencer directed three one-act children's plays, chosen to accommodate the talent of her student actors. She added experienced adults to complement her cast. She announced that the proceeds from her show would go toward the founding of a children's theatre that would be separate from the Kanawha Players. When audiences showed support for the idea, the Junior League "volunteered to put on the subscription campaign" to initiate the new organization in the fall.[11]

After her successful year of theatre activities, Spencer once again looked to her own training. In the summer of 1932, she attended classes at Emerson College in Boston, where she was put in charge of the children's play, *The Stolen Prince*.

By October 1, 1932, two hundred season tickets had been sold for the new Charleston Children's Theatre,[12] and Spencer was hired as the director, with a salary of $50 per play.[13] She opened the season that fall with a bill of one-act plays, and followed that with a Christmas production of Edna St. Vincent Millay's *The Princess Marries the Page*.

Spencer reported that directing these plays was a frustrating experience for her, since the children had no dramatic training and showed little respect for the art form. But, during rehearsal for the third show, *Snow White and the Seven Dwarves*, Spencer learned an important lesson about her work with children. She discovered that, for child actors, the "reality [in the play] . . . is what is in an actor's imagination," and not in what is actually happening to the child actor on stage. [14] This realization made Spencer more comfortable with her directing style, and she felt that this show "was the Children's Theatre's finest effort to date."[15] The theatre also earned a good profit.

Because of the Depression, the bank that held the funds for the Charleston Children's Theatre was closed in the winter of 1933. Spencer was faced with paid subscriptions, but no money to finance the final play of the season.

Spencer met the challenge by writing her own play. She dramatized her favorite sections of Mark Twain's *Tom Sawyer*, which had just passed into public domain. She then recruited prominent Charlestonians to portray the adults in the play. These well-known people, along with some talented children, attracted a large audience for the premiere on May 19, 1933. The run was extended to three performances and a profit of nearly $200 was realized.[16]

In a speech given in 1933, Spencer, reflecting on her career to that point, noted that she loved what she was doing and that her "idea of Utopia would be a world full of Children's Theatre directors."[17] Spencer would create this utopia for herself by seeking out other children's theatre directors and producers both nationally and internationally throughout her life.

In that same speech Spencer articulated her developing theories about children's theatre. She noted: (1) that every child had dramatic imagination that when properly trained would make him "a creative member of society"; (2) that she was developing a permanent "sense of artistic appreciation" in children; (3) that there is "actual reality in the situations created for children on stage" (as Spencer had seen with Shylock many years before); and (4) that a "whole cast of children, interpreting the most ordinary of dramas, will lend the play an air of fantastic simplicity so far removed from the conception of grown people, and yet so perfectly clear and satisfying to the children, that the finished product is little short of miraculous.''[18]

With the success of its first season, the Children's Theatre increased its 1933–1934 season to five plays, with one of the plays to be produced by the Junior League. But "there were few plays worthy of the name left for the Children's Theatre to offer for the next season, and this was a matter of growing concern to all volunteers who had become interested in the Children's Theatre."[19] Spencer's search for new plays during the next two years led to some discoveries.

In the summer of 1933, Mrs. Frazier Groff, a friend of Spencer's who was helping with costumes at the theatre announced: "If Spencer can write a play, so can I." Groff cleared the rights and adapted Eric P. Kelly's *The Christmas Nightingale*.[20] It was directed by Spencer and presented by the Charleston Children's Theatre on December 29, 1933.

Mimi Pickering, a local Junior League member, wrote a play for the AJLA play-writing contest. Pickering's *Cinderella* won this national contest, and a picture taken of the March 1934 production by the Junior League at the Charleston Children's Theatre appeared in *Junior League Magazine* in June 1934.[21] Spencer was starting to get national recognition.

Spencer next located a playwright friend, Grace Dorcas Ruthenburg, in Louisville, who had written *Rip Van Winkle* for Sue Hastings' Marionettes. The author allowed the Children's Theatre to adapt it. This play, which was produced by the Junior League at the Charleston Children's Theatre on November 9, 1934, was also honored with a picture in *Junior League Magazine*.[22]

Spencer's next discovery was to have long-term implications on her children's theatre work. "A neighboring Junior Leaguer had uncovered a dramatization of ALADDIN, and its author proved to be a son-in-law of a new personality on the scene, a Mrs. Chorpenning, who had just written a honey of a JACK AND THE BEANSTALK."[23] *Jack and the Beanstalk* was presented in April 1935, and Spencer began a lifelong association with noted playwright, Charlotte B. Chorpenning.

Spencer had found some excellent plays, but getting them published was not an easy task. She sent her *Tom Sawyer* to a publisher, "confident that he 'would certainly snap up this masterpiece.' But the firm said it couldn't risk a children's play in those financially perilous times."[24]

The children's theatre people did have a network where they lent plays to each other, but usually no one had more than one play available at any one time, and Spencer felt that this was a cumbersome practice. So, she decided to investigate the feasibility of starting a publishing house for children's plays. Her attraction to publishing was not unusual, for two of her brothers were in the business. One was the owner and publisher of *The National Horseman*, and another was the owner and publisher of the former *Kentucky Farmer's Home Journal*.

Spencer traveled to New York and talked with Helenka Adamowska, the children's theatre consultant for the AJLA, who had begun to build "a small and discriminating Manuscript Library,'' for the active Junior League children's theatre program. Adamowska offered Spencer ''the best scripts'' out of the Junior League library. And according to Spencer, Adamowska helped her set royalty policy:

> We agreed, between us, to set our standard royalty at $15.00, which seemed a scornful sum to the big publishing houses, but which we thought would place a dignified value on the author's work, without working a hardship on volunteer budgets. We also agreed to adjust even this $15.00 royalty, in cases of multiple performances given for welfare.[25]

This $15 royalty remained the fixed amount for plays published by Spencer's press for twenty-eight years.[26]

In 1935 Spencer resigned as the director of the Charleston Children's Theatre to devote her full attention to establishing a publishing house exclusively for children's plays. However, she did not abandon the theatre, but continued to serve on its advisory board and direct shows sponsored by the Junior League. She also provided the theatre with new plays from her publishing house for try-outs and premieres. Through Spencer's efforts, the Charleston Children's Theatre was created on a firm foundation. It continued to grow even after she stepped aside, and it is still in existence today.

Spencer's children's theatre experiences helped her determine the direction she wanted for her publishing firm. On August 8, 1935, she wrote to Adamowska:

> The more I think of it, the more I realize that nothing will quite take the place of my Press. It has a unique service to offer, and it must not be done in a piece-meal way, or under the protection of larger movements. It is a thing in itself, and must stand on its own merits, and must be independently and boldly known as a Children's Theatre Press, serving the needs of Children's Theatres as definitely as Samuel French serves the needs of adult theatres. And for me, that clarifies much. It means that if I have a competitor in the field, it is Samuel French and not you.[27]

Spencer also wanted her press to be known for its graciousness and gentility. In a letter to her printer she noted:

> [T]he personality of my Press is one of courtesy and friendliness, re-enforced by plays of genuine value. This writing-paper, for example, is the keynote of my whole Press. It does not holler for attention. It commands attention by its pride and beauty and richness. That is what this circular must do. If you allow any commercial flavor to creep in, you defeat my purpose.[28]

This gentility did not keep Spencer from getting tough when needed:

> I am not going to jeopardize the hardly-won prestige of my Press by using the everlasting, one-and-only type you foist off on everybody. . . . If you cannot rearrange, re-type, and re-block it so as to look like an invitation to a tea party, you absolutely may not print it at all.[29]

So that her purpose was obvious to all, Spencer chose the name, The Children's Theatre Press. By Spencer's own account, its beginning in 1935 was humble:

Nobody had any money those days, but I had a little red Remington typewriter that my brother had given me for Christmas, and an attic room on Fort Hill with a desk in it. And my family had credit with a Charleston printer, who was good enough to print my first four plays, with no assurance that he would ever get paid. It took me two years to pay him, and by that time I had found two more plays to be printed, so I went back in his debt again.[30]

The first four plays were: *Jack and the Beanstalk* by Charlotte B. Chorpenning; *The Christmas Nightingale* by Eric P. Kelly, dramatized by Phyllis Groff; *Rip Van Winkle* by Grace Dorcas Ruthenburg; and Spencer's own adaptation of *Tom Sawyer*.

From the beginning Spencer personally kept the press' records in small notebooks. Each play was entered in order of publication with a list of all producers and playscript purchasers. Spencer's records begin with *Jack and the Beanstalk* and end with Suzan Zeder's *Step on a Crack*.

Spencer also established an advisory board to read the plays, offer advice and lend endorsement. Her first board consisted of Helenka Adamowska, Eric P. Kelly, Charlotte Chorpenning, Dorothy L. McFadden and Virginia Howard Murray.[31]

The first catalogue of the Children's Theatre Press was printed in September 1935. Following the mailing of this catalogue Spencer wrote to Adamowska: "I had reams of fun getting it up. That's one thing about the publishing business— it's Fun, whether there is any money in it or not."[32]

The first production sold was Spencer's *Tom Sawyer*. Although she reduced the royalty charge for this first production—since it was her own play and she did not want the producer's "budget cramped by an unreasonable royalty"[33]— she was outspoken in her belief that admission should be charged for all children's theatre so that the playwrights could make money and so that children, as paying customers, would value the experience more. According to Spencer:

If a play is worth giving for welfare children, it should be worth giving for privileged children. If it is worth giving for privileged children, it is worth being paid for. And my aim in life is to encourage more and more formal, paid productions. That is why I started my Press.[34]

In early 1936, the playhouse where the Charleston Children's Theatre had been performing was destroyed by fire. The only remaining theatre in town was the 1,200-seat Shrine Mosque. Spencer again took to her typewriter and adapted *Mary Poppins* for the stage.[35] And in May 1936 this show filled the hall and paid the large rental fee.[36]

Spencer also registered a complaint about the lack of funds available after the playhouse fire:

I see no honor in giving plays to a million children, if the plays are cheap and skimpy and untheatrical. I see no glory in giving children's plays at all, unless those plays are of such quality as to make the children love the theatre all their lives.[37]

In the fall of 1936, Spencer left Charleston for a year and toured with Junior Programs, Inc. of New York to acquaint herself with children's theatre producers around the country. She reportedly appeared as narrator in several touring productions of the Edwin Strawbridge Lyric Theatre, which was sponsored by Junior Programs.[38]

Even while touring, Spencer supervised the press. She edited her fifth publication, *Heidi* by Lucille Miller, and she also worked to expand the scope of the press to include plays appealing to high school and junior high producers.[39]

While on tour, Spencer began corresponding with Ann B. Joder, the editor of *Players Magazine*. At first their letters regarded the press' advertisements in this publication; but their correspondence soon changed its focus. On August 17, 1937, Spencer wrote to Joder:

If so many of your subscribers are interested in children's plays, I wonder if you could not devote a page of each issue to Children's Theatre news. No other magazine in the country carries any Children's Theatre information, except *Junior League Magazine*, which confines its column to Junior League plays. . . . I happen to know there is a demand for such material as this, for I am in touch with all kinds of children's play producers.[40]

In September 1937 Joder commissioned Spencer to write "Children's Theatre Notes" for *Players Magazine*. In return, Spencer asked Joder to pass on any correspondence generated by her column, because she was "keenly interested in the personalities behind this movement," and wanted "to keep in touch with them as much as possible."[41] Spencer edited the column until November 1938.

Through the press, Spencer continued to "encourage new playwrights, and new trends in playwriting."[42] One of these new playwrights was Rosemary Musil, a housewife from Elmhurst, Illinois. After Musil had written a mediocre fantasy play for children, Spencer encouraged her to write in a different style; and Musil heeded her advice. Spencer later bragged that Musil's realistic plays, *Seven Little Rebels* (1938), *The Ghost of Mr. Penny* (1939) and *Five Little Peppers* (1940) were "unquestionably the best of their kind in all the Children's Theatre repertoire."[43]

In 1939 Spencer herself wrote another play, *Little Women*, based on a scenario by Robert St. Clair. The play premiered at the Charleston Children's Theatre in December 1939.

That same year, Spencer worked literally to broaden the horizons of American children's theatre. To that end she wrote to the Council of Foreign Affairs in New York City: "I am very much interested in seeing the Children's Theatre movement spread abroad, and would like to enlist your good offices in the matter." Spencer then asked for ways to contact foreign children's theatre specialists, because she believed that children's theatre's "potentialities as an instrument of international good will are so striking, that . . . it would serve a splendid purpose in all countries."[44] Nothing came of this correspondence, but Spencer would ultimately see her idea fulfilled.

In November 1940 Spencer "embarked upon an extremely ambitious publishing programme, which [was to] take [her] two years to pay for."[45] She tightened her budget severely, cut her advertisements in *Players Magazine* and added four new plays.

By this time Spencer was very active in children's theatre activities on a national level, and her influence on the developing repertoire of children's plays was great. In December 1940 she gave a speech, entitled "Plays for the Children's Theatre," at the national conference of the American Educational Theatre Association (AETA). Spencer was a member of the AETA children's theatre committee. A list of "Forty-five Plays for Children" was issued by the committee at that meeting; twenty-four of these plays were either published or represented by the Children's Theatre Press.[46]

Spencer believed that AETA could provide a unified voice for children's theatre producers and she worked to solidify the place of children's theatre within the organization. In a letter to Virginia Lee Comer, then the Children's Theatre consultant for the Association of Junior Leagues of America, Spencer noted:

It has always seemed to me that there should be a closer identity between the various groups who make up the Children's Theatre movement, and I think that year by year, this Conference [the AETA annual convention] is making real progress in that direction.[47]

In April 1943 Spencer wrote to Joder discussing an important happening in her life:

I must tell you that The Children's Theatre Press will shortly suffer a change of address, owing to the editor's imminent marriage. This is a very unexpected development, and the Press, never having made any allowance for this emergency, is having a hard time adjusting itself. Fortunately, the man in the case is a pretty swell guy, and though he is not the least bit theatrical—or even literary—(he's a business man!)—he accords the Press a place of some importance in the world, and in the life of his future wife.[48]

The "man" was Clarence A. Campbell, the widowed father of one of Spencer's Vassar friends. They were married on May 22, 1943, and Spencer moved the press to Grosse Pointe Shores, Michigan, her husband's hometown, on June 1, 1943.

In December 1943, Spencer attended the funeral of her brother, Harlow Phelps, who had been killed in World War II. On her way back to Michigan, she was notified that her husband had died of a heart attack. Spencer was deeply affected by these two deaths, by the death of her father a short time before, and by the subsequent illness of her mother.

In April 1944, Spencer traveled back and forth to Charleston to be with her mother. The following month she wrote to Joder: "The Press is due for a shake-up, in more ways than one—which will probably be jolly good for it."[49]

During all this, Spencer continued her AETA work and, in August 1944, attended the first Children's Theatre Conference at Northwestern University. This conference was called by Winifred Ward, who was on the Northwestern faculty. Spencer gave a speech entitled "When We Choose a Children's Play" at the opening of one of the panel discussions, and she also met privately with Ward to discuss the formation of a national children's theatre organization independent of AETA. Spencer was part of the unanimous vote wherein it was decided to retain affiliation with AETA, but to become the Children's Theatre Committee (CTC) of AETA.

Following this meeting, Spencer became the editor of the Children's Theatre News Letter. She believed that this was an important project:

[The News Letter is] . . . the only tangible thing our new organization has yet to offer, and on this News Letter will depend our membership, our programme and attendance at Conferences, our potential strength as a unified group, and all our wonderful possibilities for the future.[50]

Spencer edited two issues of this newsletter in 1945, but, much to her chagrin, these were the last issues printed until 1951.

In May 1945, after an extensive search throughout the bluegrass country, Spencer moved to Anchorage, Kentucky, a small community near Louisville. Spencer called her spacious new surroundings "Cloverlot."

One of the bedrooms of her home was turned into an office for the press, and an old servant's cabin and barn were used to store the press' books. Spencer was joined at Cloverlot by her mother and her sister, Daysie DeSpain, who became the custodian for the press, a job which entailed reading and proofing playscripts. These surroundings reinforced the gentility that Spencer had wanted to give her press. Soon, for many people, the press and Cloverlot became synonymous, and it became "a hospitable meeting-ground for distinguished Children's Theatre visitors from distant places."[51]

The press' staff was also augmented by Polly Colgan, who started as the secretary and eventually became the assistant editor, as well as a good friend of Spencer.

By now, the press was becoming a convenient way for Spencer to meet people and influence them. For example, in 1946 she wrote to all of her clients "urging their attendance" at the Seattle Children's Theatre Conference that summer.[52]

The press' first new catalogue since 1941 was issued in the fall of 1946. It included six plays by Chorpenning, four by Musil and some plays by new playwrights: *Marco Polo* by Geraldine Brain Siks and *The Land of the Dragon* by Madge Miller. A new advisory board included Chorpenning, Ward, George W. Savage and Ernest Bavely of the National Thespian Organization.[53]

It was also about this time that Spencer once again initiated the creation of a community children's theatre. Noting that "it was a shame a city the size of Louisville didn't have a children's theatre," Spencer, then Children's Plays Chairman for the Louisville Junior League, teamed with Ming Simpson Dick;[54] and, "with a $300 grant from the Junior League," they formed the Louisville Children's Theatre.[55]

Both Spencer and Dick knew that the theatre would not succeed if local leaders did not think of it as "their theatre."[56] In order to judge the response of the Louisville community, they hired the Edwin Strawbridge dance company to perform *Daniel Boone*. "The company's visit was a huge success, and the Strawbridge troupe went on to open each Louisville Children's Theatre season through 1951."[57] The founders believed that this performance each year lent a "high level of theatrical achievement" to their season—something that perhaps the child actors "could never accomplish."[58]

Now known as Stage One: The Louisville Children's Theatre, this organization has grown to become one of the premier children's theatre organizations in the country. Spencer's work at the the very beginning reportedly gave the theatre an important boost: "Through her connections with national and international children's theatre organizations, her presence lent dignity, credibility and professionalism to the Louisville Children's Theatre."[59] Spencer remained on the board of directors from its inception until her death.

By this time, other organizations also wanted to list Spencer as one of their backers. In 1947 she was asked to become a corporate member of the American National Theatre and Academy (ANTA). She agreed to become a member only if there was some children's theatre representation on ANTA's staff. Spencer and the chairman had previously agreed that Children's Theatre needed "some kind of professional standard set for it" and that ANTA could provide this.[60] Spencer wrote:

Please forgive me for being so militant about it. I have been in Children's Theatre through its lean, fumbling, learning years, and I hope sometime to see it emerge from the experimental stage. This is the kind of contribution ANTA could make, if there were someone among you all to call it to your attention.[61]

Spencer finally agreed to become a member of the corporate board, after ANTA, at Spencer's request, supported Monte Meacham's new Children's World Theatre project. By 1960 Spencer was on the ANTA board of directors and executive committee.

A recurring problem during this time was the dissatisfaction of many children's theatre workers throughout the country with their affiliation with AETA. In a letter to a colleague, Spencer recommended that there be no break with the parent group. She felt that the children's theatre volunteers needed the support and status of the AETA educators.[62]

The main problem was that AETA had to sanction everything CTC did—even when it was approved by the CTC membership at a convention. Spencer tried to make improvements by expressing her disapproval of this to AETA. She also asked that all AETA regional meetings have a session on children's theatre and a children's theatre committee on their planning council to "encourage interest and develop leaders in the region."[63]

In addition, Spencer sent a list of the most pressing problems with AETA to Campton Bell (a good friend of Spencer's who was then the chair of the Children's Theatre Committee) so that he could discuss them at the AETA council/CTC meeting. One of these was a suggestion from Ward that CTC become a division or section of AETA, rather than just a committee.

In the summer of 1950 Bell asked Spencer to represent Children's Theatre and AETA at the Midcentury White House Conference on Children and Youth. Spencer, Chorpenning and Burdette Fitzgerald prepared a paper for the conference entitled "The Value of the Theatre in the Emotional Development of Children."[64]

At the conference, Spencer was assigned to a work group studying "The Significance of the Aesthetic Experience in the Development of Healthy Personality in Children and Youth."[65] Spencer introduced a resolution urging the scientific study of child audiences for all the arts. It was adopted unanimously by the Arts Work Group, but it did not reach the general assembly. Undaunted, Spencer continued to lobby privately for this project.

It was during this busy time that Spencer first met Aurand Harris, who was to become her most published playwright. She first saw him at an AETA meeting in Washington and wrote to a friend that "though . . . none of us found an opportunity to talk with him, he seemed very likeable, and I for one wanted to know him better."[66]

Spencer and Harris both participated in a play analysis session in 1949 and, when Spencer wrote to thank Harris for his assistance, she got right to the point. Her letter reveals much about her views of children's theatre, as well as her honesty and directness when working with others:

Aurand, I was quite in earnest about wanting you to write a good play for the Press, and hope an idea has come to you by now. There is a highly individual charm about your plays, and you have more theatrical know-how than the average playwright whose mind works for Children's Theatre. However, your plays seem to me short on Purpose. It is not enough to spend three acts just giving a boy one happy day at a circus. He should be a better boy for the experience. . . . I hope you'll understand what I mean, and will not take offense. I have the feeling that we cannot afford to let a playwright of your talent waste his truly remarkable skill on trivial themes.

I do not know you well enough to say these things to you, but I have wanted to talk with you about this matter ever since seeing your CLOTHESLINE at Seattle, and more so after reading CIRCUS DAY. I fear I may never know you well enough, if I do not cut across conventions now, and ask you, p-l-e-a-s-e—

To write me a play with a purpose.[67]

And so Harris did; he wrote *Simple Simon*. Spencer saw *Simple Simon* as a play that would give children of other countries a positive view of America, because, according to her, it represented "a real advance in the art of playwriting for children, and indeed in our whole purpose of interpreting the democratic message. . . . "[68]

Thus, a close personal and working relationship developed between Spencer and Harris. The press, while under Spencer's control, published fifteen of Harris's plays.

In the summer of 1951, Spencer took a three-week trip to England for a vacation, but also to make some contacts that would be advantageous to the press. On her trip she visited Gerald Tyler, chairman of the Children's Theatre of Brighouse, England.

Two outcomes of this trip particularly excited Spencer: first, she "was urged by several people to establish a branch of the Children's Theatre Press" in England;[69] and second, she learned from John Allen, former director of Children's Theatre, Ltd., that an international children's theatre conference was proposed for Paris in December 1951.

At the 1951 CTC conference in Los Angeles, Spencer presented a paper entitled "Children's Theatre in England," relating the experiences of her trip and urging all CTC members who were traveling abroad to "meet our English-speaking colleagues, as there is much to gain by sharing our philosophies."[70] This speech was published in the *Educational Theatre Journal* in December 1951.

Spencer later spoke about the international connections she was making at this time:

I began . . . seeking acquaintance with foreign producers, for selfish reasons—to find a broader market for American children's theatre plays . . . but this is no longer my purpose. It lost its importance early on, as the larger ramifications of international exchange began to reveal themselves. . . .

[O]ur new international associations have led us to take our profession seriously, for the first time in our happy, care-free young lives. It is ironic that we had to learn this abroad.[71]

Spencer was also a part of the first children's theatre delegation at a 1952 United Nations Educational, Scientific, and Cultural Organization (UNESCO) meeting.

While involved with these international activities, Spencer did not neglect the press. In fact, she was pursuing a new publishing area by contacting leaders in the field and encouraging them to write textbooks. Spencer had already published Ward's revised edition of *Theatre for Children*, and she had made an agreement to publish Ward's book, *Stories to Dramatize*.

When she worked with playwrights and authors, Spencer always prodded and cajoled them to do their very best work. And when she was pleased with the results, she was always enthusiastic in her support. Note for example her response to the manuscript of Ward's *Stories to Dramatize*:

I . . . consider it the most important contribution to Creative Dramatics since the publication of Ward's *Creative Dramatics*. It is really more important than *Playmaking*, for it dramatizes the principles expounded in *Playmaking*, and offers a concrete demonstration of *Playmaking*'s whole thesis. I honestly don't see how Creative Dramatics has lived without it.[72]

Spencer also contracted to publish Chorpenning's *Twenty-One Years with Children's Theatre*. Spencer had great respect for Chorpenning—as a playwright, researcher and friend—and had published thirteen of her plays, some of which were taken over from Dramatists Play Service. Spencer encouraged Chorpenning to write this book so that future generations would "not be satisfied to just continue," but would "develop and surpass what has been done."[73]

Their correspondence regarding the book started in 1951. By June 6, 1953, Spencer was getting impatient to see the book in print, in part because Chorpenning's health was failing, and in part because she was worried that the recent spate of publications about creative dramatics might send the field too much in that direction. She wrote to Chorpenning:

For the sake of the Conference, . . . I feel it is of burning importance to get this book in circulation right away, so as to reaffirm our belief in the polished, formal production for children. Most of our articulate writing lately has been in the other direction, and we are in danger of going down a beguiling by-path, if we do not rally our forces. I am counting on this book to do it.[74]

When the final manuscript was delivered on September 26, 1953, Spencer wrote to Chorpenning that she had been "utterly unable to put [the manuscript] . . . down—" and that the book would lend the field "stature, and pave the way for better understanding ahead."[75]

In 1953 CTC changed from an AETA committee to a separate division of the association; Spencer became the first director of the division.

As director of CTC from 1953–1955, Spencer oversaw many changes in the national organization. Those of which she was most proud include: (1) the development of "minimum standards for judging children's theatre manuscripts"; (2) a draft of an "Interpretation of Terms" to establish criteria for formal play production and creative dramatics; (3) the formation of a Radio-Television Committee to improve "the quality of mass media entertainment for children"; (4) the creation of sixteen regional units charged to uphold standards in remote localities; (5) the development of an annual exhibit competition, with an award given in Chorpenning's memory; and (6) the establishment of new international contacts through the International Theatre Institute.[76] At the conclusion of her tenure as director, Spencer wrote that CTC had "a national programme whose scope is really on a par with AETA's own."[77]

As Spencer worked through her various projects on the national and international level, and as she worked with writers and experts in every aspect of the children's theatre field, her own philosophies about theatre for and with children changed from her early years with the Charleston Children's Theatre. Most notably, she came to agree that children should not be used as actors in plays for children, "except in isolated cases," until they reached the age of twelve—an idea championed by the CTC Definition Committee. She advocated the use of creative dramatics to teach the younger child "how to use his mind and his imagination, so that creating a characterization will come from within his own soul instead of being imposed on him by a director."[78]

Even after Spencer left office, CTC leaders often wrote to her for advice and sent her copies of organizational memos. Responding to one such query in 1956, Spencer had the following advice about future directions for the organization:

> The sound way to grow in stature and in breadth is from the roots. . . .
> This means giving really earnest study ourselves to the high standards we so glibly invoke at our meetings. It should give us cause for thought, for instance, that the most significant contributions to our field have been made not by ourselves, but by the seasoned professionals. . . .
> Far from *giving* workshops or institutes, we should be *taking* them, from people who know a great deal more than we do. Instead of putting out special publications for anybody, we should be accumulating material to think with, giving it a chance to ripen into something fit for publication.[79]

Spencer was embarrassed that she could offer no suggestions for reaching these goals; but before long she was to make just such a suggestion for a new project for the organization.

During the years of her work with CTC and AETA, Spencer developed a close personal and working relationship with Campton Bell; and together they influenced much policy for both organizations. On September 17, 1957, after Bell had been turned down by three foundations for a grant for CTC, Spencer wrote to him:

> I've got an idea by the tail, but it falls in your department.
> What's to prevent you setting up a "Children's Theatre Foundation," to which we can all make deductible contributions each year; to which some of us might even leave bequests? It would start with, say a capital fund of $1000, taken from CTC's Ways and Means account. . . . but its income could be administered by CTC's own self-appointed directors.
> Some of us are getting old and feeble, all of us live dangerously, and our mortality rate is high. Two authors have consulted me recently about how to leave their royalties to the best advantage. I myself anticipate willing the Press to CTC, though I don't intend to die until 2000. . . . We could be building up our own Foundation, and maybe saving some personal tax money in the bargain.
> My ignorance about money is only exceeded by the depth of the ocean, but something tells me this is practical.[80]

Bell answered:

Dear Madwoman. I think you have a brilliant idea by the tail, and as usual, I will cut through jungles and spear wild beasts to help you pull it off. I'm not sure I should be the trustee, since my life is hanging by a thread. You be the trustee, and I'll be tape-cutter and thrash-abouter.[81]

To which Spencer replied, "if your life is all that shaky, maybe the Foundation could make a lot of money by insuring you."[82]

But they proceeded with a new plan—because, as Spencer would say later, Bell "was too impatient to wait" the year it would take to work through channels.[83] Bell responded with a practical solution: that they get two other trustees, Winifred Ward and Jed Davis, and that they incorporate the foundation themselves.[84]

The foundation was incorporated on April 10, 1958 with the following goals:

To promote and encourage the production of plays for children, to cultivate interest and education in creative drama, to foster the professional training of children's theatre writers, artists, producers, and creative drama leaders, by appropriate educational processes, publications, and demonstrations.[85]

From the beginning, Spencer wanted the money to come "from *Children's Theatre people*, to be used in CTC's cause" [emphasis hers].[86] Spencer herself gave all her income from *Tom Sawyer*, from 1958 on, to the foundation. She also donated honoraria and gifts she received, and she signed over stocks and personally wrote to playwrights asking them to donate or will their royalties to the foundation.

After Bell's death, when Spencer was asked to chair the foundation, she replied: "I am not officer material. I am a witch, *and only operate out of sight*" [emphasis hers].[87] The Children's Theatre Foundation continues today as an important resource to the children's theatre community.

Spencer also had a prominent role—albeit behind the scenes—in the formation of the *Association Internationale de Theatre pour l'Enfance et pour la Jeunesse* (ASSITEJ). According to Spencer:

Indeed the whole idea of this International Children's Theatre Association, in its present form, was more or less breathed into life on my front porch one lazy summer evening in 1963, when Gerald Tyler, who was visiting me from England at the time, with his wife Emily, casually remarked, in his low-keyed British way—"By the way, the British Children's Theatre Association is thinking of inviting several other countries to take part in its annual meeting next spring, in London. Do you think the United States would be interested?"[88]

This U.S. presence took on an added urgency, when a small group of countries held a preliminary meeting in Paris in November 1963 and drew up a constitution to present in London. Urged on by letters from Tyler for a strong American representation with voting power to waylay a takeover by this small group of countries, Spencer wrote to Jed Davis, then director of CTC, and said: "To be quite crass about it, I believe the British sponsors look hopefully to the American delegation for officer material—and if so, we must send a man. Is it remotely possible that you might go yourself?"[89]

Spencer also asked Davis to appoint a delegation—not just some delegates— and to possibly extend an invitation for a meeting in the United States in the future. Spencer sent Polly Colgan to represent her. But she still wished that, "for this purpose, she [Colgan] could be a man."[90]

When the U.S. delegation returned, Spencer learned that she was a member of the ASSITEJ Executive Committee: "It fell to me, then, quaking in my orthopedic shoes, to represent the United States in actually bringing this organization into being."[91]

Spencer traveled to Venice in September 1964, for the first meeting of the preparatory committee, to try to write a constitution. Spencer was named English secretary of the committee. Her description of that meeting illustrates the political maneuvering in this new international organization:

Our chairs were placed in a circle, like a little United Nations. . . . The only two missing [countries] were Russia and East Germany, who had been unable to get visas to a Western country, for this occasion. . . .

Only three of us represented amateur children's theatre work—England, Canada, and the United States. The other seven spoke for the professional element and let me tell you, . . . the bond of brotherhood among professionals is stronger than any political tie. Whatever the issue was, those seven professionals voted together. . . . [92]

By Spencer's account, "the hardest point fought" in the meetings "was the accreditation of the amateur versus the professional." She came to understand from this gathering the "deadly serious business" of the professional:

They were proposing that each country be allowed two votes for its professionals, one for its amateurs. "But Jose," I protested to my Belgian counterpart on the committee, "this makes second class citizens of the amateurs." "*Mais oui*," he said. "*Exactement. Isn't that exactly what they are?*"

I had my mouth open to protest this, and for once shut it without speaking. By the time I had shut it, I had taken a little step in thinking. We all know, of course, that it is possible for amateurs to do better work than professionals. It happens, in all countries. But the person who invests his life in a profession shows a greater committment [sic] to his craft than the person who invests only his pastime. It is this extra degree of committment [sic] that makes the professional a first-class citizen—and makes the amateur, no matter how excellent he may be, a secondary one.[93]

But Spencer relates that she did not back down from that political challenge, and that much was gained from the interchange:

But beautiful as it [Venice] was, it was no match for the beautiful spirit of concord [*sic*] that emerged finally from all our strife for amazingly, out of all the fussing and feuding and fighting, by the last day we had grown to be colleagues in a very real sense, groping our way together toward what was best for all. Nobody's mind was changed by anything anybody said—but all minds were changed by our own individual ferment, the friction produced, and as we went our separate ways, each of us carried away a little bit of each other.[94]

On the flight home, it became clear to Spencer that "the first order of business for the children's theatre in America, was to develop a strong professional movement." She believed that this could best be done "by drawing upon the resources of our uniquely American educational drama system, and our richly American amateur theatre," rather than by relying on government subsidies or on the New York theatre.[95]

Spencer believed that diplomacy was not her strong point, and, by her account, she gradually worked other Americans into positions of power with ASSITEJ. But she always believed that her work with ASSITEJ was important:

I will tell you without modesty that I have been an important influence in it, just by being who I am. I have humanized eleven countries, by being a lame old lady who cannot climb stairs without assistance. . . . In council I ask no quarter, nor am I given any. This is mutually understood, and this is as it should be. But outside the council room, I am most tenderly cared for by my foreign colleagues in a unanimous demonstration of their human quality.[96]

Beginning in the 1950s, Spencer began placing an increased emphasis on the publication of plays from other countries. Between 1957–1966, the press imported twelve plays from Europe—four by Alan Cullen from England, three by Arthur Fauquez from Belgium, three by Alan Broadhurst from England and two by Erik Voss from Holland. The first play imported during this time was Cullen's *Niccolo and Nicollette*. Spencer liked this play because it had an original story and characters; it was not borrowed from "the traditional children's literature which had been our [Americans'] crutch"; and because it showed "that our deadly earnestness about Theme was leading us to go all pretentious and didactic."[97]

But Spencer's favorite import was *Reynard the Fox*, a satire by Arthur Fauquez. She believed that publishing this play was "a bold, risky thing to do," because "it was the first time anyone ever thought of a play for children whose hero was a rogue, who lied onstage."[98]

When both author and publisher sought out producers for this play in America, they were disappointed with superficial interpretations of the play; Spencer and Fauquez were not interested in just "someone wearing a beak on his nose and calling himself a crow."[99] So Spencer called on designer Irene Corey, of the the Everyman Players, to tackle the visual elements of the play. A subsequent production of *Reynard the Fox* by this company (produced by Orlin Corey) called positive attention to the play; and Irene Corey's "detailed instructions for makeup" were included in the published script.[100]

Spencer often told groups that after "REYNARD, other playwrights have found a theatre way to speak to children about some of the real issues that confront them."[101] According to Spencer, plays such as *Androcles and the Lion* and *The Ice Wolf* have "arisen, by natural processes, from the minds of authors who are looking at the children's world with a new kind of critical honesty, and using the theatre to prepare children for hard truth."[102]

Spencer also stated that she published these foreign plays "because they demand more of our producers than our American playwrights have dared to ask," and because they "are quite different."[103] Spencer thought that this was quite a gamble since she did not know of many producers "who would be able or willing to meet the requirements of such difficult material."[104] But Spencer was pleased when American producers chose the plays and when new producers, who had never dealt with children's plays, took on the challenge. To reflect this change in the range of publications Spencer changed the name of The Children's Theatre Press to Anchorage Press, The International Agency of Plays for Young People, as of the 1966–1967 season.

In February 1968, Spencer went to Russia to attend an ASSITEJ meeting which coincided with a ten-day festival of children's theatre plays. But Spencer's ASSITEJ participation was not limited to meetings in other countries. She served on the Executive Committee of the U.S. Center for ASSITEJ in the late 1960s and early 1970s, as honorary chairman from 1975–1977, and as chairman of the 1972 ASSITEJ Congress Executive Committee.

Spencer was also instrumental in inviting the ASSITEJ Congress to meet in the United States in 1972. When asked what the U.S. advantage was in this invitation, she answered: "To show America off to good advantage." But she insisted that to do that we must believe, as she did, in the "American way" of doing children's theatre:

Heaven knows, the American children's theatre has many drawbacks. But for all its shortcomings, the American children's theatre has a freedom and variety, a freshness and vigor that is peculiarly its own. It has an administrative ingenuity that enables it to stage children's theatre productions in more than 2000 American cities, and pay the bills. . . .

Best of all, it has a close association with the adult theatre.[105]

Spencer was proud to report that nearly six hundred people from twenty-five countries attended the 1972 ASSITEJ meeting in Albany. Nine productions were presented—seven from the United States and Canada—and they were "seriously reviewed" by major newspapers, leading Spencer to believe that "critics will review us, if we take ourselves seriously enough to create works of art, and give them productions that deserve their serious judgement [sic]."[106]

In the mid–1970s Spencer began preparations to sell the press and retire. Spencer carefully chose her successor, picking Orlin Corey to take over Anchorage Press as publisher. Corey and Spencer had worked together on various projects from 1958 on, and Spencer was particularly impressed with him because, according to her, he "always made the selection of plays his prime interest."[107]

The press was transferred to Corey on February 1, 1977, and proceeds from the sale were donated to the Children's Theatre Foundation. Spencer was to continue for a short time as editorial consultant on scripts.

Upon retirement Spencer commented on the materials she published:

Altogether the Anchorage Press published 114 plays, plus eight text-books. Some of the plays "were mistakes," . . . but 104 are still in print.

While the total output is "no great shakes in terms of big-time publishers, I'm really rather proud of what I have been able to accomplish."[108]

Spencer died at her beloved Cloverlot on February 9, 1977, and she was buried in the Lexington Cemetery. A request was made that "expressions of sympathy be sent to the Children's Theatre Foundation."[109]

Spencer received many honors during her life. In 1976, she received the Jennie Heiden Award from the Children's Theatre Association of America, the national organization that grew out of the Children's Theatre Conference of AETA. Spencer was granted the award for exceptional service to children's theatre, and she was honored at the annual national theatre convention with a "Sara Spencer Day."

In addition, Spencer was the first recipient of the Southeastern Theatre Conference (SETC) Award for Distinguished Service to Southern Theatre; she was named a Fellow of the American Theatre Association; and she was named as one of fifteen famous Kentucky women by the Women's Chamber of Commerce of Kentucky. These awards were in addition to an honor she received in 1966, when she was given the Thanksgiving Award from Clarke College in Dubuque, Iowa.

Several awards exist today to honor Spencer's accomplishments. SETC presents the Sara Spencer Child Drama Award to a member of that organization who has shown excellence in children's theatre. The American Alliance for Theatre and Education (AATE), the national professional child drama organization, presents the Sara Spencer Award to children's theatres that exhibit sustained, exceptional achievement. The Children's Theatre Foundation honors Spencer by annually sponsoring a noted speaker at the AATE annual national conference; this session is known as the Sara Spencer Event.

Spencer was a complicated woman with an eye on the whole world and her fingers in many pies. She once was criticized for using the analogy that she was the godmother who led Cinderella (children's theatre) out of the ashes into the respect of her stepsisters (theatre art).[110] Looking back on her many accomplishments, that is an appropriate description.

NOTES

1. Orlin Corey, letter to the author, September 20, 1987.

2. Biographical information gleaned from a November 7, 1987, interview with her cousin Margaret Patterson; Spencer's letters and speeches; a TS copy of Joan Kay, "Speaking of People: Children's Plays Will be Getting New Publisher," an article that appeared in the *Courier Journal*, February 3, 1977; and a TS of an untitled obituary. The latter three items are located in a collection of Spencer materials housed in the Child Drama Collection, Hayden Library, Arizona State University: "Professional Papers and Records of Sara Spencer, Publisher and Editor of the Children's Theatre Press (1935–1962) and Thereafter Called Anchorage Press, Inc. The Collection Consigned to the CTAA Archives by the Anchorage Press, Inc. of New Orleans, 1983." Hereafter this collection will be cited as "Spencer Collection."

3 Sara Spencer, "Theatre for Louisville," TS of a speech delivered to the Louisville Branch, AAUW, Louisville, December 7, 1953. Spencer Collection.

4. Sara Spencer, "The Challenge of Children's Theatre," TS, n.d. Spencer Collection.

5. Ibid.

6. Sara Spencer, "A Theatre Is Born," TS from an article written for *Thespian Magazine*, March 1936. Spencer Collection.

7. Spencer, "Challenge of Children's Theatre."

8. Sara Spencer, TS of a speech prepared for the West Side Women's Club, Charleston, West Virginia, 1931. Spencer Collection.

9. Sara Spencer, "Memoirs of a Children's Theatre: It Develops a Director," TS, n.d. Spencer Collection.

10. Spencer, "Theatre Is Born."

11. Ibid.

12. Ibid. The Charleston Children's Theatre was sometimes also referred to as the Children's Theatre of Charleston, West Virginia.

13. Sara Spencer Campbell, "The Charleston Children's Theatre," Anchorage, Kentucky, TS, September 21, 1952. Spencer Collection.

14. Spencer, "Theatre Is Born."

15. Sara Spencer Campbell, "Charleston Children's Theatre."

16. Ibid.

17. Sara Spencer, "The Children's Theatre," TS, speech prepared for the University Women's Club, October 28, 1933. Spencer Collection.

18. Ibid.

19. Sara Spencer Campbell, "Charleston Children's Theatre."

20. Ibid.

21. *Junior League Magazine*, June 1934, p. 50.

22. *Junior League Magazine*, January, 1935, p. 50.

23. Sara Spencer, "Royalties," TS of a speech prepared for the Junior League, n.d. Spencer Collection.

24. Joan Kay, "Speaking of People."

25. Spencer, "Royalties." It was then common practice for the Junior League to sponsor free performances for underprivileged (welfare) children.

26. In 1963 the royalty was raised for new releases of the press, but the early plays

were still offered for $15. *Jack and the Beanstalk* still had a $15 royalty in 1977, when Spencer sold the press.

27. Sara Spencer, letter to Helenka Adamowska, August 8, 1935. Spencer Collection.

28. Sara Spencer, letter to Quinby, between sessions, n.d. Spencer Collection.

29. Ibid.

30. Spencer, "Challenge of Children's Theatre."

31. The names of the advisory board were found inside the front cover of Grace Dorcas Ruthenberg's *Rip Van Winkle* (Charleston, West Va.: Children's Theatre Press, 1935).

32. Sara Spencer, letter to Helenka Adamowska, September 21, 1935. Spencer Collection.

33. Sara Spencer, letter to Edward A. Wright, December 14, 1935. Spencer Collection.

34. Sara Spencer, letter to Helenka Adamowska, September 13, 1935.

35. *Mary Poppins* was never published by the press. Spencer could never get the rights released from the publisher. She made it available in manuscript form to amateur producers through 1950. Spencer said this was the one project left hanging in her life and if she could ever get the release she would "make a million dollars on it." (Sara Spencer, letter to Winifred Ward, November 28, 1951. Spencer Collection.)

36. Sara Spencer, "The Children Come of Age," TS of a speech prepared for the Southern Speech Teachers Conference, Atlanta, 1938.

37. Sara Spencer, "What Price Glory," TS, n.d. Spencer Collection.

38. Dorothy Schwartz, as recorded in notes of an interview by Orlin Corey, TS, n.d. Spencer Collection.

39. Sara Spencer, letter to "Mr. Joder," March 26, 1937. Spencer Collection. Initially Spencer mistakenly wrote to "Mr. Joder." The editor's name was Anne Joder.

40. Sara Spencer, letter to "Mr. Joder," August 17, 1937. Spencer Collection.

41. Sara Spencer, letter to "Mrs. Joder," November 26, 1937. Spencer Collection.

42. Sara Spencer, "Play Selection," TS of remarks for panel discussion [for the AETA conference], Chicago, December 1939. Spencer Collection.

43. Sara Spencer, "Playwriting for Children in the Present Day World," TS of a speech prepared for the West Virginia Children's Theatre Council Spring Conference, Charleston, West Virginia, May 9, 1942. Spencer Collection.

44. Sara Spencer, letter to Council of Foreign Affairs, New York City, May 30, 1939. Spencer Collection.

45. Sara Spencer, letter to Mrs. Joder, November 12, 1940. Spencer Collection.

46. "Forty-Five Plays For Children: Recommended by the Children's Theatre Committee of the American Educational Theatre Conference," Washington, D.C., December 1940. Spencer Collection.

47. Sara Spencer, letter to Virginia [Lee Comer], November 30, 1940. Spencer Collection.

48. Sara Spencer, letter to "Mrs. Joder," April 19, 1943. Spencer Collection.

49. Sara Spencer, letter to "Mrs. Joder," May 8, 1944. Spencer Collection.

50. Sara Spencer, letter to Hazel Robertson, September 28, 1944. Spencer Collection.

51. Mrs. Dan Hallenberg, "Cloverlot," Anchorage, Kentucky, TS, n.d. Spencer Collection.

52. Sara Spencer, letter to George W. Savage, March 25, 1946. Spencer Collection.

53. The list of the advisory group found inside the front cover of Madge Miller's *Land of the Dragon* (Anchorage, Ky.: Children's Theatre Press, 1946).

54. Carol Thompson Sgroi, "The Louisville Children's Theatre: A History," Ph.D. diss., Southern Illinois University at Carbondale, 1979, p. 63.

55. Ibid., p. 16.

56. Ibid., p. 34.

57. Stage One: The Louisville Children's Theatre, "Celebrating Our Fortieth Season," TS, n.d. In files of researcher.

58. Sgroi, "Louisville Children's Theatre," p. 66.

59. Ibid., p. 32.

60. Sara Spencer, letter to George Freedley, April 10, 1947. Spencer Collection.

61. Ibid.

62. Sara Spencer, letter to "Margaret [Edmonds], Dear," Tuesday. Spencer Collection.

63. Sara Spencer, letter to "Norman," October 3, 1950. Spencer Collection.

64. TS copy available in Spencer Collection.

65. Sara Spencer, letter to "Mr. Whitney," October 9, 1951. Spencer Collection.

66. Sara Spencer, letter to "Burdette [Fitzgerald], Dear," Monday night. Spencer Collection.

67. Sara Spencer, letter to Aurand Harris, January 6, 1950. Spencer Collection.

68. Sara Spencer, "Children's Theatre—The Road to Understanding," TS copy of a speech prepared for the Theatre Section of the Third National Conference of the United States Commission for UNESCO, New York City, January 28, 1952. Spencer Collection.

69. Sara Spencer, "Children's Theatre in England," TS report prepared for the Seventh Annual Children's Theatre Conference, Los Angeles, July 26, 1951. Spencer Collection.

70. Ibid.

71. Sara Spencer, "Our New International Associations—Where Are They Leading Us?," TS of a speech prepared for the AETA convention, Chicago, December 30, 1966. Spencer Collection.

72. Sara Spencer, letter to Winifred Ward, Friday night. Spencer Collection.

73. Sara Spencer, letter to Charlotte Chorpenning, Sunday. Spencer Collection.

74. Sara Spencer, letter to Charlotte Chorpenning, June 6, 1953. Spencer Colllection.

75. Sara Spencer, letter to Charlotte Chorpenning and Alice, September 27, 1953. Spencer Collection.

76. Sara Spencer, "The Children's Theatre Conference: Annual Report of the Director," Anchorage, Kentucky, TS, November 28, 1955. Spencer Collection.

77. Ibid.

78. Sara Spencer, "Definition of Terms and Objectives of the Birmingham Meeting," TS of introductory remarks for a sectional meeting of the Children's Theatre Conference, Birmingham, Alabama, March 13, 1954. Spencer Collection.

79. Sara Spencer, letter to Paul Kozelka, November 15, 1956. Spencer Collection.

80. Sara Spencer, letter to Campton Bell, September 17, 1957. Spencer Collection.

81. Sara Spencer, "The Children's Theatre Foundation," TS of a speech prepared for the Children's Theatre Foundation luncheon, Lawrence, Kansas, August 21, 1964. Spencer Collection.

82. Ibid.

83. Ibid.

84. Ibid.

85. Ibid.

86. Sara Spencer, letter to Jed Davis, March 31, 1960. Spencer Collection.

87. Sara Spencer, letter to Albert Mitchell and Maurice Forkert, February 24, 1964. Spencer Collection.

88. Sara Spencer, TS of speech prepared for the D.C. District AETA Conference, Washington, D.C., October 12, 1969. Spencer Collection.

89. Sara Spencer, letter to Jed Davis, January 13, 1964. Spencer Collection.

90. Sara Spencer, letter to Gerald Tyler, January 14, 1964. Spencer Collection.

91. Sara Spencer, "Children's Theatre," TS of a speech prepared for the Northwest Drama Conference, Seattle, Washington, February 10, 1967. Spencer Colllection.

92. Sara Spencer, "Venice," TS of a speech prepared for the Southeastern Theatre Conference, Louisville, Kentucky, March 19, 1965. Spencer Collection.

93. Sara Spencer, "Script Selection," TS of a speech prepared for a Director's Workshop, D.C. Chapter AETA, Gallaudet College, Washington, D.C., September 30, 1967. Spencer Collection.

94. Spencer, "Venice."

95. Ibid.

96. Sara Spencer, "New Directions in Children's Theatre Scripts," TS of speech prepared for the Summer Speech Conference, University of Wisconsin-Madison, July 14, 1966. Spencer Collection.

97. Ibid.

98. Kay, "Speaking of People."

99. Ibid.

100. Ibid.

101. Spencer, "New Directions."

102. Ibid.

103. Sara Spencer, "Where Are Our New International Associations Leading Us?" TS of a speech prepared for the AETA convention, Chicago, December 30, 1967. Spencer Collection.

104. Ibid.

105. Sara Spencer, TS of a speech prepared for SETC Conference, Mobile, Alabama, March 8, 1969. Spencer Collection.

106. Sara Spencer, handwritten notes, n.d. Spencer Collection.

107. Kay, "Speaking of People."

108. Ibid.

109. Untitled obituary.

110. Sara Spencer, "CTC Annual Report of the Director," TS [draft], Palm Beach, Florida, September 24, 1955. Spencer Collection.

11

The Children's Theatre Company and School: Raising the Curtain

JOHN V. HICKS

The Children's Theatre Company and School of Minneapolis is one of the most significant theatres in this country. From its inception in 1961, the organization has grown into an institution which, today, is one of the most prolific producers of dramatic literature for children in the United States. It employs a unique style of production that is internationally recognized for its artistic merit, and is housed in a theatre complex that rivals most in the nation—a facility which serves as a symbol and an acknowledgment that this organization has revolutionized attitudes toward the art of theatre for children and young people in America. The Children's Theatre Company also embraces the active participation of an artistic elite, who previously had no affiliation with live children's theatre. These include Edward Albee, Ray Bradbury, Dr. Seuss and Tomie dePaola.

The Children's Theatre Company and School of Minneapolis originated in the Moppet Players, organized in 1961 by Beth Linnerson. Initially, the Moppet Players consisted of a group of volunteers led by Linnerson. Linnerson worked as a waitress in a small restaurant, called "Mama Rosa's," in what was then called the Seven Corners area of Minneapolis. Linnerson and her close friend, Martha Pierce, encouraged Tony Rosa, the proprietor of the restaurant, to let them develop entertainment for children. With his approval, the women created a modest, but successful, theatre for children.[1]

Rosa donated one side of one room in the restaurant for the theatre. With the exception of this space and a $100 donation, the theatre developed from the love, dedication and energy of a local group of scavengers. Linnerson and Pierce, who became the co-directors for the Moppet Players, were greatly influenced by the work at Karamu House in Cleveland, Ohio; and thus their activities took on a social work bias. In its first year, the Moppet Players created entertainments in which underpriviledged youth from the area participated in every aspect of the production. They presented magic shows and mounted original scripts based on popular children's stories. Neighborhood children attended performances on Saturday afternoons for a twenty-five cent admission fee. The entire operation depended upon volunteer labor and donated materials and supplies. In its first year at Mama Rosa's, the Moppet Players developed an eager clientele.[2]

In an effort to find a permanent home for the Moppet Players, Linnerson located an abandoned firehouse owned by the University of Minnesota. This badly vandalized building stood in a poverty-ridden area, which served as the terrain for several youth gangs. Linnerson contacted the director of cultural affairs for the Pillsbury-Waite Settlement House, an organization, which, in the early 1960s provided social services to the people of the impoverished Seven Corners area. Linnerson expressed her interest in establishing a children's theatre in the firehouse, and, in the summer of 1962, the Moppet Players became officially affiliated with the Pillsbury-Waite Settlement House.

The University of Minnesota leased the firehouse to the settlement house; and the settlement house provided the Moppet Players with a board of directors and the facility. The board consisted of influential citizens who provided the theatre with important connections and, in many cases, an automatic line of credit. It is important to note that the settlement house served only as an umbrella for the theatre. Because it was affiliated with United Way, the settlement house could not actually provide funding. It provided a certain administrative credibility, but the theatre had to be self-supporting.[3]

The last major resource crucial to the development of the Moppet Players came in the person of John Clark Donahue. Donahue had known Linnerson while he was a student in visual arts at the University of Minnesota. In the summer of 1962, Linnerson invited Donahue to visit the new firehouse to discuss the possibility of doing social work through the arts in that neighborhood. "It was understood that everything would be volunteer. There was no money. It was an idea."[4]

Donahue's orientation to the arts was in direct contrast to Linnerson's. Linnerson had a burning desire to use theatre to help children develop the ability to be social. In contrast, Donahue was ultimately concerned with artistic excellence; social work was of interest only if it did not interfere. It was the juxtaposition of these two individual biases which led to the unique success and subsequent demise of the Moppet Players.

The Moppet Players officially began activities in the summer of 1962, with renovation of the firehouse. The renovation was the theatre's first social project involving neighborhood children. Donahue recalls:

One of the first things I did was to create, with the children of the neighborhood, a mural called "The Procession of the King" on a wall into which a wet mixture of plaster and concrete on lathe was pressed pebbles and pieces of colored glass from the street outside. And that, combined with colored enamels was the first beautification project.[5]

Almost everything involved in transforming the run-down firehouse into a theatre was donated. Minneapolis Paints donated 120 gallons of paint and 100 yards of burlap to cover walls. Schools donated old desks, kindergarten chairs and tables.[6] Donahue jokingly reminisces:

The audience sat on little chairs that were gotten from the Minneapolis Public Schools Warehouse which were old bentwood kindergarten chairs which were painted in more of this colored enamel paint brilliantly anticipating the Guthrie Theatre and its multicolored seats, albeit not so comfortable.[7]

All of this was done by "children of the neighborhood, penniless artists, occasional wanderers-by, perhaps an interested group like American Friends Service."[8]

By mid-November 1962, the firehouse had undergone a transformation, and the Moppet Players acquired an operating budget of $2,859 through various donations and fund-raising activities. On November 9, 1962, *The Reluctant Dragon,* adapted from the story by Kenneth Graham, opened to an invited audience, with preshow entertainment provided by the Minnesota Symphony. The theatre consisted of a 150-seat auditorium and a stage with an opening fourteen feet wide, nine feet tall and twelve feet deep. Admission was fifty cents.[9]

Despite a meager financial premise, *The Reluctant Dragon* brought the first monetary compensation to the Moppet Players' staff, and it received positive reviews from both public and press. In all the Moppet's work, there was no shortage in the press's willingness to write about "a doe-eyed blond girl" starting a children's theatre group. The press regularly reviewed the Moppet Players productions, lending artistic credibility as well as promotional benefits.[10]

The success of *The Reluctant Dragon* anticipated an equally successful season. The Moppet players produced four additional plays: *Winnie-the-Pooh, The Peterkin Papers, The Swineherd* and *The Merry Pranks of Tyl.* All but the last were original adaptations by local artists. In addition, the Contemporary Dance Playhouse, under the direction of Loyce Houlton, presented a Christmas adaptation of Bemelmans' *Madeline,* which was held over one week due to popular demand. Houlton participated in productions throughout the history of the Moppet Players and continued in the work of the Children's Theatre Company. As a result, the use of dance in drama emerged as a major stylistic component of Donahue's work at the Children's Theatre Company.

In January 1963, Martha Pierce began both a theatre workshop program and a series of after-school classes. Forty children registered for the theatre workshops and participated in all aspects of the Moppet Players' productions. In addition, over one hundred children enrolled in two eight-week sessions of after-school classes. The classes included art, creative dramatics, dance, puppetry, pottery and stage movement. All teachers worked on a strictly volunteer basis. Ten teachers from the Minneapolis Art School volunteered as a result of a fund-raising open house held by the Moppet Players' staff.[11]

Over a three-year period, the Moppet Players survived on donated funds and services. Members of its board of directors often made donations to compensate for deficits. Yet, with each new year, budgets increased, and the theatre's entire level of operation grew more complex, requiring the services of a business manager. In July 1963, Mike Schulte joined the Moppet Players as full-time business manager. Other staff members acquired official titles: Linnerson served as coordinating director, Donahue as director of theatre, and Sue Lynch (replacing Martha Pierce) as director of educational activities.[12]

In the 1963–1964 season, the Moppet Players presented five plays: *The Emperor's New Clothes*, *The Three Billy Goats Gruff and Budulinek*, *The Nightingale*, *Ozma, Ruler of Oz* and *Hansel and Gretel*. The Contemporary Dance Playhouse produced *Shoe Fly Pie for Christmas*. All productions received critical and public acclaim, and the theatre workshop and after-school classes experienced equal success.

In the fall of the 1963–1964 season, Donahue directed a benefit for the Moppet Players which afforded him the opportunity to work with Wendy Lehr, an aspiring young actress. Her participation in this event appeared of no great significance at the time; however, in later years, Lehr emerged as the maternal figure for the Children's Theatre Company, participating in every aspect of the theatre's operation and as the theatre's primary teacher and actress.[13]

By the middle of the 1963–1964 season, problems surfaced which eventually led to the dissolution of the Moppet Players. Concerning finances, the board noted that the Moppet staff seemed "confused about expectations and demands of the Pillsbury Citizens Service since it doesn't supply financial support." The theatre grew too rapidly for the support capabilities of the settlement house. Because of its affiliation with United Way, the settlement house did not supply funds and, in addition, restricted the theatre in its fund-raising activities. The settlement house became a liability for the Moppet Players. A sub-committee of the board stated: "One of the problems is that Beth Linnerson has created a Topsy which has outgrown her."[14]

To complicate matters, the staff continued to disagree on the goals of the Moppet Players. Linnerson continued to stress the arts in a social context. Her bias, however, was beginning to lose relevance. The University of Minnesota began renovations in the Seven Corners area, lessening its deprived, poverty-ridden status and decreasing the need for social programs. Donahue, by then functioning as artistic director, stressed artistic excellence. The two did not find a ground for compromise, and the conflict reached emotional levels.[15]

While the Moppet Players implemented its first season, the board took action to solve the theatre's administrative and financial dilemmas. In August 1964 the board hired John Davidson as administrator of the Moppet Players.

Davidson's influence began to resolve the social-work-versus-art conflict, because his goals and strategies, while motivated by sound fiscal and business practices, leaned toward Donahue's artistic bias. The changes which Davidson believed were necessary were not compatible with Linnerson's social work bias. Linnerson was slowly losing hold of her dream, and the tables turned in Donahue's favor as the 1964–1965 season began.[16]

The 1964–1965 season consisted of: *Ali Baba and the Forty Thieves*, *The Bremen Town Musicians*, *The World of Mother Goose* and *The Princess and the Pea*. The Contemporary Dance Playhouse also produced its annual Christmas production.[17]

In early September, the board gave its unanimous consent for the incorporation of the Moppet Players, and, on January 1, 1965, the theatre separated from the Pillsbury-Waite Settlement House. The theatre held a series of benefit performances and raised $2,605 to finance the transition.[18]

In December, the board asked for Linnerson's resignation as coordinating director of the Moppet Players in exchange for a position on the board. Linnerson rejected that proposal, incorporated the Moppet name as belonging to her and, in the fall of 1965, left for St. Paul to continue doing theatre in a social work context.[19]

The Moppet Players acquired a great deal in a short time. From its meager beginnings in one side of a pizza parlor, it established itself as a major social and artistic resource and the first full-time children's theatre in the state of Minnesota.

The work of the Moppet Players created many traditions and programs which lived on in a new organization, the Children's Theatre Company of Minneapolis. The Moppet Players established the practice of producing original adaptations of popular works for children; Donahue and Houlton promoted the use of dance in drama; educational programs complemented theatre production for children; and the theatre acquired an influential board of directors, who remained with the theatre—some through its entire evolution.

Donahue's participation in the Moppet Players was of crucial significance. It was ironic that Donahue would take the opportunities presented by Linnerson and enlarge upon them to create a significant arts organization. It would seem that this achievement resulted from his unique ability to make the connection between the static world of the graphic arts and the kinetic world of the performing arts.

On July 7, 1965, Donahue (as artistic director), Davidson (as managing director) and the Moppet Players' board of directors joined the Minnneapolis Institute of Art and took on a new name, the Minneapolis Children's Theatre Company.[20]

From 1965 to 1975, under this parent organization, the theatre experienced substantial growth. The institute provided a stable foundation, conducive to the expansion of programs—a situation which was sorely lacking under the Pillsbury-Waite Settlement House.

The institute adopted the Children's Theatre with a $29,700 budget. The theatre was then required to generate enough income to meet expenses. Consequently, the real fiscal responsibility remained with the board of directors. Under the institute, the board became the advisory committee. Davidson recalls that committee members covered deficit spending out of their own pockets for the first few years.[21]

The institute imposed few fund-raising restrictions. It provided salaries for Donahue, Davidson and one office attendant, all administrative services, printing, publicity and, most important, a new and larger theatre space.[22] The new performance space included an auditorium with 646 seats and a proscenium stage with ample backstage space.[23]

What the Children's Theatre Company of Minneapolis accomplished in ten years, from 1965 to 1975, was remarkable. It developed from a small, privately supported troupe to a nationally recognized company, with a high level of financial support from government and national foundations. Its budget grew by more than ten times its original figure, and its staff tripled. It received numerous awards in recognition of its artistry, its contributions to dramatic literature and its accomplishments related to arts management. It performed for delegates from other countries. And, by the end of this period, it became a full-fledged department of the Minneapolis Society of Fine Arts, with a theatre facility unrivaled by any other in the country. The key to this success was Donahue's gift as an artist and administrator, working within a wealthy community devoted to the support of the arts and a children's theatre of quality.

From 1965 to 1975, the theatre produced over fifty original plays for children. But five plays by Donahue most clearly represent the philosophy and unique style of theatre for which the company is acclaimed. *Good Morning Mr. Tillie*, *Hang on to Your Head*, *Old Kieg of Malfi*, *How Could You Tell* and *The Cookie Jar* all have certain common stylistic qualities.

The plays reflect Donahue's visual arts background. They subordinate language and rely on strong visual images to provide the catalyst for meaning. The plays rely less on past conventions of mythology and legend and more on twentieth-century concepts of technology, television and consumerism to reveal their artistic truth. Most important, Donahue and his staff developed aesthetic and technical expertise in translating storybook images into three-dimensional space. In production, all plays emphasized the use of mime, dance and music—a total integration of all the arts.

The Children's Theatre Company produced *Good Morning Mr. Tillie* in its first season, along with four other original adaptations of classic fairy tales. Donahue mounted the production in black and white, with actors in clown-face. He then used color, in contrast, to suggest character transformation. When Mr. Tillie conquered his fears, the stage broke into color, accompanied by the music of Vivaldi. The play anticipated Donahue's developing style in its use of flashback, montage, slow motion and other cinematic techniques, with scenes fading into one another, as in dreams. *Good Morning Mr. Tillie* was the first play to become part of the theatre's permanent repertory. The title role was played by a young boy named Myron Johnson, who, later, taught mime and dance at the Children's Theatre Company.[24]

In its first season, the Children Theatre proved itself worthy of its sponsor's support. All productions played to full houses and received critical acclaim.

In its second year, the Children's Theatre Company expanded its entire level of operation. The theatre increased its budget, the number of productions, number of performances and ticket prices, and it developed new sources of contributed income such as the Minnesota Arts Council.

The Children's Theatre Company also developed important collaborations with area artists. *The Emperor's New Clothes*, produced in the second season, used four singers from the Center Opera Company, a composer who agreed to conduct the theatre's newly formed chamber ensemble of youth musicians and a professional violinist to serve as concertmaster.[25] This type of collaboration, utilizing artists of renown in a given area, continued throughout the theatre's history, and is an important factor in the artistic achievements of the Children's Theatre Company.

In the summer of 1968, the theatre staff participated in a pilot program, which eventually led to an alternative education program of national repute at the Children's Theatre Company. The coordinator of federal and special projects for the Bloomington, Minnesota School System hired Donahue and Lehr to participate in teaching two days of workshops on language arts, music, art, creative movement and physical education.[26]

The Bloomington pilot project served as an example for the Minneapolis Public School System, which was already considering some sort of accredited education program for the arts. In the summer of 1969, the Children's Theatre School held its own official classes, which were accredited by the Minneapolis Public School System. The theatre offered four hours of classes per day, from June 21 until August 1. Thirty junior and senior high school students, chosen by audition, participated. The faculty consisted of staff from the Children's Theatre Company, the Contemporary Dance Playhouse and the Guthrie Theatre. The school, which was called Arts Opportunity Center, had funding provided by the Minnesota State Arts Council.[27]

This summer project proved successful, and a program in alternative education continued in the fall. The fall program provided classes for twenty-five students, once again chosen by audition, from five pilot schools. Students attended classes in the institute auditorium, Monday through Thursday from 3:15 to 4:30, and 1:30 to 4:30 on Fridays. The school system offered English credits to participating students. Classes consisted of ballet, modern dance, pantomime and voice production. Minneapolis Public Schools provided transportation, as well as equipment and supplies.[28]

In September 1970, the theatre received funding for the Children's Theatre School from the Minneapolis Urban Arts Program. The money had two major components: the National Endowment for the Arts provided an annual grant of

$25,000 to be used for educating children and, in addition, the Minneapolis Public School System obtained a Title III grant, providing tuition money and aid for participating students.[29]

These funding sources cemented the affiliation between the Children's Theatre Company and the Minneapolis Public Schools. Together, they built a program of alternative education that became a model for the nation.

The school system released its students from the public schools from 1:30 to 3:30, Monday through Friday and bussed them to the institute, where they studied theatre for credit. As many as one hundred students enrolled in one of two programs. The performance program included courses in movement, dance, mime, karate, singing and instrumental music and various acting classes. The technical program included courses in drawing, sculpture, scenery, costumes, makeup, wigs and props.[30] These programs continued until 1982. However, as federal support for the arts waned in the 1980s, many students became responsible for their own tuition.[31]

With its growing recognition, the theatre received invitations to present its work to professionals around the nation. In 1970 the Children's Theatre Company performed *Good Morning Mr. Tillie* in Washington, D.C., for the American Education Association.[32] More important, the company presented *Hang on to Your Head* at an international children's theatre conference in Albany, New York, in 1972. *Hang on to Your Head* provoked heated controversy among the delegates to the conference, and the response was intense and polarized. Natalia Sats (of the Soviet Union) marched down the aisle and asked for five minutes to denounce the production as "immoral, reactionary, revisionist." Many felt the play presented alienation between parent and child. Donahue proposed, however, that frequently there is an alienation between parent and child, and that parents must learn to be less concerned with dirt on children's knees and more concerned with their souls and the joy that exists in the small, everyday activities of life. But while delegates were opposed in their opinions of the play's thematic content, all agreed that the production displayed technical brilliance unsurpassed by any other company at the conference.[33]

During its years under the Society of Fine Arts, the theatre also received financial recognition of historic significance. By 1975 the Rockefeller Foundation had donated a total of $900,000 to the Children's Theatre Company and School. In 1972 the foundation awarded $250,000 to promote investment in human resources. Up to that time, this was the largest grant ever given to a children's theatre in this country. Also in 1972, the foundation provided a $500,000 "brick-and-mortar" grant. The Kennedy and Lincoln Centers were the only facilities ever previously given this type of assistance. A spokesman for the Rockefeller foundation explained the large bequests: "We felt that this was the most important theatre anywhere, a theatre of international importance."[34]

In 1972, due to its dynamic growth and recognition, the Children's Theatre Company became a department of the Minneapolis Society of Fine Arts, on a parallel basis with its other departments: the College of Art and Design and the Institute of Art. The reasons for this new status were simple. A tension surfaced while the theatre company was growing as a department within the Institute of Art. The theatre became the largest department in the institute, with, by 1970, an operating budget of $102,847. However, the primary patrons of the institute generally preferred to see money going to the museum rather than to a theatre. This created an internal challenge to the institute.[35]

In 1973, the Children's Theatre Company prepared to move into a new $4.5 million facility, designed by Kenzo Tange as part of a larger complex for the society and its various departments. Planning for the complex began in 1965, when the theatre was not yet a significant consideration. In 1969, the architects began to acknowledge the theatre's growth, and they incorporated into the plan a multipurpose museum auditorium for the use of all of the departments of the society. In the early 1970s, as a result of the recognition of the theatre from international artistic institutions and financial support from the Rockefeller Foundation, a $4.5 million theatre facility, for the use of the Children's Theatre Company, was incorporated into the overall design plan. A ground-breaking ceremony for the theatre complex took place on January 31, 1973.[36]

The 1974–1975 season was the first in the company's new home, and the structure seemed to be a physical manifestation of all that had been accomplished in nine short years. The facility is composed of three major areas: (1) the auditorium and lobbies, (2) the stage and backstage support areas, (3) and the theatre school and administrative offices.

The fan-shaped auditorium provides continental seating for 745 people, in fifteen main floor rows, two rows of cantilevered balconies and a soundproof, late-viewing room. No seat is located farther than sixty-two feet from the stage.

The stage, behind the sixty-six foot wide proscenium, is spacious, measuring forty feet deep, ninety feet wide and ninety feet high. If necessary the scene shop door can be opened to add an additional eighty-two feet of playing space.

The sound and light booths are located at the rear of the auditorium; they house sophisticated, state-of-the-art amplification and control systems.

The backstage areas, consisting of four levels, include: the scene shop, which is at stage level and separated from the stage by a soundproof door; the dressing and green rooms on the basement level; and the costume shop and dance rehearsal rooms on the upper two levels.

By the summer of 1975, at the conclusion of its first season in the new facility, the theatre was operating on a $580,000 annual budget; a familiar problem then surfaced. The theatre, once again, had outgrown its sponsor's support capabilities. Inflation created cutbacks in private, foundation and government contributions to the Society of Fine Arts, and the cost of every aspect of the society's operation had doubled. Through the years of planning and construction, costs rose dramatically. For several years, the society purposely created sizeable deficits in order to begin and to expand programs, because they believed that these programs would increase public interest and, then, support. All three institutions were encouraged to add programs, enlarge present ones and increase the size of their operations to complement the new and larger facility.

Inflation and recession during the construction forced the society to borrow money at high interest rates, while contributions decreased. Once the building opened, costs to run it were far over projections. Foundations cut back, and the Rockefeller's support of the theatre came to an end.[37]

The society then demanded that the theatre reduce its budget by half. Donahue was unwilling to do this, because he believed that such a move—which would require laying off over half of the forty-person staff and reducing technical capabilities—would compromise the artistic work of the theatre. The conflict reached a deadlock, and emotions flared, with neither side willing or able to compromise.

Donahue, who had worked hard to acquire the stature of the theatre, was extremely vocal in justifying his firm stance:

In medical terms, you'd say you can either perform radical surgery or let the patient die. The latter case is true here. It would simply be impossible for us to chop here and there because our investment is not in materials, but in human resources. How do you think we put together such lavish productions? Surely not through lavish spending but by getting people who know how to make something look good.

These people are no longer eighteen. They have grown and developed here and now we have something unique: a familial situation, a spine which cannot be shrunk. Now that our people are grown up, we can't simply send them back into each other's attics. We cannot cut them off.

Which brings us to the second point: why was this theatre custom made for us? Every member of our staff is represented in the structure of this building. When they built this theatre there was no other theatre company involved, and it is stated in the by-laws that a high quality theatre and school would be here. Now that must have specifically meant us, or why would they have so thoroughly followed my suggestions?[38]

Later, in 1981, Donahue reflected on this crisis:

During that time they said to me, bring us your core people. And, I said, there are no core people. We are all in this together. We have to have it this way or we are going to close down and I held a vote on it and 98% of the staff raised their hand and said either we have it the way we have worked for and believe is right or we will dissolve because we won't have the dignity or integrity without it.

And I went to the board meeting, I'll never forget this, with the society trustees in the board room, and the room filled up with our staff.

They all came. It was suggested that some of them could be gotten jobs in industry and other places. And, one of the actresses stood up and said, "I want to make it clear that I do not want a job, I don't need a job. I need to work at my art, and this is the place where I want to work at it. Unless I can have it this way, I'm not interested." And it caused a sensation and I was called up and told that they were set up and it was just incredible the attacks that came from community leaders of the highest so-called influence.

But we did it, and we did it boldly and easily because we knew that is how it had to be. Now, of course, a different tune is being sung.[39]

Stephen Ayers, one of the chief administrators for the theatre, supported Donahue's stance:

The Society does not understand the nature of a performing arts organization. For example, the resources of a museum are its objects, but the resources of a theatre are its artists. The difference can be built from that basis. Each picture can stand on its own, but in a theatre you can create experiences. The process must be complete. If someone leaves, someone has to cover his position. In the process there is implicit growth.[40]

While independence seemed the only alternative, some society members intensely opposed this option. The theatre was the most public institution under the society, and more people visited the theatre than visited the museum. During the primary fund-raising period for the new facility, the theatre managed to find places to mount productions, while the museum closed down. The theatre became the public front of the society. The theatre also had important educational resonance. While the museum held some Saturday classes, it did not affect large numbers of people; the theatre was the only reason some people came into the facility.[41]

In addition, certain board members were also concerned with the status of the new facility should the Children's Theatre Company become independent. Should the company continue to use the new facility, negotiations and contract work would be extensive.

On July 2, 1975, a proposal for the theatre's independence was accepted. The conditions for independence were centered on two issues: fund raising and incorporation. The theatre incorporated on July 30, 1975, and initiated a fund raising campaign on September 21. The theatre raised $125,000 to guarantee its season. To secure the theatre's independence, the Rockefeller Foundation assisted both the society and the theatre in the following areas: the development of an accounting system with internal and administrative controls; the refinement of budget procedures and the development of cash-flow forecasts; a review of assets and balances to be transferred from the society to the theatre; and a review of employee benefits and separation and lease agreements.[42] On January 1, 1976, the Children's Theatre Company became officially independent of the Society of Fine Arts.[43]

During the latter half of the 1970s, the theatre achieved two primary goals that helped insure its artistic and financial solvency. The first of these was to raise artistic standards by promoting the active participation of internationally recognized artists and writers who had no previous affiliation with children's theatre.

In the 1979–1980 season, the Children's Theatre Company produced the first dramatic adaptation of any work by Theodore Geisel (Dr. Seuss). Geisel offered the rights to *The 500 Hats of Bartholomew Cubbins* as a gift to the theatre, after he saw the Children's Theatre Company production of *The Little Match Girl*. He was impressed with the production values at the Children's Theatre Company, and he felt his work would be treated well. Geisel reserved the right to write the lyrics and edit the libretto. The theatre presented fifty-five performances of the production to a total of 46,000 patrons, an attendance record at the Children's Theatre Company.[44]

In the following season, the theatre formed another, similar collaboration and produced the first dramatic adaptation of Tomie dePaola's *The Clown of God*; and dePaola himself designed the sets and costumes for this production.[45]

In 1982, the National Advisory Council to the Children's Theatre Company and School was formed. This council consisted of artists who are leaders in their respective fields. Members of this council have included: Edward Albee, Ray Bolger, Nancy Ekholm Burket, Laurent de Brunhoff, Tomie dePaola, Joel Grey, Linda Kelsey, Michael Langham, Tanya Moiseiwitsch and Maurice Sendak. Donahue stressed that the formation of this council would not inhibit the unique style of production that had grown out of the Children's Theatre Company and for which it was so acclaimed. He saw it, rather, as a broadening device for children's theatre artists to combine their own special skills and methodologies with those of other artists. Donahue saw these collaborations as the first step toward achieving his goal of getting major authors to write and adapt fairy tales, which would be translated to the stage by world-renowned directors.[46]

With government and private funding for the arts ever decreasing, the Children's Theatre Company continued to develop programs for product development and revenue. In 1980, the theatre developed a wide line of products, consisting of book bags, stationery, books, dolls and commemorative plates. These were offered for sale through a catalog, as well as through private shops and shops connected with art museums and cultural organizations.[47]

But the most important development in the area of revenue diversification, and certainly the most experimental one, concerned the theatre's growing participation in the area of television. On May 4, 1981, the Children's Theatre Company signed a contract with MCA/Universal and its subsidiaries, MCA Videocassette, MCA Video Disc and Universal Pay Television.[48]

MCA/Universal outbid thirty other companies for the rights for video production and distribution of the Children's Theatre Company production of *The Marvelous Land of Oz*, for pay cable, cassette, disc, network and theatrical release. In return, the Children's Theatre Company received both a flat fee and a guarantee of a percentage of the profits. In 1983, MCA/Universal and the Children's Theatre Company completed *Wind in the Willows* and *The Red Shoes* for distribution. Other productions produced for video distribution included *Alice in Wonderland* and *Puss in Boots*.[49]

The 1980s brought radical changes in the educational structure of the Children's Theatre School. By 1981, the Children's Theatre School had developed one of the most extensive programs in alternative education in this country. David Rockefeller, Jr., expressed his admiration of this work:

> The high quality of instruction provided by this institution may be hard to emulate. But, it must be remembered that the pursuit of excellence is an important factor in teaching any of the arts. It is part of the educator's job to maintain standards of excellence and craftsmanship in addition to accepting and understanding students' work.[50]

The Rockefeller Brothers Fund granted the Children's Theatre Company $25,000 to conduct a feasibility study for Donahue's newest education idea, the learning lab.[51] This lab was to be an advanced school for children, ranging in age from four to eighteen. The intention was to satisfy educational needs that conventional schools failed to meet. The grant provided financial support for the theatre to begin preparations on several levels: to design the learning lab; to explore finances, commitments and allegiances; and to plan a curriculum.[52]

The performance and technical schools remained the primary education programs at the school, with students continuing to take classes on a time-release basis from individual public schools.

In 1982, the Children's Theatre School ended its affiliation with the Minneapolis Public Schools and established a private conservatory school, with fifty full-time students enrolled for both academic and theatre arts training. An academic staff was hired to supplement the artistic staff.

The conservatory school, which included students in grades four through twelve, stressed an interdisciplinary approach that attempted to help students integrate learning. Students at all levels participated in the design of the educational programs.

Competency areas included reading, writing, computation, information finding, oral presentation, reasoning, media expression, creative problem solving and democratic participation. While students were not graded, progress evaluations were made for each of the competency areas, and diagnostic tests were given as desired or needed. Students were also given standardized tests in math, science, language arts and social studies by the end of grade 10 and the PSAT in grade 11. In grade 12, students prepared a senior project which culminated in an original work of art, presentation, writing or other media approach.[53] The program was fully accredited by the North Central Association of Colleges and Schools.

In 1984, amidst a swirl of controversy not directly related to his artistic work at the Children's Theatre Company, Donahue resigned as artistic director.[54] Jon Cranney was appointed acting artistic director upon Donahue's resignation and, in 1985, after a national search, Cranney became the artistic director of the Children's Theatre Company and School.

Donahue's resignation, and the difficulties that contributed to his departure, had a profound impact on the operation of the Children's Theatre Company and served as the catalyst for financial turmoil within the organization. Private and public funding sources for the theatre became tenuous, because Donahue was synonymous with the Children's Theatre Company and School of Minneapolis. However, the community once again rallied to the theatre's support. The organization encompassed a large family of artists and administrators, some of whom, like Wendy Lehr, had remained with the theatre from the beginning. The theatre survived the difficult departure of Donahue, but not without some loss.

In 1986, the Children's Theatre Company and School discontinued the conservatory school and halted any further exploration concerning the learning lab. Increasing production costs and insufficient tuition revenues required that the organization cut back on its menu of programs and, thus, return to its primary focus, the artistic excellence of its mainstage productions. The mission of the Children's Theatre Company, as adopted by its current board of directors, is to "provide a professional quality theatre experience for young people and their families as audience."[55]

The 1985–1986 season closed with record attendance of 248,000, including 67,000 students attending weekly matinees. This constituted a 40 percent increase in attendance from the previous year, the largest single increase in the theatre's history. The company played to 89 percent capacity, and earned revenues accounted for 72 percent of the total budget.[56]

In 1985, the Children's Theatre Company launched a new program at the Ordway Theatre in St. Paul, to provide smaller, more intimate productions for younger children. This has given the company the opportunity to develop a larger audience from St. Paul.

The Children's Theatre Company is also still aggressively developing programs for revenue diversification. These include the development of a line of products, the addition of the Ordway Music Theatre Series and, most important, the use of television technology for financial and artistic benefit.

The Children's Theatre Company has recently undergone the most radical change in its entire history: the loss of its founder and long-time artistic director, John Clark Donahue. However, attendance and financial records indicate a positive outlook for the future. While it is impossible to predict how such a dynamic administrative change will affect the work of the Children's Theatre Company, the dedication of its artists, administrators and supporters is of major significance. Continuity of human resources has been maintained in all areas of the operation. The number of veterans in the organization is astonishing, and the value of this organization cannot be overestimated. It is responsible for the consistency of artistic quality at the theatre as well as the financial level of operation that the theatre has acquired. It is this constituency which perhaps insures the Children's Theatre Company's place in history.

NOTES

1. Programs and ideas of major relevance did not begin to develop until the Moppets became affiliated with the Pillsbury-Waite Settlement House. The history of the Children's

Theatre Company of Minneapolis cannot be divorced from, or extended beyond, John Clark Donahue's participation in the theatre's activities. Therefore, the real history of the Children's Theatre Company begins with Donahue's entrance into the Moppet Players in 1962–1963. However, for the sake of continuity, the year 1961–1962 is discussed in as much depth as available resources have permitted. Information on the 1961–1962 season is primarily the product of interviews with people affiliated with the Moppet Players. Written documentation is limited to a few flyer brochures and newspaper articles announcing productions.

2. Mailer/brochure, held by the Pillsbury House, Minneapolis, Minnesota.

3. Interview with Mike Schulte, former business manager of the Moppet Players, March 17, 1981.

4. Interview with John Clark Donahue, January 8, 1981.

5. Donahue interview.

6. Minutes of the board meeting of the Pillsbury-Waite Settlement House, September 11, 1962, held by the Pillsbury House, Minneapolis, Minnesota.

7. Donahue interview.

8. Ibid.

9. Minutes of the board meeting, October 23, 1962.

10. Dan Sullivan, "Adults Could Learn: Moppets' Play Rich with Rare Innocence," *Minneapolis Sunday Tribune*, November 18, 1962, p. 17B.

11. Minutes of the board meeting, January 22, 1963.

12. Minutes of the board meeting, November 17, 1963.

13. Mike Steele, "Wendy Lehr—the Graceful Hurricane," *Minneapolis Tribune*, October 25, 1970.

14. Minutes of the board meeting, April 14, 1964.

15. Donahue interview.

16. Interview with John Davidson, August 6, 1981.

17. Moppet Players' season flyer 1964–1965, held by Pillsbury House, Minneapolis, Minnesota.

18. Minutes of the board meeting, September 8, 1964 and November 10, 1964.

19. Minutes of the board meeting, January 12, 1965.

20. "Art Institute Forms Children's Theatre," *Minneapolis Tribune*, July 7, 1965. The Minneapolis Institute of Art is a department of the Minneapolis Society of Fine Arts.

21. Davidson interview.

22. Proposed draft of agreement between the advisory committee, the institute and the Minneapolis Society of Fine Arts, n.d., Children's Theatre Company Archives.

23. "Present Space Descriptions, Appendix H," 1970, Children's Theatre Company Archives.

24. John Clark Donahue, *The Cookie Jar and Other Plays* (Minneapolis, Minn.: University of Minnesota Press, 1975).

25. Letter to Ward, Robinson and Clark from John Clark Donahue, May 7, 1968, Children's Theatre Company Archives.

26. Letter to Wendy Lehr from Wallace Kennedy, May 20, 1968, Children's Theatre Company Archives.

27. "Announcement from the CTC," May 29, 1969, Children's Theatre Company Archives.

28. Minutes of the staff meeting, September 4, 1969, Children's Theatre Company Archives.

John V. Hicks

29. Mike Steele, "Urban Arts Program Is a Model for Nation," *Minneapolis Tribune*, May 16, 1976, p. 1D.

30. John Donahue and Timothy Mason, "Thoughts on the Arts," 1973, TS, p.1.

31. Interview with Wallace Kennedy, August 20, 1981. Interview with John Clark Donahue, August 19, 1981.

32. Letter to Mrs. Walter Mondale from Mel Kurnow, Public Relations Director, July 20, 1970, Children's Theatre Company Archives.

33. Mike Steele, "Two Area Groups Cause Stir at Theatre Congress," *Minneapolis Tribune*, July 2, 1972.

34. Mike Steele, "Rockefeller Fund Continues Aid," *Minneapolis Tribune*, October 13, 1974.

35. Interview with Dixon Bond, August 11, 1981.

36. Letter to John Donahue from Clinton Morris, February 11, 1973, Children's Theatre Company Archives.

37. Bonnie Leslie, "MSFA & CTC: Trouble Within the Shrine," *Minnesota Daily*, July 18, 1975, pp. 11–14.

38. Ibid.

39. Interview with John Donahue, conducted by A. C. Powell, past member of the board, February 18, 1981, pp. 16–17, Children's Theatre Company Archives.

40. Leslie "MSFA & CTC," p. 12,

41. Interview with Dixon Bond, January 1, 1981.

42. Letter to Steve Ayers from Arthur Young & Co., December 9, 1975, Children's Theatre Company Archives.

43. Agreement between the Children's Theatre Company and the Minneapolis Society of Fine Arts, January 1, 1976, Children's Theatre Company Archives.

44. Mike Steele, "Children's Theatre Company Coup: Seuss Work Adapted for Stage," *Minneapolis Tribune*, April 20, 1980, p. 1G.

45. Mike Steele, "Tomie dePaola: Designing Sets Is a Dream Come True," *Minneapolis Tribune*, February 22, 1981.

46. Interview with John Donahue, November 21, 1982.

47. Interview with Sarah Lawless, November 23, 1982.

48. A recorded interview with John Donahue by Bill Powell, February 18, 1981, Children's Theatre Company Archives.

49. The Children's Theatre Company case statement for 1986–1987 indicates that video production at the Children's Theatre Company was encouraged as part of a $6 million grant to PBS.

50. CTC school flyer, 1981, Children's Theatre Company Archives.

51. Letter to John Donahue from the Rockefeller Brothers Fund, February 20, 1980, Children's Theatre Company Archives.

52. Ibid.

53. "The Children's Theatre School," a paper written by staff of the Children's Theatre Company and School, 1982, Children's Theatre Company Archives.

54. For a complete account see *Minneapolis Tribune,* April 29, 1984.

55. The Children's Theatre Company case statement for 1986–1987.

56. Ibid.

12

Aurand Harris: Playwright and Ambassador

Rachel Fordyce

The strengths or weaknesses of children's theatre have always been linked, in part, to the strengths and weaknesses of the plays available for production; and the cry for good scripts has never ceased.[1] The contemporary children's theatre scene includes only a small number of writers who have contributed more than one play of note to the repertoire. By far the most prolific of these is Aurand Harris. To date, Harris has written thirty-seven plays for children and young adults, and is noted as a director, teacher, and spokesperson for children's theatre.

James Aurand Harris, the only child of Myrtle Sebastian and George Dowe Harris, was born on July 4, 1915, in Jamesport, Missouri.[2] His father was a physician; his mother, a graduate of Northwestern University, was trained in theatre and speech, and was also an active and well-known director, teacher, and amateur actress who maintained her own studio. From an early age Harris was drawn to things theatrical, no doubt in part due to his mother's influence but, also, because of the variety and high quality of the theatre with which she surrounded him.

Harris's acting career began at age four, when he played a bumblebee in a local musical production; before seven he had written his first "little dramatic piece." His education was augmented with speech, dance, and musical training. In high school he was involved in dramatic and oratorical contests, to the extent that when he graduated he was named "the best actor and the best orator in the state of Missouri."[3]

During his formative years, Harris not only studied with his mother but also at the Horner Conservatory in Kansas City. In 1930, the summer Harris turned sixteen, he performed in Kansas City in *Opportunity Revue*, "a vaudeville show which was produced with local and professional talent in many of the larger cities throughout the United States. Primarily a publicity venture [for RKO Studios], the show was ostensibly designed to discover new talent for the motion-picture industry."[4] Along with another talented performer from his hometown with whom he worked frequently, Harris acted in comic double entendre skits four times a day between showings of Frank Buck's film, *Bring 'Em Back Alive*— a remarkably enriching experience for a young actor.

During the Depression, Harris was forced to stay close to home; consequently he began his college education, in 1933, at Trenton Junior College in Missouri. He continued it at the University of Kansas City where he graduated in 1937. During these years he wrote and performed several plays that were produced locally. Although this early work was well received, it was still very much a learning experience for him. With these plays he learned much about the craft of play writing: that action is vital to good drama, that a good playwright must have a sensitive ear for dialogue and the nuances of sound and diction patterns, and that "theatricality in writing and acting—the need to create characters and situations which are larger than life and capable of being projected honestly to an entire audience" is important.[5]

During this period Harris began to develop a sense of audience and the limitations and demands of the stage; he also learned a considerable amount about scene design and construction. These skills have been beneficial in creating dramatic plays, plays that actually play. Harris says that when he creates characters, he goes over their lines again and again, acting out all of the parts much as if he were performing.[6] He is always acutely aware of the technical limitations of the stage. An obvious advantage of having this background is that it has allowed him to create widely differing types of plays, including musicals, historical plays, adaptations from Shakespeare and original plays that feature mime, puppetry, slapstick and courtly display—to name a few.

In 1937, Harris began work on a master's degree in speech and drama at Northwestern University in Evanston, Illinois. More important than classroom instruction to his education, though, were the people and the prevailing atmosphere at Northwestern during this time. This is the period when Winifred Ward's career as a practitioner of children's theatre was beginning to have an impact, and interest throughout the country was focused on her teaching of creative drama and her children's theatre productions at Northwestern. Simultaneously, noted playwright Charlotte Chorpenning was writing and producing children's plays at the Goodman Theatre in Chicago. Moreover, there was a strong drama program in the Evanston schools where the value of drama was recognized and its use encouraged. Harris not only absorbed this atmosphere but also worked for Ward and with fellow graduate students Kenneth Graham, Geraldine Brain Siks, Campton Bell, Walter Kerr and George Eells, all of whom would leave their mark on the field of drama as educators, playwrights or critics.

Having finished his masters degree at Northwestern in 1939, Harris began a grueling two years of teaching in Gary, Indiana. This involved preparing a large range of classes for widely different age groups, while constantly directing and writing plays and skits for students to perform. Surviving that, Harris served as head of the drama department at William Woods College for three very productive years, during which he wrote and had performed *Ladies of the Mop* and *Once Upon a Clothesline*. The latter won an award from the Seattle Junior Programs. In 1945, Harris moved to New York, thus ending what might be viewed as formative years, years rich in the variety of their experiences and uniform in leading Harris toward a career as a playwright for children.

Harris was always sure about what field he would enter; it only remained to be seen whether he would be an actor, a director, or a playwright, as each was a viable possibility at one point in his life. After deciding to become a playwright, and bolstered by further experiences at Columbia University, at the the New School for Social Research with John Gassner, by the many play-writing competitions he won and by the publication of his first plays for adults, Harris ultimately had to decide for what audience he would write.

Given his early success with adult plays (*Madam Ada* and *Hide and Seek* were produced on national television, and the latter was staged by the Theatre Guild), one might have expected Harris to continue to write for an adult audience. But, in fact, Harris found that those principles and standards he most admired were more often associated with theatre for young people than for adults. Harris liked to write plays with much physical action. Moreover, when he was beginning his career as a playwright there was little room for fantasy in the theatre. The theatre of the 1950s was steeped in naturalism, as was the case with most Broadway plays at that time. Quite simply, Harris realized that children were his audience, that he liked writing plays for them, and that the appreciation was reciprocated. So began a long career as a professional playwright for children that has also included stints as a director and as a teacher of playwriting. What is of interest here, however, is the body of Harris' work.

A CANON OF PUBLISHED PLAYS BY AURAND HARRIS

PLAY	INTENDED AUDIENCE	PUBLISHER
Once Upon a Clothesline	Children	Baker's, 1945
Ladies of the Mop	Adol/Young Adult	Baker's 1945
The Moon Makes Three	Adol/Young Adult	French, 1947
Madam Ada	Adult	French, 1948
Seven League Boots	Children	Baker's, 1948
The Doughnut Hole	Young Adult	French, 1948

Circus Day (*Circus Wind*, rev.)	Children	French, 1949/60
Pinocchio and the Indians	Children	French, 1950
Freely adapted from the book by Carlo Collodi		
And Never Been Kissed	Adol/Young Adult	French, 1950
Adapted from the book by J. M. Proffitt		
Simple Simon, or Simon Big Ears	Children	Anchorage, 1953
We Were Young That Year	Young Adult	French, 1954
Buffalo Bill	Children	Anchorage, 1954
The Plain Princess	Children	Anchorage, 1955
The Flying Prince	Children	French, 1958 Anchorage, 1985
Based on stories told by Vikramaditya of Ujjain		
Junket	Children	Anchorage, 1959
Adapted from the book by Anne H. White		
Pocahontas	Children	Anchorage, 1961
Adapted from historic records		
The Brave Little Tailor	Children	Anchorage, 1961
Adapted from the Brothers Grimm		
Androcles and the Lion	Children	Anchorage, 1964
Rags to Riches	Children	Anchorage, 1966
Adapted from stories by Horatio Alger		
Pinocchio and the Fire Eater	Children	McGraw-Hill, 1967
Brief adaptation from the book by Carlo Collodi		
A Doctor in Spite of Himself	Children	Anchorage, 1968
Freely adapted from the play by Moliere		
Punch and Judy	Children	Anchorage, 1970
Just So Stories	Children	Anchorage, 1971
Adapted from three tales by Rudyard Kipling		
Ming Lee and the Magic Tree	Children	French, 1971
Steal Away Home	Children	Anchorage, 1972
From the book by Jane Kristof		
Peck's Bad Boy	Children	Anchorage, 1974
Adapted from stories by George W. Peck		
Yankee Doodle Dandy	Children	Anchorage, 1975
Star Spangled Salute	Children	Anchorage, 1975

| *Robin Goodfellow* | Children | Anchorage, 1976 |

Adapted from English folk tales and Shakespeare's *A Midsummer Night's Dream*

A Toby Show	Children	Anchorage, 1978
Arkansaw Bear	Child/Adol	Anchorage, 1980
Yankee Doodle Dandies	Children	Anchorage, 1981

Three scenes from *Yankee Doodle Dandy*

| *Treasure Island* | Children | Anchorage, 1983 |

Adapted from the novel by Robert Louis Stevenson

| *The Magician's Nephew* | Children | Dramatic, 1984 |

Adapted from the book by C. S. Lewis

| *Ride a Blue Horse* | Children | Anchorage, 1986 |

From the life and works of James Whitcomb Riley

| *Huck Finn's Story* | Children | Anchorage, 1987 |

Publishers: Anchorage Press, New Orleans, Louisiana.
Baker's, Boston, Massachusetts.
Dramatic Publishing, Chicago, Illinois.
McGraw-Hill, New York.
Samuel French, New York.

Harris' plays fall into four, roughly defined categories: original plays; adaptations from literary sources; adaptations of ancient and modern tales, *fabliaux*, *Marchen* and legends; and plays based on historical, heroic or mythical characters. They are as different as *And Never Been Kissed,* a play about a girl who, by hook or crook, refuses to reach sweet sixteen without having been kissed, and *Punch and Judy,* a *grand guignol* with somewhat more serious proportions than one would expect in a children's play and certainly a more serious theme than one would find in a typical Punch and Judy show in the Tuileries on a summer afternoon.

In general, Harris' plays demonstrate a concern for the relationship between form and content, character and dialogue, tone and atmosphere, theme and plot. This regard for balance almost suggests a neoclassic decorum that, in the extreme, can produce lifeless statues instead of vibrant characters. But action is always foremost in Harris' plays, and this is as true of the early plays as of the late, and as true of the farces, with which one typically associates action, as with the more serious plays.

Yet Harris' plays are so wide-ranging by type, that their very diversity makes it difficult to hang any labels on the author. And this diversity is one of Harris' greatest assets.

Equally diverse is Harris' treatment of characters and subject matter. For example, as with his serious discussion of death in *The Arkansaw Bear,* he often explores subjects before they have become popular or even generally acceptable for child audiences. In another vein, his play, *We Were Young That Year*, though

somewhat dated by modern standards, is significant as one of the earlier plays
for children to employ a female narrator.

Pocahontas is another example of an early play with sophisticated treatment
of a female character. The play focuses on the role of a woman in history, and
it is significant that the main character is not sentimentalized. Harris based the
play on the many legends about Pocahontas, and he created a well-tempered and
believable character. His practice of doing considerable research and his adher-
ence to historical fact is underscored with the inclusion of a glossary of authentic
Powhatan Indian words at the end of the play.

Concerning the subject matter of Harris' plays, one critic observes:

Harris has always been favorably disposed to stories, subjects, or characters which have
not already been dramatized. He has chosen with an eye for the unusual, but always
weighing his choice against his belief that directors are often hesitant to produce totally
unknown titles because parents of young audience members are much more likely to take
their children to productions with recognizable titles.[7]

This attention to the development of original or fresh subject matter for children,
and to a balance between the aesthetic and the practical, is apparent throughout
Harris' career, though it manifests itself in different ways.

For example, when Harris chose to adapt *The Magician's Nephew*, he dramatized a lesser work of a well-known author. This is not one of C. S. Lewis'
better books in the Narnia series, nor is it one of his most popular. Its weakness
as a book—that it wanders from episode to episode without unity or tautness of
plot—is minimized in the play setting, which, by definition, can cover much
less territory than the book. Harris uses the novel's picaresque structure to
advantage; he captures the most dramatic scenes and lets the dross go by the
wayside. Where Lewis fails to realize his characters fully, Harris redeems them
by highlighting them in the most interesting scenes from the book.

In addition to the diversity in Harris' plays, some things can also be said about
his consistency as a playwright. In the field of children's theatre, Harris is both
a challenger and an upholder of tradition. Like the active, imaginative, and
thoughtful children he writes for, his plays are robust. His work extols curiosity,
an inquiring mind and the desire to know and to understand. This tendency on
the part of characters to explore is reflected in the way Harris also seems to
enjoy playing with ideas, images and sounds. Particularly, he savors active and
expressive language, and he enhances characters and plot through the richness
of the language, sound patterns and rhythms.

Nowhere is Harris' playfulness with the language more apparent than in the
use of rhyme. Practically all of his plays from the early 1950s onward are infused
with rhyme—sometimes to heighten the comic or lyrical effect, sometimes to
accompany song, sometimes for repetitive effect.

The discussion of rhyme in any play for children is a ticklish one; those people
who employ it most often tend to write doggerel (or worse), and those who

eschew it are not convinced there is any merit in its use. Given this pejorative burden it is questionable why a playwright, particularly a good one, would employ a device some critics scorn.

One obvious answer is that Harris appears to be writing for two kinds of critics, and they are potentially quite different. For example, the adult critic may question the literary merit of the following, while the child critic enjoys it for the breeziness of diction that, in this case, instantly updates a Punch and Judy show for them:

> I love you, I love you.
> I love you divine.
> Save me your chewing gum,
> You're sitting on mine.[8]

Likewise, children delight in Harris' use of internal rhyme and alliteration:

Androcles: Free? I am free.

Lion: The way the world should be!

Androcles: Free—to find my family—to work the best I can—to raise my head—to be
a man.
To find out who I am.[9]

Harris rarely uses the sophisticated rhyme of double and triple syllables, but he does use complicated assonance and consonance, both of which invariably enhance the tone of his plays. His use of internal rhyme is particularly effective. By its very nature, internal rhyme does not rely on meter; it can be used anywhere in a line, and it has no rules to follow. Unfortunately, this lack of structure makes it difficult to appreciate the amount of effort a poet must use to hone such lines.

As rhyme is used in many of Harris' plays to set tone and carry action, music is used to set the rhythm and pace. From *Simple Simon* forward, fourteen of Harris' plays rely heavily on music. Plays like *Yankee Doodle Dandy* and *Star Spangled Salute: A Patriotic Musical with Traditional American Songs* could be considered reviews. But in plays like *Steal Away Home, Treasure Island* and *The Magician's Nephew* the music is so thoroughly integrated into the plot and action that it is as much a fabric of the play as the dialogue. Moreover, Harris has been particularly fortunate in the people he has worked with on the scores for his plays, most notably William Penn, Kevin Dunn and Mort Stine.

Harris' work is also characterized by inventiveness of plot and character (even when he may be adapting from another source), innovative use of established theatre convention and a high regard for literary standards (even when dealing with a somewhat hackneyed theme or time-honored plot). *Rags to Riches,* an amalgamation of two well-known dime novels by Horatio Alger, is a typical example of all three of these characteristics.

The play is a pastiche of high-keyed incidents, asides, suspended animation, slapstick, misconstrued verbal cues and the obligatory curses and coincidences. Typical characters include the honest-but-poor hero, the good-but-helpless quasi-saint harassed by the blundering and malevolent bully, the evil old crone, the rich benefactor, and, of course, his pretty daughter. The number of musical citations for contemporary catches and art songs rivals the classic of the form, *The Knight of the Burning Pestle*. The elaborate choreography and use of mime in a tea scene between the unpolished hero and the refined heroine rival the universally admired tea scene in *The Importance of Being Earnest. Rags to Riches* is not a Sunday school lesson come true in the triumph over evil. This use of an older theatrical form is a polished, well-researched reenactment of melodrama that becomes, in effect, one of the few farces written for children.

Given that Harris is so widely acclaimed, it should be possible to pinpoint reasons, other than mechanical ones, for his success. Many critics of literature, whether dramatic or otherwise, still agree in principle with Horace that the purpose of literature is to entertain and to educate. Disagreements arise only in determining the proportion between entertainment and education. Equally unstable is the definition of the phrase "to educate," which is often interpreted to mean "to moralize."[10] In a Harris play, the latter does not apply. He does not moralize. That, in itself, probably accounts for a portion of his popularity with young people. Heavy-handed moralizing is never a substitute for a strong, well-conceived theme.

But the major ingredient contributing to the critical acclaim of Harris' plays appears to be the balance of these works. Consciously or unconsciously, Harris carefully balances entertainment and education, and the result is plays with general appeal. If he uses slapstick, as he does effectively in *Punch and Judy* and *Rags to Riches* for instance, it is for reasons of historical accuracy as much as to amuse and further the action.

Only rarely, as may be the case with *A Toby Show*, does a Harris play rely exclusively on entertainment for its impact. This fast-paced show, written with a grant from the National Endowment for the Humanities, is, in fact, a celebration of the arts as they were purveyed in rural communities at the turn of the century and up through the 1920s. Neither a chatauqua nor a vaudeville, or even just a cross between, *A Toby Show* is the old-time tent show that includes a three-act play with lively *entr'acte* pieces and a band or orchestra. Harris' *A Toby Show* relies heavily on stock characters and jokes, fast curtains, slick repartee, much music and spectacle. By comparison, *Huck Finn's Story*, a recent Harris publication, is austere in the extreme. In this play Harris has limited himself to a bare stage and five actors who play numerous roles. Where theatricality is the driving force of *A Toby Show*, substance and content characterize *Huck Finn's Story*.

While Harris' reputation is based on the generally high quality of the plays written throughout his career, two of his works, *Androcles and the Lion* and *The Arkansaw Bear*, are generally acknowledged as superior. These plays have influenced the field greatly, and will probably remain in the children's theatre repertoire for a long time. The content is rich and imaginative; the characters and plots are well developed; the music and the spectacle are integral to the plots; and they are eminently playable. But the lasting quality of both plays must be attributed to their themes.

Androcles and the Lion is certainly one of the most joyful reenactments of the *commedia* tradition written in this century, and one of the most fascinating aspects of the play is that it has a serious theme couched in an outwardly light-hearted play.

Like *Punch and Judy* and *Steal Away Home,* both written a decade later, the theme of *Androcles and the Lion* is freedom: freedom to be oneself, freedom to be unrestrained physically, freedom to think and to know without having the thoughts, wills and actions of others imposed upon you. However serious this all sounds, the play is, in reality, wonderfully amusing, and the theme is not sugar-coated. If balance is the mark of Harris' success, then *Androcles and the Lion* is one of his most even-handed plays.

Another significant aspect of Harris' work is that, without intending to be a controversial figure, he has introduced controversial topics into his plays; and because of his faithfulness to theme and characters and the truth behind the issues he raises, his audiences should grow a little because of what they have viewed. Harris seems motivated to deal with issues that are important to a child, even though children are not universally acknowledged to have deep feelings and concerns about "mature" topics.[11]

To date, *The Arkansaw Bear* is probably Harris' most controversial play. Its story—about a young girl forced to deal with the death of her beloved grand-father—is more difficult to deal with than most, because many people have trouble accepting both the outward manifestation of death and its implications. Furthermore, the willingness and ability of a playgoer to reach beyond the subject matter and action of the play (and beyond his or her trepidations about a fearful subject) to understand a play's essence is not generally associated with a child audience. Yet with *The Arkansaw Bear,* it has become obvious that Harris is capable of dealing with mature themes for child audiences, and that the audience is able to make a leap of faith to understand and appreciate this play.

It is unlikely that *The Arkansaw Bear* would have been, or could have been, produced prior to 1970.[12] Either motivated by squeamishness, prudence or moral reticence, many authors and playwrights eschewed difficult subjects for children. When they did discuss them, their works were not always met with a warm reception. In the early 1970s, amidst an atmosphere where, for example, some teachers were pasting miniature diapers on the pictures of the naked main char-acter in Maurice Sendak's *In the Night Kitchen,* the treatment of a topic as controversial as death was extremely rare. The consensus of opinion was that children either could not handle such a difficult or remote topic, or that it made them too uncomfortable.

But the lesson in *The Arkansaw Bear* is a lesson about life, wherein the main character learns about the cyclical nature of life, that death is only one aspect of the cycle, and that even in death one can live on in the memory of friends or family.

Structurally, *The Arkansaw Bear* is a play within a play. Its external, realistic framework is about a young girl, Tish, whose grandfather is dying and whose mother and great aunt are unwilling to let her see her grandfather, to participate in his death, to discuss the meaning of what is happening. In frustration, even rage at not understanding the unknown, Tish steps out of the situation at home, goes to her private tree, wishes on the first star of the evening and precipitates the play into a fantasy world. Here, fantasy is an elaborate metaphor for the real world.

Once Harris shifts the action of the play to the world of fantasy, he is free to have his characters allude to what is going on in the real world and to try to make sense of reality. The major theme in the play, that life and death are "part of the great pattern . . . , the great cycle of life" and that "in every ending there is a new beginning," is stated early, as the fantasy begins.[13] But it is not necessarily accepted wholesale by the audience any more than the main characters are able to accept it at this point.

Tish's deepest wish is expressed when she says " I wish I knew why." And this realistic wish is probably the most universally understood thematic idea in the play. With potential sorrow, carefully tempered by wit, imagination, compassion and comprehension on the part of the main characters, Harris illustrates the universality of death. Ultimately in the play, understanding, not a temporal life or final death, triumphs.

After a long and illustrious career, Harris is still active as a playwright, teacher and director. In addition to working as guest artist and teacher at various theatres and universities throughout the country, in 1987 he was invited to the People's Republic of China. At the invitation of the American-Chinese Cultural Exchange Foundation, Harris' *The Plain Princess*, translated by Ye Xiao, was presented in commemoration of the fortieth anniversary of the Children's Art Theatre of Shanghai, with Harris himself directing. This singular honor makes Harris the first U.S. playwright for children to have his plays produced in China.

It is understandable why Harris is asked constantly to be the ambassador for theatre for young audiences. His plays are produced more than those of any other children's playwright, and he is probably the single most influential writer the field has produced.

NOTES

1. For discussions of this dilemma see Constance D'Arcy Mackay, *Children's Theatre and Plays* (New York: Appleton-Century, 1927); Moses Goldberg, *Children's Theatre: A Philosophy and a Method* (Englewood Cliffs, N.J.: Prentice-Hall, 1974), pp. 26–78; and Winifred Ward, "Children's Theatre: Help Wanted," *Theatre Arts* 44 (August 1960), pp. 53, 55.

2. Biographical material is based on personal and telephone interviews with the author between 1985 and 1987 and earlier work by Coleman Jennings. For a much more complete biographical history of Harris, see "The Playwright and the Plays," in *Six Plays by Aurand Harris,* ed. Coleman A. Jennings (Austin: University of Texas Press, 1977), pp. 3–29. Included in appendix 2 of this volume is a list of awards Harris has won, through 1976.

3. Ibid., p. 6.

4. Ibid.

5. Harris, as quoted in ibid., p. 7.

6. Telephone interview with Harris, January 11, 1987.

7. *Six Plays,* p. 25.

8. Ibid., pp. 160–61.

9. Ibid., pp. 86, 51.

10. For an extended discussion of sententious children's theatre and its use to inculcate moral and political propaganda, see Jack Zipes, "Taking Children Seriously—The Recent Popularity of Children's Literature in East and West Germany," *Children's Literature: The Great Excluded,* 2 (1973), pp. 173–91.

11. Several major sources discuss those qualities that constitute a good play for children. These include, among others: Kenneth Graham, "An Introductory Study of Evaluation of Plays for Children," Ph.D. diss., University of Utah, 1947; Lowell Swortzell, "Five Plays: A Repertory of Children's Theatre to be Performed by and for Children," Vol. 2, Ph.D. diss., New York University, 1963.

12. There was a spate of excited discussion during the late 1950s and through the 1960s about what was "suitable" for a child audience. Much of the discussion came to the boiling point over Arthur Fauquez' *Reynard the Fox,* a play with a somewhat unscrupulous but very entertaining hero who, his detractors asserted, did not represent an appropriate role model for children. Three theses during this period are the clearest and most extended discussions of the moral implications of these issues: Dorothy Aldrich, "A Study of Child Audience Reaction to a Controversial Character in a Children's Play," M.A. thesis, University of Pittsburgh, 1962; Sara Soller, "The Attenuation of Evil Characters and Plot Elements in Children's Theatre Scripts Adapted from Five Fairy Tales," M.A. thesis, University of Kansas, 1967; and Bill Kingsley, "Happy Endings, Poetic Justice, and the Depth and Strength of Characterization in American Children's Drama: A Critical Analysis," Ph.D. diss., University of Pittsburgh, 1964. The latter is useful for its discussion of taboo subjects in children's dramatic and fictional literature, particularly death.

13. Harris, *Androcles and the Lion* (New Orleans: Anchorage Press, 1964), p. 11.

Bibliographical Notes

Anyone seeking to learn about the history of American children's theatre is immediately confronted with three problems: first, the confusion as to the definition of the term, *children's theatre* (in various publications it can mean theatre or drama by, with or for children); second, the vast diffusion of children's theatre activity throughout the fields of education, social work and recreation—as well as the theatre; and, third, the somewhat limited historical research that has been done to date. As such, the researcher needs to approach the task with the knowledge that only a few secondary sources are available and that in-depth research will require the synthesis of scattered and sometimes disparate data to be found generally in primary source materials.

Theatre, Children and Youth, by Jed H. Davis and Mary Jane Evans (New Orleans: Anchorage Press, 1982), offers a general introduction to U.S. children's theatre for the newcomer to the field. While this book offers only cursory historical data, it provides a good synthesis of current trends and practices, as well as lengthy notes and bibliographies that illuminate possible paths for the historian.

To date, there has been only one general history of the field written, *Theatre for Children in the United States: A History,* by Nellie McCaslin (Norman: University of Oklahoma Press, 1971). While this book provides important documentation of some children's theatre work in this country, it is limited in both the period it covers (1900–1970) and its lack of detail. For the serious scholar, McCaslin's dissertation, ''A History of Children's Theatre in the United States'' (New York University, 1957), provides a bit more detail and more thorough documentation.

McCaslin's *Historical Guide to Children's Theatre in America* (Westport, Conn.: Greenwood Press, 1987) offers a condensed version of the historical data from her previous volume (updated to the 1980s) and a section on profiles of theatres and organizations past and present. As the title indicates, it is best used as a guide to the history of the field, though it too focuses entirely on twentieth-century activity.

In the last thirty years several bibliographies of U.S. children's theatre have been compiled. *Children's Theatre and Creative Dramatics: An Annotated Bibliography of Critical Works* (Boston: G. K. Hall & Co., 1975), by Rachel Fordyce, includes over two thousand entries, with separate categories for children's theatre and creative drama. This work provides an overview of books and journal articles about children's theatre history, but the alphabetical arrangement (by author) makes it difficult to track historical subjects. Fordyce also combines citations of minor journal and magazine articles with the more important books.

Other bibliographies include three republished by the University Press of America in 1983. Wesley Van Tassel's *Children's Theatre: A Selected and Annotated Bibliography* is a helpful, if confused, collection of sources ranging from journal articles to unpublished theses and dissertations. Carol Jean Kennedy's *Child Drama: A Selected and Annotated Bibliography 1974–1979* picks up the chronology where Van Tassel's bibliography ends. Mary Eileen Klock's *Creative Drama: A Selected and Annotated Bibliography* provides a list of important creative drama resources not noted in the others.

A Preliminary Checklist of Children's Plays in English, 1780–1855 (New York: Theatre Library Association, 1987), compiled by Jonathan Levy with Martha Mahard is a recent addition to the material covering pre-twentieth-century children's theatre. Given the often-stated view that children's theatre did not begin in earnest in this country until the twentieth century, this "checklist" points the historian to new and important avenues of investigation.

Levy's helpful bibliography also lists important resources for the historian. Some collections of plays from the first part of the nineteenth century can be found in books on oratory, such as Increase Cooke's *American Orator* (New Haven: Sidney's Press, 1811). Important sources for dialogues include *School Dialogues* (Boston: Thomas & Andrews, 1797) by Samuel Morse, and *New School Dialogues* (New Haven: S. Babcock, 1851) by John Lovell.

Eliza Follen's *Home Dramas for Young People* (Boston: James Munroe & Co., 1859) and Mary Cobb's *Poetical Dramas for Home and School* (Boston: Lee & Shepard, 1873) provide a good glimpse of late nineteenth-century activity.

Several early twentieth-century play anthologies also give a fair perspective of the practices of the time. Stuart Walker's work for family audiences is covered in several volumes edited by E. H. Bierstadt. See particularly, *Portmanteau Plays* (Cincinnati: Stewart Kidd, 1917) and *Portmanteau Adaptations* (Cincinnati: Stewart Kidd, 1921). Theatre critic Montrose Moses edited three volumes of plays and comment: *A Treasury of Plays for Children* (Boston: Little, Brown & Co., 1921), *Another Treasury of Plays for Children* (Boston: Little, Brown & Co., 1926), and *Ring Up the Curtain* (Boston: Little, Brown & Co., 1932). The anthologies edited by Constance D'Arcy Mackay suggest the wide range of the then prevalent dramatic literature for children. These include, among others, *Patriotic Plays and Pageants for Young People* (New York: Holt, 1912) and *Forest Princess and Other Masques* (New York: Holt, 1916).

Some of Clare Tree Majors' simplistic fairy tale adaptations are included in her *Playing Theatre: Six Plays for Children* (New York: Oxford University Press, 1930). And a selection of children's plays written for professional productions by the Federal Theatre Project are anthologized, with comment, in Lowell Swortzell's *Six Plays for Young People from the Federal Theatre Project (1936–1939)* (Westport, Conn.: Greenwood Press, 1986).

An overview can be found in *Dramatic Literature for Children: A Century in Review*

(New Orleans: Anchorage Press, 1984) edited by Roger L. Bedard. This book contains an essay tracing the development of plays to be performed for child audiences plus an appendix listing play anthologies of historical interest.

The philosophies and practices of settlement house drama work have been treated, in part, by some who were involved in these activities. While many of these accounts are anecdotal and subjective, they offer a valuable glimpse at an important thread of children's theatre activity. For information on the early years of Hull House, the most famous of these, see Jane Addams' *Spirit of Youth in the City Streets* (New York: Macmillan, 1909) and *Twenty Years at Hull House* (New York: Macmillan 1910). The work of the Henry Street Settlement is covered in Lillian Wald's *The House on Henry Street* (New York: Holt, 1915). *The Children's Educational Theatre* (New York: Harper, 1911), by Alice Minnie Herts, discusses the work of an organization noted by some as the "first" American children's theatre.

Important first-hand insight into the development of the theory and practice of recreational drama can be found in Neva Boyd's writings as collected by Paul Simon (editor) in *Play and Game Theory in Group Work* (Chicago: University of Illinois Press, 1971). See also Charlotte Chorpenning's "Putting on the Community Play," *Quarterly Journal of Speech Education*, 5 (1919).

By far the most extensive and focused historical research in American children's theatre completed to date, has been written as Ph.D. dissertations. Several of the chapters in this book were based on such work, including:

Abookire, Noerena. "Children's Theatre Activities at Karamu House in Cleveland, Ohio: 1915–1975." New York University, 1982.

Bedard, Roger L. "The Life and Work of Charlotte B. Chorpenning." University of Kansas, 1979.

Heard, Doreen B. "A Production History of the New York City Children's Theatre Unit of the Federal Theatre Project, 1935–1939." Florida State University, 1982.

Hicks, John V. "The History of the Children's Theatre Company and School of Minneapolis 1961–1981." University of Wisconsin–Madison, 1982.

Rodman, Ellen. "Edith King and Dorothy Coit and the King-Coit School and Children's Theatre." New York University, 1980.

Salazar, Laura. "The Emergence of Children's Theatre and Drama, 1900–1910." University of Michigan, 1984.

Other Ph.D. dissertations covering important aspects of children's theatre history include:

Gamble, Michael W. "Clare Tree Major: Children's Theatre 1923–1954." New York University, 1976.

Graham, Kenneth L. "An Introductory Study of Evaluation of Plays for Children's Theatre in the United States." University of Utah, 1952.

Guffin, Jan. "Winifred Ward: A Critical Biography." Duke University, 1975.

Jennings, Coleman. "The Dramatic Contributions of Aurand Harris to Children's Theatre in the United States." New York University, 1974.

Parchem, Georga Larsen. "The Paper Bag Players, A Theatre for Children 1958–1982: Development, Creative Process and Principles." Ohio State University, 1983.

Popovich, James E. "A Study of Significant Contributions to the Development of Creative
    Dramatics in American Education." Northwestern University, 1955.

Information from a computerized data base, entitled "Graduate Research in Creative
Drama and Theatre for Children and Youth," is available from the department of drama
at the University of Texas–Austin. The file contains over five hundred entries, listing
theses and dissertations, many of which cover historical aspects of the field.

Archive collections are particularly important for historical research in children's theatre. Although most relevant data is scattered throughout many sources there are at least
two library collections of more than usual interest to the children's theatre researcher.
The children's theatre collection at Arizona State University includes primary source
materials of many noted twentieth-century children's theatre workers, including playwrights, publishers, theorists and educators. This collection also includes the organizational records of the national children's theatre organization (which has had various names
since its inception in 1944) and an extensive collection of early publications in the field.

The Winifred Ward Collection at Northwestern University includes Ward's personal
correspondence and records. Because of Ward's pivotal role in the development of the
profession, materials and information about virtually every other important figure in the
field in mid-century can also be found among her papers.

Many good resources exist, and those described above may prove a good introduction
to the history of the field. But the children's theatre historian is generally met with the
task of filling in pieces of a story that has not been completely told. Happy hunting!

Index

198 Index

About the Contributors

EDITORS

ROGER L. BEDARD is an associate professor of theatre and coordinator of the M.F.A. program in Child Drama at Virginia Polytechnic Institute and State University in Blacksburg, Virginia. He currently serves as Executive Secretary for the American Alliance for Theatre and Education. His publications include *Dramatic Literature for Children: A Century in Review* (editor) and numerous articles on children's theatre history. Bedard received his Ph.D. from the University of Kansas, M.F.A. from the University of Oregon and B.A. from the University of Northern Iowa.

C. JOHN TOLCH is a professor of theatre and drama at the University of Wisconsin–Madison. He earned his Ph.D. from Ohio State University. Long active in national and international children's theatre activities, plays directed by Tolch have been presented at the Kennedy Center for the Performing Arts in Washington, D.C., and at an international play festival in Sibenik, Yugoslavia. He is a former editor of *Children's Theatre Review* and former vice-president for research and publications for the Children's Theatre Association of America.

CONTRIBUTING AUTHORS

NOERENA ABOOKIRE received her Ph.D. in theatre education from New York University, and she currently serves as Magnet Schools and Experimental Curriculum Specialist for the Cleveland School of the Arts, in Cleveland, Ohio.

Much of her professional career has been devoted to writing, producing and directing theatre with and for inner-city youth.

CHARLES E. COMBS received his B.A. and M.A. from San Jose State University and his Ph.D. from the University of Wisconsin–Madison. His teaching experience ranges from elementary to college level, and he has conducted or administered numerous summer youth theatre programs. A former editor of the *Children's Theatre Review* and the *Youth Theatre Journal*, Combs is now editor of the *New England Theatre Journal*. He is currently an associate professor and director of theatre at Plymouth State College, Plymouth, New Hampshire.

RACHEL FORDYCE was trained at Northwestern University and the University of Pittsburgh, receiving her Ph.D., M.A. and B.A. from the latter institution. She is currently assistant vice-president for academic affairs at Eastern Connecticut State University. Author of two books, *Creative Dramatics: An Annotated Bibliography of Critical Works* (1975) and *Caroline Drama: A Bibliographic History of Criticism* (1978), and numerous articles, Fordyce is past executive secretary of the Children's Literature Association, an original member of the board of directors of the association, and a contributing editor to *Children's Literature: An International Journal*.

DOREEN B. HEARD is the artistic director of the Florida Children's Repertory Theatre, a professional company based in Orlando. She also currently teaches at Valencia Community College. She formerly taught at Illinois State University, California State University–Northridge, and Florida State University. Her writing appears in *Theatre Journal*, *Children's Theatre Review* and several other publications. She received an M.F.A. in child drama from the University of North Carolina at Greensboro and a Ph.D. from Florida State University.

JOHN V. HICKS received his Ph.D. from the University of Wisconsin–Madison in theatre history. He holds a B.F.A. from Kent State University and an M.A. from the University of Cincinnati. He currently resides in New York City and owns and operates Baby Wranglers Casting Inc., and agency specializing in the casting of babies and children for television, print and film. He is currently writing a book on children and the commercial industry.

KATHERINE KRZYS earned her B.A. in children's theatre at California State University–Hayward, where she studied under Jeanne Hall. An accomplished storyteller and puppeteer, Kryzs has taught at California State University–Hayward, Contra Costa College and the Mesa, Arizona Public Schools. She was the editor of *Professional Theatre for Young Audiences*, volume 2. She received the M.F.A. degree in child drama from Arizona State University.

JONATHAN LEVY is a professor of theatre arts at the State University of New York–Stony Brook and currently a visiting scholar at Harvard University. He received his A.B. degree from Harvard, did graduate work at the Universities of Rome and Venice, and received his M.A. and Ph.D. degrees from Columbia University. His writings include fiction, light verse, reviews and translations from French and Italian, plus more than twenty plays and libretti for adults and children. His current publications include *Preliminary Checklist of Early Children's Plays in English: 1780–1855* (with Martha Mahard) and *A Theatre of the Imagination*, a book of essays on children and theatre.

JENNIFER SCOTT MCNAIR received her B.A. (*magna cum laude*) from the University of Alabama, Birmingham, and is currently completing an M.F.A. degree in child drama at Virginia Tech, in Blacksburg, Virginia. She has worked as an actress, puppeteer and creative drama teacher in a variety of professional and educational settings. Her publications include "Living Japan" (*UAB Phoenix*), an article describing her experiences as a member of a theatre company visiting Japan. McNair was named the 1988 Winifred Ward Scholar by the American Alliance for Theatre and Education,.

ELLEN RODMAN (Ph.D., New York University) is currently a partner in LN Productions, which has a children's television series under option at Hanna Berra and several television movies under development. She has held executive positions at NBC, Group W and Children's Television Workshop. From 1974–1979 she was children's entertainment reviewer at the *New York Times*, and in 1976 she co-authored the *New York Times Guide to Children's Entertainment*. Active in several professional organizations, including the International Radio and Television Society, Women in Communications, the National Academy of Television Arts and Sciences and Broadcasters Promotion and Marketing Executives, Rodman is cited in several editions of *Who's Who*.

LAURA GARDNER SALAZAR is an associate professor in communications at Grand Valley State University. She is a graduate of the University of Michigan professional theatre program, where she studied directing. Salazar, who has been active in programs and projects of both the national and international children's theatre associations, was awarded the 1985 Children's Theatre Association of America Research Award for "The Emergence of Children's Theatre, 1900–1910." Her article, "The Emergence of Children's Theatre, A Study of America's Changing Values and the Stage," appeared in volume 2 of *Theatre History Studies*.